Florence

WHAT'S NEW | WHAT'S ON | WHAT'S BEST

www.timeout.com/florence

Contents

Published by Time Out Guides Ltd
Universal House
251 Tottenham Court Road
London W1T 7AB
Tel: + 44 (0)20 7813 3000
Fax: + 44 (0)20 7813 6001
Email: guides@timeout.com
www.timeout.com

Managing Director Peter Fiennes
Financial Director Gareth Garner
Editorial Director Ruth Jarvis
Deputy Series Editor Dominic Earle
Editorial Manager Holly Pick
Assistant Management Accountant Ija Krasnikova

Time Out Guides is a wholly owned subsidiary of Time Out Group Ltd.

© **Time Out Group Ltd**
Chairman Tony Elliott
Financial Director Richard Waterlow
Group General Manager/Director Nichola Coulthard
Time Out Magazine Ltd MD Richard Waterlow
Time Out Communications Ltd MD David Pepper
Time Out International MD Cathy Runciman
Production Director Mark Lamond
Group IT Director Simon Chappell

Time Out and the Time Out logo are trademarks of Time Out Group Ltd.

This edition first published in Great Britain in 2008 by Ebury Publishing
A Random House Group Company
Company information can be found on www.randomhouse.co.uk
10 9 8 7 6 5 4 3 2 1

Distributed in US by Publishers Group West
Distributed in Canada by Publishers Group Canada

For further distribution details, see www.timeout.com

ISBN: 978-184670-083-5

A CIP catalogue record for this book is available from the British Library

Printed and bound in Germany by Appl

The Random House Group Limited supports The Forest Stewardship Council (FSC), the leading international forest certification organisation. All our titles that are printed on Greenpeace approved FSC certified paper carry the FSC logo. Our paper procurement policy can be found at www.rbooks.co.uk/environment

Time Out carbon-offsets all its flights with Trees for Cities (www.treesforcities.org)

Florence Shortlist

The **Time Out Florence Shortlist** is one of a new series of guides that draws on Time Out's background as a magazine publisher to keep you current with what's going on in town. As well as Florence's key sights and the best of its eating, drinking and leisure options, the guide picks out the most exciting venues to have recently opened and gives a full calendar of annual events. It also includes features on the important news, trends and openings, all compiled by locally based editors and writers. Whether you're visiting for the first time, or you're a regular, you'll find the *Time Out Florence Shortlist* contains all you need to know, in a portable and easy-to-use format.

The guide divides central Florence into six areas, each of which contains listings for Sights & Museums, Eating & Drinking, Shopping, Nightlife and Arts & Leisure, with maps pinpointing all their locations. At the front of the book are chapters rounding up these scenes city-wide, and giving a shortlist of our overall picks in a variety of categories. We include itineraries for days out, plus essentials such as transport information and hotels.

Our listings give phone numbers as dialled within Florence. Area codes must be dialled in full, whether dialling from within the city or from elsewhere in Italy. To call from outside Italy, use your country's exit code, followed by 39 (the international dialling code for Italy), and then follow this with the number given. Some listed numbers (normally starting with '3') are mobiles, indicated as such.

We have noted price categories by using one to four euro signs (€-€€€€), representing budget, moderate, expensive and luxury. Major credit cards are accepted unless otherwise stated. All of the listings in this guide have been double-checked, but places do sometimes close or change their hours or prices, so it's a good idea to call a venue before visiting. While every effort has been made to ensure accuracy, the publishers cannot accept responsibility for any errors that this guide may contain.

Venues are marked on the maps using symbols numbered according to their order within the chapter and colour-coded according to the type of venue they represent:

❶ Sights & museums
❶ Eating & drinking
❶ Shopping
❶ Nightlife
❶ Arts & leisure

Map key

Regional border	⌇⌇⌇⌇
Province border	‒ ‒ ‒
Autostrada	▬▬▬
City wall	▭▭▭▭
Place of interest and/ or entertainment	▨
Railway station	▬
Park	▭
Hospital/university	▨
Ancient site	▨
Car park	🄿
Tourist information	🄸
Pedestrianised area	▨
Electric bus route	🄐

Time Out Florence Shortlist

EDITORIAL
Editor Anna Norman
Proofreader Patrick Mulkern

DESIGN
Art Director Scott Moore
Art Editor Pinelope Kourmouzoglou
Senior Designer Henry Elphick
Graphic Designers Gemma Doyle,
   Kei Ishimaru
Digital Imaging Simon Foster
Advertising Designer Jodi Sher
Picture Editor Jael Marschner
Deputy Picture Editor Katie Morris
Picture Researcher Gemma Walters
Picture Desk Assistant Marzena Zoladz

ADVERTISING
Commercial Director Mark Phillips
International Advertising Manager
   Kasimir Berger
International Sales Executive
   Charlie Sokol
Advertising Sales (Florence)
   The Florentine
Advertising Assistant Kate Staddon

MARKETING
Head of Marketing Catherine Demajo
Marketing Manager Yvonne Poon
**Sales & Marketing Director, North
   America** Lisa Levinson
Marketing Designers Anthony Huggins,
   Nicola Wilson

PRODUCTION
Production Manager Brendan McKeown
Production Controller Caroline Bradford
Production Co-ordinator Julie Pallot

CONTRIBUTORS
This guide was researched and written by Julia Burdet, Maddalena Delli,
Anna Norman and Nicky Swallow. Listings were checked by Heather Sockol.

PHOTOGRAPHY
All photography by Gianluca Moggi, except: page 45 Anna Norman; 60 akg-images/Erich
Lessing; 18, 19, 66 Jonathan Perugia; 115 Ministero per i Beni e le Attivita Culturali and
Dipartimento della Protezione Civile.

The following images were provided by the featured establishments/artists: pages 65,
164, 168, 175.

Cover photograph: Alberto Biscaro/Masterfile.

MAPS
JS Graphics (john@jsgraphics.co.uk).

About Time Out

Founded in 1968, Time Out has expanded from humble London beginnings into the
leading resource for those wanting to know what's happening in the world's greatest
cities. As well as our influential what's-on weeklies in London, New York and Chicago,
we publish more than a dozen other listings magazines in cities as varied as Beijing
and Mumbai. The magazines established Time Out's trademark style: sharp writing,
informed reviewing and bang up-to-date inside knowledge of every scene.

Time Out made the natural leap into travel guides in the 1980s with the City Guide
series, which now extends to over 50 destinations around the world. Written and
researched by expert local writers and generously illustrated with original photography,
the full-size guides cover a larger area than our Shortlist guides and include many
more venue reviews, along with additional background features and a full set of maps.

Throughout this rapid growth, the company has remained proudly independent, still
owned by Tony Elliott nearly four decades after he started Time Out London as a single
fold-out sheet of A5 paper. This independence extends to the editorial content of all
our publications, this Shortlist included. No establishment has been featured because
it has advertised, and no payment has influenced any of our reviews. And, for our critics,
there's definitely no such thing as a free lunch: all restaurants and bars are visited and
reviewed anonymously, and Time Out always picks up the bill.
For more about the company, see www.timeout.com.

Don't Miss

Michelangelo's David p10

Sights & Museums

Florence may be building a
state-of-the-art tram system
and farming out museum extension
commissions to some of the world's
most cutting-edge architects… but
that's not fooling the millions of
visitors who come here for one
thing – the Renaissance art.

UNESCO estimates that Italy is
home to around 60 per cent of the
world's most important works of
art, over half of which are located
in Florence, and with the lion's
share created in the golden age of
Medici patronage. Kick-started by
the boy prodigy Masaccio and the
visionary Giotto, and epitomised
by Michelangelo, Leonardo and
Brunelleschi, this explosion of
artistic invention and architectural

brilliance brought to the city the
masterpieces that still grace its
squares and alleyways, museums
and churches. Without even setting
foot inside those great shrines
to art the Uffizi, the Accademia
and the Bargello, the glimpses
of Brunelleschi's miraculous
dome, Cellini's impossible bronze
Perseus and Alberti's faultless
façade of Santa Maria Novella are
constant reminders that to come to
Florence is to enter a honey-stone
coloured time warp.

New kids on the block

Florence may be living off its past,
and change can be slow in coming
here, but these are exciting times
for the city. As well as the major

tram project, several important new works are in progress and pending. Sir Norman Foster has designed the enormous underground terminal of the high-speed Milano–Roma train link, due to be completed in 2010-11 with an arched glazed roof that will hark back to the railway stations of the 19th century. Controversial designs for the new Uffizi exit (p69) by Japanese architect Arata Isozaki were finally given the green light in August 2007. The exit, which will feature a high canopy made out of steel, stone and polycarbonate, is now expected to be completed in 2013, ten years after its original deadline. Meanwhile, the planned extension to the Museo dell'Opera del Duomo (p64) involving Spanish architect Santiago Calatrava has suffered a series of setbacks and has yet to get off the ground. In another development, feasibility studies are being carried out and public reaction tested about the prospect of a finished façade for San Lorenzo church, based on Michelangelo's original designs (see box p97).

Some of the city's new museums have more niche than mass-market appeal – the Interactive Museum of Medieval Florence (p94) being a case in point. Other new openings have become part of mainstream itineraries. The Museo Leonardo da Vinci (p104), which opened a couple of years ago, has been a great success, as has the new Alinari photography museum (p86 and box p86), while the long awaited Villa Bardini (p133) and adjacent Giardino Bardini (p128) are well worth a detour.

Museums & galleries

Many of Florence's unrivalled museum repertoires have private collections at their core, either of a mega-family such as the Medici, who started the Uffizi and Palazzo Pitti, or of a lone connoisseur,

SHORTLIST

Best new sights
- Giardino Bardini (p128)
- Museo Leonardo da Vinci (p104)
- Museo Nazionale Alinari della Fotografia (p86)
- Villa Bardini (p133)

Must-see museums
- Bargello (p112)
- Galleria dell'Accademia (p103)
- Museo dell'Opera del Duomo (p64)
- Museo di San Marco (p104)
- Uffizi Gallery (p69)

Greenest oases
- Giardino Bardini (p128)
- Giardini di Boboli (p128)
- Giardino di Semplici (p104)

Most crucial chapels
- Cappella dei Bardi & Cappella dei Peruzzi (p117)
- Cappella Brancacci (p132)
- Cappelle Medicee (p95)
- Cappella Tornabuoni (p87)

Most momentous architecture
- Biblioteca Mediceo-Laurenziana (p99)
- Campanile (di Giotto) (p62)
- Chiesa di Santo Spirito (p133)
- Cupola del Duomo (p61)
- Façade of Santa Maria Novella (p87)
- Palazzo Rucellai (p84)

Most-famous Last Suppers
- Cenacolo del Conservatorio di Fuligno (p96)
- Cenacolo di Ognissanti (p87)
- Cenacolo di Sant'Apollonia (p96)

Best vantage points
- Campanile (p62)
- Cupola del Duomo (p61)
- Forte di Belvedere (p143)
- Piazzale Michelangelo (p152)

such as the Horne and Stibbert museums. Others were founded to preserve treasures too precious to expose to the elements, such as the Accademia, the Bargello and Museo dell'Opera del Duomo.

Administratively, they fall into three categories: state, municipal or private. The state museums are the Pitti museums, the Uffizi, the Accademia, the Bargello, Museo di San Marco, the Opificio delle Pietre Dure, Cappelle Medicee and Museo Archeologico. The main municipal museums are Cappella Brancacci, Cenacolo di Santo Spirito, Museo di Firenze di com'era, Palazzo Vecchio and Collezione della Ragione.

Art lovers should be aware that works of art are often lent to other museums or to exhibitions, and restoration can be carried out with little or no notice, so it's always a wise idea to call first if you want to view a specific piece. Ticket offices normally have lists of artworks not on show.

Orientation

The city centre is compact and easy to get around, with most major sights within walking distance of any other central point. It's practically impossible to get lost, with the ever-visible Duomo and the River Arno and its four central bridges acting as reference points. The majority of the main sights and museums are clustered north of the two central bridges in the area around the Duomo (p58), with most other important sites circling this rectangle in the Santa Maria Novella, San Lorenzo, San Marco, Santa Croce and Oltrarno zones.

Tickets

There are no major free museums in Florence; entrance is usually between €4 and €6.50. Churches don't generally charge for entry,

though some charge an admission fee for specific chapels and others may ask for donations. For one week of the year (the Settimana dei Beni Culturali; p33), entrance to all the state museums is free. This is generally in late spring/ early summer, but exact dates vary.

For general information on the state museums and for booking, call Firenze Musei (055 294 883), which strongly recommends booking for the Uffizi and the Accademia, and, at busy times of year, for the Pitti museums. This could save you a minimum two-hour queue or possible disappointment at busier times. (Michelangelo's *David* draws such a long queue for the Accademia, that authorities are seriously considering moving the iconic statue to a newly planned development at the Stazione Leopolda (p149), in order to farm the tourist overflow to outer districts.) Sometimes when booking you'll be given an earliest slot in several days' time, or even longer, so if you're on a short visit it's best to book ahead of the trip (from abroad call +39 055 294 883). Booking costs €3 and tickets are collected from a window beside the normal ticket office. Pay when you pick up the tickets. Don't expect to be able to book there directly; you'll be told to phone the central number. Last issuing times for tickets vary (and we have given the closing time in our listings, not last admission). Try to get to the ticket office at least an hour before the museum closes.

Opening hours

Florence may be home to more works of art per square metre than any other place on earth, but the millions of visitors waiting to see the most important of these works have to be squeezed into only six

Ponte Vecchio

DON'T MISS

days of the week: the Uffizi, the Accademia and the Galleria del Palatina in the Palazzo Pitti are all closed on Mondays. There are some complicated variations to the *'lunedì chiuso'* rule; if you're lucky and it's the first, third or fifth Monday of the month, you could go to the Galleria dell'Arte Moderna, the Bargello or the Museo di San Marco, or if it's the second or fourth, the Cappelle Medicee and the minor museums of the Palazzo Pitti. So if you're planning a long weekend, make sure to book must-see museums for the weekend, or resign yourself to visiting a smaller, less well-known museum or church. Half days are also an unexpected spanner in the planning works: the closing time for at least half of the city's museums is 1.50pm.

Tours

Many of Florence's tour companies offer standard itineraries, with English-language options covering the main sights by foot or by bus. The reputable Association

of Tourist Guides (055 210 641/ www.florencetouristguides.com), the Association of Florentine Tourist Guides (055 422 0901/ www.florenceguides.it) and the Cultural Association of Guides (055 787 7744/www.firenze-guide. com) all offer a wide choice of standard tours. There are also some specialist companies offering a little more variety. Walking Tours of Florence (055 264 5033/ www.artviva.com) organises a morning jaunt into Tuscany and a 'views tour', CAF (055 283 2000/ www.caftours.com) runs a Florence by Night tour, and Context Florence (06 4820911, www.contextflorence .com) uses expert scholars rather than tour guides, and limits groups to six. A new option is an official bus tour. City Sightseeing Firenze (piazza Stazione 1, 055 290451) runs two lines of one- and two-hour lengths, departing from Santa Maria Novella train station and Porta San Frediano (9.30am-6pm Mon-Sun, €20, €10 concessions, no credit cards).

Filipepe

WHAT'S BEST

Eating & Drinking

Florentines are as traditional in their eating habits as they are in their approach to many other things, so the city's gastronomic scene has been dominated for years by homely *trattorie* and *osterie* offering hearty *cucina casalinga* (home-style cooking). However, the boundaries are widening, and there are now plenty of restaurants where the *mamma* figure has been replaced by a younger generation of cooks doing a creative take on her traditional recipes. Some of these are cool, contemporary spaces while others maintain the rustic look and feel of their predecessors; not all are totally convincing. Add to this a growing number of ethnic eateries (again, of varying standards) and a clutch of top-notch restaurants offering 'gourmet' dining and it's fair to say that there's now more variety to Florence's eating out scene than ever before.

The local cuisine

While the locals all have their favourite neighbourhood eaterie where prices are reasonable and the food is the genuine article, the main problem for tourists is the high number of shoddy imitations, which make choosing where to eat your *ribollita* and *bistecca* less than straightforward. With some seven million visitors passing through Florence annually, it's a seller's market and standards are not always what they should be. It pays to do a bit of research.

Although it's perfectly acceptable to order only a couple of dishes, a full-blown Italian meal goes something like this: *antipasto* (hors-d'oeuvre), *primo* (pasta, risotto or soup), *secondo* (meat or fish) *e contorno* (vegetable) and *dolce* (dessert). In a traditional Florentine restaurant such as Del

SHORTLIST

Best new places
- 'Ino (p76)
- Komè (p119)
- Ora d'Aria (p120)
- Portofino (p145)
- Povero Pesce (p146)
- La Vie en Rose (p121)

Best traditional fare
- Da Camillo (p135)
- Cibreino (p118)
- Da Mario (p99)
- Da Ruggero (p153)
- Da Sergio (p100)
- Trattoria del Carmine (p138)

Firm favourites
- Bibè (p152)
- Filipepe (p135)
- Il Guscio (p137)
- Da Ruggero (p153)
- Santo Bevitore (p138)
- Trattoria del Carmine (p138)
- Le Volpi e L'Uva (p138)
- Zibibbo (p147)

Best cheap and cheerful
- Mangiatoia (p137)
- Nerbone (p100)
- Da Rocco (p121)

Perfect pizza
- Il Pizzaiuolo (p120)
- Santa Lucia (p146)
- Vico del Carmine (p154)

Best fishy flavours
- Arte Gaia (p151)
- Borgo San Jacopo (p134)
- Portofino (p145)
- Povero Pesce (p146)

Coffee and cakes
- Caffè Florian (p88)
- Caffè Rivoire (p72)
- Gilli (p75)
- Robiglio (p107)

Favourite wine bars
- Casa del Vino (p99)
- Fuori Porta (p153)
- Le Volpi e L'Uva (p138)

Fagioli (p189) or Da Ruggero (p153), the meal starts with liver-topped *crostini* or *bruschetta* drizzled with local olive oil and a platter of mixed prosciutto and salame. This will be followed with an earthy, bread or bean-based soup (*ribollita*, *pappa al pomodoro*, *zuppa di farro* or *pasta e fagioli*) or a pasta dish such as *pappardelle alla lepre* (hare) or *al cinghiale* (wild boar) and *ravioli con burro e salvia* (ricotta and Swiss-chard-stuffed ravioli with sage-infused melted butter). The rare-cooked *bistecca alla fiorentina*, a vast T-bone steak, is the city's most famous culinary claim to fame and often big enough to feed three or four hungry carnivores. Other *secondi* include *trippa* (tripe) *alla fiorentina* (stewed in with tomato), *salsicce e fagioli* (sausage and beans) and *arista di maiale* (rosemary and garlic-spiked roast pork). *Contorni* are likely to be roast potatoes and the ubiquitous (but delicious) *fagioli* – white beans best eaten with new-season's olive oil and black pepper. The Florentines don't really 'do' desserts, so finish

Time Out
Travel Guides

Italy

Written by local experts

Available at all good bookshops and at timeout.com/shop

Time Out
Guides

off with hard, almondy *cantucci* biscuits dunked in Vinsanto. There won't be room for much more.

Raising the stakes, in terms of both food and atmosphere, is now a feasible option in Florence. There are several interesting places to eat where the cooking is still based on the 'old ways', but where chefs like Benedetta Vitali at Zibibbo (p147), Arturo Dori at Cavolo Nero (p135) and Robbie Pepin at Beccofino (p134) are paying more attention to provenance, where the wine lists are long and varied and where the ambiance and presentation are part of the whole experience.

It's always a good idea to book a table for dinner, especially at weekends and in high season. Lunchtimes are less of a problem. Most restaurants start serving evening meals around 8pm.

Taking it lightly

If your stomach (or wallet) can't face yet another blow-out meal, there are alternatives. Wine bars, or *enoteche* (see p17), usually offer a range of wine-friendly snacks alongside a selection of hot and cold dishes. At lunchtimes, bars often have a short menu of *primi*, *secondi* and salads, and you can go into any *alimentari* (grocer's) and ask them to make you up a prosciutto, salame or cheese sandwich (*un panino al prosciutto/salame/formaggio*). For what is arguably the best *panino* in town, try newcomer grocer/wine bar 'Ino (p76). Another useful option is one of the city's *rosticcerie*, marvellous institutions serving good, home-cooked food at rock bottom prices to take away or, in some cases, eat in.

Eat humble pizza

A traditional Florentine pizza has a thin, crisp base. However, such a thing is hard to find nowadays as the rage for Neapolitan-style pizza

(with a puffier base) continues its stranglehold on the city. When these are good (Vico del Carmine's are a work of art; p154), they are very good, but when they are bad (soggy and stodgy), they are horrid. The locals only eat pizza in the evenings; *pizzerie* that serve at lunchtimes tend to be tourist joints. Always choose a pizzeria with a wood-fired brick oven (*forno a legna*); the electric or gas alternatives just don't cut the mustard.

Meat-free meals

While Florence can only boast a couple of dedicated vegetarian restaurants, a meat-free meal is not hard to come by, especially if you eat fish; and waiters no longer look aghast when you announce '*sono vegetariano*'. Menus will usually include several vegetable-based pasta options, and if all else fails, you can always ask for a simple plate of *pasta al pomodoro*. More contemporary restaurants often feature a vegetarian *secondo* on the menu, and there's often a good

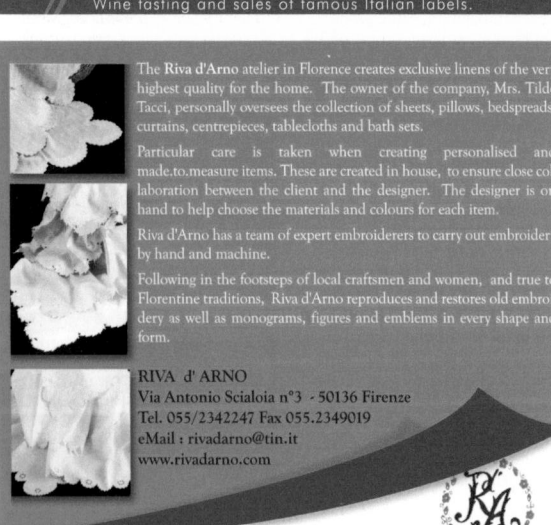

choice of seasonal vegetable side dishes. Florentines seem to be watching their cholesterol intake more and more, and fish eaters will be pleased at the increased number of *ristoranti di pesce* in town.

The wine list

Not so long ago, only the most upmarket restaurants would have a list that included wines from outside Tuscany, let alone non-Italian labels, but these days even many *trattorie* offer more than just house plonk. An increasing number of places are offering wines by the glass too. However, most budget and moderately prices restaurants do offer *vino della casa* (in litre, half and quarter litre flasks), usually an acceptable rustic plonk that suits the sort of food on offer.

The bill

Florentine restaurants these days are rarely a bargain. Prices sky-rocketed after the introduction of the euro, and have stayed high. Some more upmarket establishments now offer a multi-course tasting menu or *menu dégustazione* and this can be good value. When the bill arrives, check to see if service is included. It often isn't; a five to ten per cent cash tip is the norm. In a simple *trattoria*, just round the bill up a couple of euros. The *pane e coperto* charge is supposed to cover the cost of bread and should also reflect the standard of service; it ranges from around €1.50 to €5 in snazzy places.

Cafés and bars

Many a Florentine's day starts in the neighbourhood bar with a lethal shot of espresso and a brioche. The same bar will serve mid-morning cappuccinos (which a local will never, EVER drink after 11am), sandwiches and light meals (and more espresso) at lunchtimes, yet more espresso (and maybe a pastry)

throughout the afternoon and *aperitivi* in the evening. All this will be peppered with plenty of local chat plus newspaper reading and even card-playing. Upmarket bars will often stay open well into the night. Like the rest of the country, Florence is still in the grip of its love affair with the *aperitivo*, a ritual that usually runs from around 7pm to 9pm and involves a range of 'free' snacks thrown in for the price of your drink. The food is often filling enough to replace dinner.

The city boasts a number of traditional cafés, beautiful gilded affairs like Gilli (p75) and Rivoire (p72), where white-jacketed waiters serve morning coffees and afternoon teas accompanied by cakes, pastries or elegant *aperitivi*. You'll often pay through the nose, but it's a very civilised treat.

Wine bars

Wine bars come in various guises in Florence, from tiny, atmospheric street booths like I Fratellini (p75) (known as *fiaschetteria* or *vineria*) serving basic Tuscan wines and snacks, to upmarket *enoteche* offering a vast range of labels from all over Italy and beyond, and more sophisticated edible goodies. Le Volpi e l'Uva (p138) is one of the best for sampling wines from small producers, while Fuori Porta (p153) is a classic offering a vast range both by the bottle and glass.

I scream…

Florence boasts some top-notch *gelaterie*, with Grom (p76) and Vestri (p123) among the best. Between them they produce enough flavours to give a *gelato*-holic a different-flavoured daily dose for several months. Some are better than others; always look for a sign saying *produzione propria* or *artigianale* for home-made ice-cream. See also box p73.

Via Strozzi

Shopping

A seismic shift in the character of shopping in central Florence has taken place over the last few years, due to the fact that an entire chunk of the historic centre has been invaded by big-name Italian and international designer clothes stores. The joke in town is not about banks being converted into bars but about banks turning overnight into Bulgari. Epitomising this new look is the recently opened, sparkling Chanel boutique, the only shop to have a window (or, in fact, three) on the hallowed ground of piazza della Signoria.

While sentimental locals are deeply dismayed by this 'branding' revolution and by the loss of beloved shopping institutions, visitors looking for something more unusual, original or characteristic of Florence need only shop between the lines. Slipping off the main shopping arteries into narrower streets and alleyways, out of the central tourist honeypot or across the river will still reveal a richly woven patchwork of small, independent and unique *botteghe* (artisan workshops); so intrinsic are these to Florence's cultural and commercial heritage that we've included a walking itinerary based on them – see pages 40-43 The Artisan Way.

Where to shop

Food and gift shops – as well as the latest fad to hit the city: vintage boutiques (see box p140) – are dotted all around the central areas,

Via Tornabuoni

while the other categories of shops have gradually gravitated towards each other to form clusters. Designer clothes shop are concentrated in via della Vigna Nuova, via Tornabuoni and via Strozzi (all to the west of the Duomo). These three adjoining central streets are home to Gucci, Armani, Prada, Roberto Cavalli, Salvatore Ferragamo, Pucci, Hermes, Louis Vuitton, Max Mara and Fendi as well as the newly opened Burberry, Bulgari, Dolce & Gabbana and Bottega Veneta shops. Other recent flagship store arrivals in the area are Tommy Hilfiger and local designer Michele Negri, whose cavernous vaulted shop also has a bar, a novelty in Florence. In nearby via Roma are designer emporia Raspini (nos.25-29r, 055 213077, www.raspini.com) and Luisa (nos.19-21r, 055 217826, www.luisaviaroma.com), with more rich pickings for label lovers.

Lungarno Details p19

The spokes leading off the hub of piazza della Repubblica are the best place to root out mid-range togs, with Sisley, Liu Jo and a new Zara opposite its sister store. Also here are the two main department stores, La Rinascente (p79) and COIN (p75).

For budget fashion options head to via de' Neri, borgo San Lorenzo and via Cerretani. Via Porta Rossa, via dei Pucci, via del Corso, borgo degli Albizi, borgo San Jacopo and the streets around via Guicciardini in the Oltrarno, meanwhile, are good bets for one-offs from independent shops and boutiques, such as Ethic (p122), A Piedi Nudi nel Parco (p121) and Quelle Tre (via de' Pucci 43r, 055 293284).

Via del Corso and via Porta Rossa are the streets from which to kick off the Italian shoe trail; check out the bargain Otisopse (p78) and Peppe Peluso (p79) before upping the ante by a hundred euros or two at Bologna (p75), Calvani (via degli Speziali 7r, 055 2654043) and Marco Candido (piazza del Duomo, 055 215342).

The areas around the churches of San Lorenzo and Santa Croce are practically bursting with leather shops selling generally bog standard jackets, bags and accessories, though they can yield the odd surprise. Via Por Santa Maria and via della Vigna Vecchia are better options for swankier, seasonally changing designs.

For traditional jewellery, the ponte Vecchio's 16th-century shops are the obvious starting point. The adjacent lungarno Accaiuoli and borgo San Jacopo, and via Santo Spirito, offer quirkier baubles at Graziella (p78), Angela Caputi (borgo SS Apostoli, 055 292993) and Aprosio e Co (p138).

Grand antiques shops line via Maggio, via dei Serragli and via Romana, while another street known for its antique shops – via dei Fossi – has several new contemporary interior design studios and galleries.

The Oltrarno, and in particular the area around piazza Santo Spirito, is still a buzzing hub for the city's artisans, despite the fear that many of their age-old skills are dying out (see pp40-43 The Artisan Way). A stroll around the area reveals the workshops of furniture and picture restorers and experts in marquetry, inlay, gilding, carving, bookbinding and paper-making. Handmade paper, especially of the colourful marbled breed, is a classic Florentine souvenir, and while most of the workshops are in the Oltrarno, tiny wood panelled shops selling paper gifts, such as Il Papiro (p109), spring up all round the city.

Multi-floor stores with the biggest selections of books, calendars and magazines are to be found in the main thoroughfares around piazza del Duomo, though there are several specialist gems in every *quartiere* of the city. Some, such as BM American British Bookstore (p90), McRae Books (via de' Neri 32r, 055 2382456) and Paperback Exchange (p78) stock English-language new or second-hand titles.

To market, to market

The most central of the gift and clothing markets is the Mercato Nuovo (p77), also known as the Mercato del Porcellino, in the covered Loggia del Mercato Nuovo (9am-7pm Mon-Sat). The city's main market is held in the streets around San Lorenzo (8.30am-7pm Mon-Sat), touting leather goods, clothes and souvenirs, while the main food market is inside the 19th-century covered building in the piazza del Mercato Centrale (which features heavily in the culinary itinerary on pages 44 to 46). Foodies can also check out the Sant'Ambrogio market in piazza Ghiberti (7am-2pm Mon-Sat). The fleamarket (Mercato delle Pulci) is round the corner in piazza dei Ciompi (9am-7pm Mon-Sat) and

once a month an antiques and bric-a-brac market is held in piazza Santo Spirito (8am-6pm 2nd Sun). The Fierucola (8am-6pm 3rd Sun), also in the piazza, is the place to go for organic and locally produced food, wine, clothing and gifts. Biggest of all, however, is the Tuesday morning market at the Cascine, a riotous mess of 300 or so stalls.

Opening times

Supermarkets and larger stores in the city centre generally stay open throughout the day (*orario continuato*), but most shops still operate standard hours, opening from 3.30pm to 7.30pm on Monday, and 9am to 1pm then 3.30pm to 7.30pm from Tuesday to Saturday. Clothes stores sometimes open a bit later (around 10am), while food shops usually open earlier in the morning, close at 1pm, reopen at 5pm and are closed on Wednesday afternoons. Many of the central stores stay open for at least part of Sunday; several more open on the last Sunday of the month. In summer, shops usually close on Saturday afternoons instead of, or as well as, Wednesdays. Small shops also tend to shut completely for anything from a week to a month for an annual summer break, usually in August.

Taxing matters

Non-EU residents are entitled to a VAT (IVA) refund on purchases of €155 and over, at shops participating in the 'tax-free shopping' scheme, identified by a purple sticker. On presentation of your passport, the shop will give you a 'cheque' to be cashed at the Tax Free Cash Refund desk at the airport on your way home. You'll need to show your passport and the unused goods, and there's a three-month time limit.

Plasma p25

Nightlife

A new one-size-fits-all arrangement has turned nightlife in Florence on its head in recent years. The *aperitivo* phenomenon that has taken Florence by storm has led to a much more Anglo-Saxon pattern of early evening socialising; as the lure of free buffets at hybrid bar-restaurant-clubs has worked its magic, bars are now packed from 7pm till late. The late-night club is the loser in this new timetable, and, to survive, many have morphed into bar/clubs also serving early evening *aperitivi* in the hope of roping punters in for the night. Pure-bred clubbing has increasingly become occasional big-night-out entertainment, often combined with a gig or saved for one-off events at venues such as the Stazione Leopolda and paying villa parties on the hills.

Opening times and closing days of bars and clubs are notoriously vague, and phones that are answered are the exception, so be prepared to take a chance. Musical genres often vary with the day of the week – check flyers, the free local English-language newspaper *The Florentine* or the monthly *Firenze Spettacolo* for information.

The aperitivo craze

Almost any bar worth its salt now serves up a full free buffet with its drinks (which generally cost between €8 and €10). The biggest nightly event, and one of the most popular, is at Noir (previously Capocaccia; p93 and box p92), while the most atmospheric *aperitivo* affair is to be found at Slowly (p83).

Sushi and ethnic cuisine are the latest variations on the *aperitivo* theme. Both Noir and Rex (p125)

angels

restaurant and american bar

Via del Proconsolo 29/31 - Florence - Italy
tel +39.055.2398762 fax +39.055.2398123
www.ristoranteangels.it - info@ristoranteangels.it

My name is DORIS

music drink dj-set

Via de' Pandolfini 26r - Florence - Italy
myspace.com/dorisfirenze - simone@dorisfirenze.it

have their own versions, while the expert is Ferragamo's Fusion Bar Shozan (p75), serving snacks of authentic sushi and tempura.

A few of the city's hotels have also started up *aperitivo* nights, the best being those with rooftop bars. The Sky Lounge bar of the Hotel Continentale (p83) is on the fifth floor and serves cocktails and plates of delicacies to the backdrop of a sunset panorama during the warmer months. The rooftop bar of the Hotel Minerva (p173) has an equally swish buffet for its poolside *aperitivo*.

Many bars extend the evening buffet into club-night entertainment with live music or DJ sets that go on till late. Notable if you want to make a night of it are Twice (p125), Dolce Vita (p142), Colle Bereto (p82), Noir, Plasma (p154) and Rex.

Alfresco imbibing

One defining characteristic of Florentine bars has always been the outdoor element. Crowds gather in the squares that house the most popular venues, and covered seating areas, patio heaters and outside armchairs have been introduced over the last couple of years to make alfresco bar-going a year-round activity. The very central Colle Bereto has created an indoor-out oasis of sofas, cushions and bucket chairs and is popular till late. Dolce Vita is the classic outdoor bar experience, while neighbours Negroni (p142), Zoe (p142) and Il Rifrullo (p137) provide their own Oltrarno outdoor bar crawl. The crowd outside the incredibly popular Noir, meanwhile, stops the Lungarno traffic on most nights.

Summer nights

The alfresco phenomenon comes into full swing, however, from the end of May to the beginning of September, when most Florentine nightlife shifts from crowded,

S H O R T L I S T

Best recent openings
- Doris (p123)
- Plasma (p154)
- Twice (p125)

Best big club nights
- Central Park (p148)
- Full-Up (p124)
- Meccano (p148)
- Tenax (p149)
- Yab (p82)

Best for live music
- Ambaciata di Marte (p147)
- Auditorium Flog (p147)
- Sintetika (p93)

Best jazz jibes
- Astor Caffè (p80)
- BZF (p99)
- Caruso Jazz Café (p80)
- Jazz Club (p109)
- Pinocchio Jazz (p154)

Hottest latin beats
- Girasol (p148)
- Maracana Casa di Samba (p101)

Most laid-back affairs
- Art bar (p93)
- Mayday Lounge Café (p81)

Greatest gay venues
- Muna (p142)
- Piccolo Caffè (p125)
- Tabasco (p82)
- YAGB@R (p125)

Most stylish aperitivi
- Fusion Bar Shozan (p73)
- Moyo (p125)
- Noir (p93)
- Slowly (p82)

Best alfresco
- Colle Bereto (p80)
- Dolce Vita (p142)
- Negroni (p142)
- Il Rifrullo (p137)
- Zoe (p142)

overheated underground clubs to seasonal outdoor venues in piazzas, gardens and villas. Most have free admission and stay open until well into the small hours. Each summer brings new openings as well as non-appearances of some of the previous year's venues.

Temporary bars set up in streets and squares are also a hot summer phenomenon, with piazza Santo Spirito usually playing host to nightly gigs and events. Other one-off events are organised in piazza de' Pitti and the Boboli Gardens (p128) and the Stazione Leopolda (p149) is also increasingly used. The Ippodromo delle Mulina at the Cascine (via del Pegaso, bus 17C or p149) has roots, reggae, rock, dance or house music every night from 11pm till late in summer. Jazz nights at the Sant'Ambrogio Summer Festival (www.firenzejazz.it; p35) run from June to July in piazza Ghiberti, and there's a bar and restaurant at the Loggia del Pesce in piazza de' Ciompi with music ranging from bossa nova and samba to jazz and blues. For riverside seats, head for Teatro sull'Acqua (Lungarno Pecori Giraldi, Santa Croce, 055 2343460) or Lido (p124), sprawling bar-cum-clubs on the banks of the Arno.

All of the above are planned for annual opening but bear in mind that the local council grants permission to these summer-only venues on a year-by-year basis, and the situation can change at any time. Check the local press for details.

Getting in

Door policies in Florence are fairly easy-going and dress codes relaxed, though, when queues build up on more popular nights, entry can become arbitrarily selective. Most clubs charge an admission fee that includes one drink, but some still use the card system. At these venues, you're given a card that's stamped whenever you buy drinks or use the cloakroom. You then hand the card in at the till and pay before leaving. Some smaller clubs are members only, but will often give out free membership. For some gay venues you'll need an ArciGay/Lesbica membership card, which costs €14 per year – it's available at any of the venues that require it.

Going live

Florence is left off the touring itineraries of many major musical acts but it's still possible to catch the odd international name at the larger venues such as the Artemio Franchi football stadium (p150), Auditorium FLOG (p147) and even at the Teatro Verdi (p125). Conversely, the city is often chosen over mightier Italian neighbours Rome, Milan and Turin by dance and indy bands, with Tenax (p149) in particular reeling in surprising catches for its capacity. Thanks largely to the student population, Florence also has a strong local base of home-grown rock bands and beatniks providing nightly live gigs. Jazz enthusiasts should not miss the excellent programme of mostly contemporary and progressive sounds promoted by Musicus Concentus (piazza del Carmine 19, Oltrarno, 055 287347, www.musicusconcentus.com) and small clubs such as Jazz Club (p109); Pinocchio Jazz (p154) and Caruso Jazz Café (p82). Regular live Latin beats are on offer at Girasol, and Auditorium FLOG (p147) hosts the world music festival Musica dei Popoli in October/November (p37).

The best way to find out about live events is to pick up the latest edition of *Firenze Spettacolo* or *The Florentine*, or drop into a record shop to pick up flyers. To book tickets for concerts, call the venue direct or contact the Box Office ticket agency (p187).

Arena di Marte p31

Arts & Leisure

Florence's main claim to musical fame is that it was the 'birthplace of opera'. In the mid 16th century, a group of intellectuals known as the Florentine Camerata began experimenting with the setting of words to music, an evolution that was to lead to the composition of Peri and Caccini's *Euridice*; performed in the Boboli gardens for the wedding of Henry IV of France to Marie de' Medici in 1600, this is generally acknowledged to be the first opera. The city's position as a cutting-edge centre for musical activity continued right through to the early 17th century, at which point the focus shifted over to Venice and its exciting new opera houses.

The term 'cutting-edge' cannot be used for the Florentine performing arts scene today. However, there is a surprising amount going on for such a small city, with enough cultural events to satisfy most visitors once the museums begin to pall.

Classical music

The city's classical musical life revolves around its municipal opera house, the Teatro del Maggio Musicale Fiorentino (p93), which supports a full symphony orchestra, chorus and ballet company. Opera (especially Puccini or Verdi) is very much part of the Italian soul and if you get a chance to catch a performance at the Maggio theatre, take it. Productions here, often

Teatro del Maggio p27

featuring well-known singers, conductors and stage directors, are usually good and occasionally outstanding. The highlight of the theatre's year is the Maggio Musicale festival (p33), which starts in late April and continues until late June/early July. It features opera, ballet and chamber concerts by 'in-house' companies as well as big-name guest artists.

Florence's other resident orchestra is the smaller but excellent Orchestra della Toscana (www.orchestradellatoscana.it) whose home base is the Teatro Verdi (p125); its concert season runs from November to May. If you're more interested in chamber music, however, then make sure you look up the programme of concerts held in the exquisite 18th-century Teatro della Pergola (p109). Meanwhile, early music fans should try to check out the Amici della Musica's Settembre Musica season that runs in September (p37), and also scour the Pergola programme.

Theatre and dance

While it's of limited interest to non-Italian speakers, Florence's theatre scene continues to flourish, in spite of under-funding. Productions range from classics by the likes of Pirandello, Shakespeare and Goldoni at the Teatro della Pergola (p109) to alternative and fringe events hosted by small, out-of-the-way spaces such as the Teatro Studio di Scandicci (via Donizetti 58, 055 751853, www.scandiccicultura. org) and Teatro della Limonaia (via Gramsci 426, Sesto Fiorentino, 055 440852, www.teatrodella limonaia.it). If all goes according to plan, Florence will have a new theatre and performance space within the next couple of years; the 1658 Teatro Niccolini, located just steps from the Duomo and closed since 1995, is due to be restored and reopened as a state-of-the-art cultural centre by late 2009.

Dance events enjoy a large following among the locals. MaggioDanza (the Teatro del

Maggio's resident company) puts on regular full-length classical and modern productions, while contemporary work comes from ensembles such as the Virgilio Sieni Dance Company. Keep an eye open for the Florence Dance Festival (p35) in July and December and the excellent early summer Fabbrica Europa festival (p33), which also showcases theatre and music events.

The silver screen

Florence is suffering from a nosedive in cinema attendances, and several of the city centre's historic cinemas have been forced to close down, while others are under threat. One culprit is the new suburban Warner Village multiplex that's drawing local cinema-goers away from the centre of town.

The Italian dubbing industry is one of the biggest and best in the world, and most foreign films in Florence are shown in Italian without subtitles. The gorgeous art nouveau Odeon (p83), however, hosts a programme of the latest original-language films (mostly in English) with Italian subtitles on Mondays, Tuesdays and Thursdays, although as this guide went to press, rumours (and they are still just rumours) are rife about a possible closure here too, a move that would devastate the English-speaking expat community. The British Institute (p143) runs Talking Pictures on Wednesday evenings.

Movies are also usually screened in their original language at the city's important film festivals. The Festival de' Popoli (p37) is held in November/December, while the Premio Fiesole ai Maestri del Cinema (p35) takes place in Fiesole in July/August. The annual River to River Indian Film Festival (p37) is another December event where films are screened mostly in English or with English subtitles.

SHORTLIST

Best festivals
- Maggio Musicale Fiorentino (p33)
- Estate Fiesolana (p35)
- Festival dei Popoli (p37)
- Musica dei Popoli (p37)

Best for opera lovers
- Teatro del Maggio Musicale Fiorentino (p93)
- Estate Fiesolana (p35)

Most classic venues
- Teatro del Maggio Musicale Fiorentino (p93)
- Teatro Verdi (p125)
- Teatro della Pergola (p109)

Best live music venues
- Tenax (p149)
- Auditorium FLOG (p147)
- Jazz Club (p109)
- Caruso Jazz Café (p82)
- Girasol (p148)

Best for English-language film
- Odeon (p83)
- British Institute (p143)
- Festival dei Popoli (p37)
- River to River Indian Film Festival (p37)

Most beautiful settings
- Teatro della Pergola (p109)
- Piazzale Michelangelo (p152)
- Teatro Romano, Fiesole (p151)

Best for sports junkies
- Stadio Artemio Franchi (p150)
- Parco delle Cascine (p149)
- Florence Marathon (p37)

Best for dance enthusiasts
- Maggio Musicale Fiorentino (p33)
- Florence Dance Festival (p35)
- Fabbrica Europa (p33)

DON'T MISS

See the sights

Italian-style... with our Fiat 500 tours.

From €25

Experience Italy like a local with our unique, classic Fiat 500 self-drive convoy tours.

A cult symbol of Italian pride and style, our vintage Fiat 500's are your passport to nostalgic fun, generating a warm welcome wherever they go!

Take the wheel and follow the lead car for an uncomplicated and unforgettable cultural guided tour, complete with full commentary via radio relay. No map-reading, no fuss - just an authentic Italian experience.

Romantic for couples, great for groups and friends, the 500 Touring Club offers daily departures and a choice of routes and itneries.

For the independant explorer, our Fiat 500's are also available for private hire, with or without a chauffeur.

500 Touring Club

For more information please call or contact us below:
Tel. (+39) 055 286 886
UK Tel. (+44) 020 8123 8966

info@500touringclub.com
www.500touringclub.com

FIRENZE
The Club House
Via Vinegia 23 R
50122 Firenze
ITALIA

(Around the corner from Uffizi Gallery)

Summer madness

The long, hot Florentine summer sees a glut of performing arts and cinema events in open-air venues, some of them free. Alfresco bars such as the one in piazza Santo Spirito, the Parterre in piazza della Libertà and at the Rime Rampanti above piazza Poggi host almost nightly live music shows. Piazza della Signoria sees several high profile music (both classical and other) and dance events, the Boboli gardens becomes the setting for both opera and ballet performances and the atmospheric Teatro Romano at Fiesole hosts the Estate Fiesolana festival (p35) with its mixed bag of prose, opera, jazz and dance; the Florence Dance Festival summer edition (p35) is also held here. The high summer live entertainment at the Piazzale Michelangelo – mostly musical crowd-pleasers – comes with the stunning backdrop of the Arno and the glittering city lights. Classical concerts take place in churches, *piazze*, courtyards and cloisters with the odd jazz and world music line up in the mix. Open-air cinemas such as the Chiardiluna (via Monte Oliveto 1, 055 218682) and the Arena di Marte (p149) put on two screenings a night (mostly in Italian with the odd offering in its original language) of both blockbuster and less mainstream films.

Information and tickets

Some of the events and festivals mentioned above are regular fixtures while others are one-offs. Local newspapers (like *La Nazione* or the Firenze section of *La Repubblica*) carry up-to-date information, as do the English-language, fortnightly newspaper *The Florentine* and the English-language listings section of the monthly *Firenze Spettacolo*.

For opening nights of the opera at the Teatro del Maggio, tickets will often be sold out way in advance, but it's always worth turning up on the night for the chance of a return or to purchase one of the restricted-vision seats. However, tickets are also available online (www.maggiofiorentino.com) up to a week before the performance. For other classical, dance and theatre events, tickets will almost always be available on the door. For information on the main ticket agencies, see p187.

Sport and fitness

Few visitors come to Florence for its sporting life, but facilities are improving; the annual marathon (held in November; p37) attracts a growing number of participants and there are some excellent opportunities for spectators too.

Football fans should head to the Stadio Artemio Franchi (p150) on alternate Sunday afternoons from August to May to catch Florence's home team Fiorentina (now back in Serie A after a wobbly few years), known locally as Viola.

Florence is home to two race courses, both located in the riverside Cascine park. The Ippodromo Le Cascine (p149) hosts *galoppo*, or flat-racing, in April and May and September and October, while *il trotto* (trotting) takes place at the Ippodromo Le Mulina (p149) between November and March and June and July; here the driver sits in a carriage behind the horse.

Many Florentines head to the Parco delle Cascine (p149) for their daily run (or bike ride or roller blade session), but the wide, tree-lined viale Michelangelo, which winds up the hill south of the river, is another good bet; the many small lanes that lead off the viale will have you surrounded by idyllic countryside within minutes.

DON'T MISS

WHAT'S ON

Calendar

Scoppio del Carro

The following are the pick of the annual events that take place in Florence, as well as the major forthcoming one-off events. Further information and exact dates can be found nearer the time from flyers and seasonal guides available from tourist information centres (p187).

January

Ongoing **Nativities** (see Dec)

1 **New Year Concert**
Teatro Comunale, Corso Italia 12
055 597851
Put on by the Scuola di Musica di Fiesole. Call for free tickets.

Jan-Mar **Pinocchio Jazz Live Festival**
Pinocchio Jazz, p154
The best Italian jazz musicians, plus global talent, every Saturday night.

6 **La Befana (Epiphany)**
An old woman on a broomstick rewards good children with toys and sweets; naughty kids just get a sockful of coal.

February

Ongoing **Pinocchio Jazz Live Festival** (see Jan)

Throughout Feb **Carnevale**
Lungarno Amerigo Vespucci
www.ilcarnevale.com
Florentine children dress up and scatter confetti as part of the nationwide carnival celebrations.

18 **Elector Palatine commemoration day**
Piazza della Signoria (p54) to the Cappelle Medicee (p95)
A city procession on the anniversary of the death of Anna Maria Luisa – the last great figure of the Medici dynasty.

March

Ongoing **Pinocchio Jazz Live Festival** (see Jan)

8 **Festa della Donna**
International Women's Day: women are presented with yellow mimosas; in the evening, restaurants and bars get packed with girlie gangs on a night out.

Mar/Apr (date varies) **Holy Week**
Various venues
055 646051/www.rievstoricagrassina.it
Religious processions in the week leading up to Easter, often in period costume.

Easter Sunday (date varies)
Scoppio del Carro
Piazzale della Porta al Prato to
piazza del Duomo (p52), and
Santissimi Apostoli (p68)
Morning parades of costumed musicians, flag-throwers and dignitaries, culminating in a fireworks display.

April

Late Apr/early May & early Oct
Mostra Mercato di Piante e Fiori
Giardino dell'Orticoltura, via Vittorio
Emanuele 4, Other Districts
055 2625385
Spectacular horticultural shows held
for one week.

Late Apr-early July **Maggio
Musicale Fiorentino**
Teatro del Maggio Musicale
Fiorentino (p93); piazza della
Signoria (p54)
055 213535/www.maggiofiorentino.com
Florence's 'Musical May' is one of Italy's
best festivals for opera and dance, lasting around two months. It closes with
free jamborees in piazza della Signoria.

Apr/May **Settimana dei
Beni Culturali**
Various venues
055 290832
'Culture Week' means free admission
to state museums, including the Uffizi,
Bargello and Accademia.

May

Ongoing **Maggio Musicale
Fiorentino** (see Apr)

May **Fabbrica Europa**
Stazione Leopolda, p149
055 2480515/www.fabbricaeuropa.net
Innovative month-long festival of theatre, music, dance and multimedia arts.

May-July **Mese Mediceo**
Florence and province
055 6120205/www.mesemediceo.it

Galileo, Galileo...

In the late months of 1609,
Pisan mathematician Galileo
Galilei (1564-1642) first pointed
his newly invented telescope to
the night sky. His observations
confirming the Copernican theory
– which cost him the wrath of
the Vatican – are universally
acknowledged as the birth of
modern science. To mark the
400th anniversary of this event,
2009 has been declared the
International Year of Astronomy,
with events celebrating the
genius of Galileo in the Italian
cities in which he lived and
worked, including Florence.

The Florentine celebrations
are being supervised by the
Museo di Storia della Scienza
(p64), and two of the museum's
highlights – Galileo's original
telescopes – play the star role
in two successive exhibitions.
Until 30 September 2008, the
ground floor of the museum is
housing a temporary display
of Galileo's instruments, while
the two upper floors undergo
a refurbishment to reopen in
autumn 2009 as Museo Galileo.

Then from 5 March to 12
September 2009, Palazzo Strozzi
(p67) plays host to Macrocosm,
an exhibition recounting how the
universe was imagined from
antiquity to Galileo's times.

As we went to press, hopes
were fading that the other major
IYA2009 project, a Museum of
the Universe, set to occupy the
Torre del Gallo, could be open
in time; but follow Galileo's
lead and keep your eyes open,
just in case...

Artigianato e Palazzo

Original plays about the Medici family, staged in various historic locations.

6th Sun after Easter (date varies)
Festa del Grillo
Parco delle Cascine, p149
On the feast of Ascension, Florentine families picnic and chase mechanical crickets (traditionally it was live ones).

Mid May **Artigianato e Palazzo**
Palazzo Corsini sul Prato, via della Scala 115
055 2654589/www.artigianato epalazzo.it
Master artisans sell their wares at this weekend craft show in one of Tuscany's finest Italianate gardens.

May **Amico Museo**
Throughout Florence & Tuscany
www.regione.toscana.it/amicomuseo
Special and late openings and events over three weeks, to familiarise the crowds with lesser-known museums.

May **Genio Fiorentino**
Florence & around
055 2760061/www.geniofiorentino.it
Arts events over two weeks, exploring the elusive Florentine mentality, which has fostered a string of 'geniuses'.

Late May **Mille Miglia**
Across Tuscany
030 280036/www.millemiglia.it

Almost 400 vintage cars take part in this three-day, 1,600km (1,000 mile) race, which enters central Florence on a Saturday afternoon.

June

Ongoing **Maggio Musicale Fiorentino** (see Apr); **Mese Mediceo** (see May)

Oltrarno Atelier festival
Cango Cantieri Goldonetta
Firenze, p143
Five-day theatre and arts festival.

June-Sept **Outdoor cinema season**
Arena di Marte (p149), Forte di Belvedere (p143), Arena Raggio Verde (Palacongressi Firenze, viale Strozzi), Cinema Chiardiluna Arena (via Monte Oliveto 1)
Open-air cinema screenings after dusk.

June-Sept **Jazz&Co events**
Piazza della SS Annunziata, p106
www.firenzejazz.it
Jazz acts play nightly on the piazza della SS Annunziata's open-air stage.

June-July **Sant'Ambrogio Summer Festival**
Piazza Ghiberti, Loggia del Pesce in piazza dei Ciompi
www.firenzejazz.it

Florence Marathon p37

Hot, jazzy nights, with music swinging from bossanova and samba to jazz and blues tracks.

Mid June-early Sept
Estate Fiesolana
Fiesole
800 414240/www.estatefiesolana.it
Performing arts shows in scenic settings, such as the Roman theatre. The oldest open-air festival in Italy. The Vivere Jazz Festival is a highlight.

24 **Calcio Storico**
Piazza Santa Croce, p110
055 290832
See box p36.

24 **Festa di San Giovanni**
Throughout Florence
A public holiday in Florence. A fireworks display takes place in the evening near piazzale Michelangelo to honour the city's patron saint.

July

Ongoing **Maggio Musicale Fiorentino** (see Apr); **Mese Mediceo** (see May); **Outdoor cinema season** (see June); **Sant'Ambrogio Summer Festival** (see June); **Estate Fiesolana** (see June)

July/Aug **Premio Fiesole ai Maestri del Cinema**
Teatro Romano, p151
055 597107/www.comune.fiesole.fi.it
This two-week film festival pays homage to the works of one director. Recent honorands have included Spike Lee and Bernardo Bertolucci.

July & Dec **Florence Dance Festival**
Florence Dance Cultural Center, p143.
055 289276/www.florencedance.org
The month-long festival fuses some of the greatest names in contemporary and classical dance. A winter festival (p37) is held in Teatro Goldoni.

August

Ongoing **Outdoor cinema season** (see June); **Estate Fiesolana** (see June)

10 Aug **Calici di stelle**
Throughout Tuscany
www.movimentoturismovino.it
About 50 Tuscan 'Città del vino' participate in this 'wine under the stars' event.

September

Ongoing **Outdoor cinema season** (see June); **Estate Fiesolana** (see June)

All the rage

The Florentine sport of **calcio storico** certainly isn't for the fainthearted. Within minutes of the starting whistle in the 2006 semi-finals, the violence of this hybrid of football, rugby and boxing was so sudden and so severe that the game was called to an end before it had barely begun; the 2007 tournament was cancelled altogether. Although the 2008 tournament is still due to take place (fans were vocal about their disappointment over the cancelled games, with blogs and internet sites popping up by the dozen), the future of the game – which dates back to at least the early 16th century – is now looking rather uncertain. Best to watch the historical spectacle while you still can, before it's banned forever.

Also known as calcio in costume, or calcio fiorentino, calcio storico was in the past part of the training for Florence's citizens' militia, and reportedly shocked the invading armies of Charles V. It traditionally takes place in piazza Santa Croce (p110), with the final normally scheduled for 24 June.

The 50-minute match involves two teams taken from the four ancient Florentine districts (and kitted out in medieval garb) attempting to land a ball in their opponents' goalmouth – while fending off and initiating brutal physical attacks.

After the 2007 cancellation, the chief procuratore of Florence said he was considering making the rules of calcio storico a little closer to those of rugby, where you can only tackle or attack the person with the ball. Further safety precautions will dictate that all players must be a resident of their *quartiere*, to prevent the hiring of professional boxers and wrestlers. Furthermore, players will need to have criminal background checks. A friendly match took place in October 2007 to test the 2008 rules, which include teams training together in order to foster 'a love for the sport and fair play'. Fans argue, though, that the violent elements of the sport are an integral aspect of its heritage; whether the players can adhere to these new, modernising rules remains to be seen.

Sept **Settembre Musica**
Teatro della Pergola & other venues
055 608420/www.amicimusica.fi.it
A month of early music concerts, by
young or up-and-coming ensembles
with the odd bigger name.

7 Sept **La Rificolona**
Through central Florence
Children parade through the city with
candlelit paper lanterns (*rificolone*),
re-enacting a past pilgrimage of country folk. A fair is still held for the
occasion in piazza SS Annunziata.

Sept-Oct **Florence Queer Festival**
Various venues
www.ireos.org
A two-week showcase of films and
documentaries on GLBT issues, plus
theatre, literature, photography and
music events.

Late Sept-early Oct **Teatri Aperti**
Florence and metropolitan area
055 2779362/www.firenzedeiteatri.it
Seventeen theatres offer around 60
shows and events over ten days,
with the aim of disproving the notion
of theatre-going as a stuffy, passive
experience.

October

Ongoing **Florence Queer Festival**
(see Sept); **Teatri Aperti** (see
Sept)

1st wknd Oct **Musica dei Popoli**
Auditorium FLOG, p147
www.musicadeipopoli.com
This world music festival has varied
artists playing their original folk
sound, and is not to be missed.

Early Oct **Mostra Mercato
di Piante e Fiori**
Giardino dell'Orticoltura, via Vittorio
Emanuele 4
055 2625385
See April.

November

Last Sun **Florence Marathon**
Piazzale Michelangelo to piazza
Santa Croce, via the suburbs
055 5522957/www.firenzemarathon.it.

Nov or Dec **Festival dei Popoli**
Various clubs and cinemas
throughout Florence
055 244778
Drama and documentary screenings
centring around a social issue.

Nov **France Cinema**
French Institute, piazza Ognissanti
2 and Teatro della Compagnia,
via Cavour 50r
055 214053/www.francecinema.it
This festival, showcasing recent French
film releases, has grown in importance
over the past few years.

December

Dec **River to River Festival**
055 286929/www.rivertoriver.it
This annual Indian film festival shows
films mostly in English, or the original
language with English subtitles.

Dec **Florence Dance Festival**
Teatro Goldoni, p143
055 289276/www.florencedance.org
See July.

Dec-Jan **Nativities**
Various venues
Many churches set up Nativity scenes,
including the Duomo, San Lorenzo,
Santa Croce and Chiesa di Dante.

Early Dec **Christmas Market**
Piazza Santa Croce, p110
This 'Weihnachtsmarkt' has become a
destination for local shopping sprees in
the first two weeks of December.

24-26 **Christmas**
Ice-skating in piazza della Libertà and
a huge tree and an info booth in piazza
della Repubblica. The Uffizi puts up a
free themed exhibition.

24 Dec **Christmas Concert**
Teatro Verdi, p125
055 2340710/tickets 055 212320
An annual concert by the Orchestra
Regionale Toscana.

31 Dec **New Year's Eve**
Many Italians spend the night among
friends and family at home, with
a huge meal and firecrackers and
sparklers to 'burn' the past year and
welcome in the new.

www.treesforcities.org

Trees for Cities
Charity registration number 103215

Travelling creates so many
lasting memories.

Make your trip mean something for
years to come - not just for you but
for the environment and for people
living in deprived urban areas.

Anyone can offset their flights,
but when you plant trees with
Trees for Cities, you'll help create
a green space for an urban
community that really needs it.

To find out more visit
www.treesforcities.org

Leave
Your
Mark
Create a green future for cities.

Itineraries

Maurizio Balloni p42

The Artisan Way

Florence is rightly proud of its artistic and cultural wealth, with its museums, churches and monuments drawing millions of visitors from all over the world each year. But only a small minority of these visitors are aware of the more modest, but nonetheless valuable and unique, cultural and social heritage of an artisan community that has existed in the city for some 500 years.

Until the Medici moved into the Pitti Palace in the mid 16th century, the Oltrarno was a solidly working-class area with a bit of a reputation for low life. However, with the arrival of the royal family, Florentine bigwigs began to move into this district south of the Arno, building magnificent palaces in streets such as via Maggio and via Santo Spirito. With them came

the attendant cabinet-makers and restorers, wood-carvers, dressmakers and cobblers, metal workers and gilders that, added to the *botteghe* (workshops) already established in the area, made for a rich and varied pool of artisan talent that thrived for centuries.

Today's picture is very different and not all positive. The first big blow in recent times came with the 1966 flood, which drove dozens of artisans from their shops and forced many closures. Modern-day gentrification of the Oltrarno has also resulted in a rise in rents and many craftsmen being evicted from profitable residential properties. Those that remain have had to contend with increased taxes, a generally depressed market, new European health and safety standards and a lack of support

Enrico Giannini p42

Mimmo Muratore p42

from the local government. It's difficult to find apprentices these days – many young people haven't got the patience (or financial means) to put in the years it takes to learn these skills – and there's a danger that Florence's artisan tradition will simply die out.

On the bright side, an artisan community still exists in the Oltrarno (and this includes both old-timers and younger craftsmen, as well as a number of foreigners) that is fiercely proud of its trades and will do whatever it takes to carry on. Today's visitors to the area will find a delightful contrast to the grand monuments north of the river, with narrow streets dotted with shops and workshops where everything is still made by hand by master craftsmen practising skills handed down over centuries.

This itinerary focuses on an area in the western Oltrarno between **piazza della Passera** and **porta San Frediano**. Artisan *botteghe* don't keep to strict hours, but are usually open between about 8.30am and 12.30pm and 3pm to 6pm Monday to Friday. Note that the street numbers referred to in the addresses are almost exclusively red (for commercial addresses) rather than black (residential). Most artisans are happy for visitors to come to their workshops, as long as they are not too intrusive.

Breakfast at the **Caffè degli Artigiani** (p134) in charming piazza della Passera is an appropriate start to this walk, lying as it does at the heart of the artisan community. There are numerous workshops on the streets radiating out from the square, so take a bit of time to stroll around and see what you come across.

From the piazza, walk south (away from the river) along via Toscanella, a characteristically medieval street. On the left is

Borgheresi & Chiti (via Toscanella 31/r, 055 211437, www.bieci.it), which makes stars and lanterns from glass and brass. Next door is Timothy James' glass bead workshop and school. Attracted by the creative vibe of the Oltrarno, Tim and his jewellery-maker wife Lily Mordà moved to Florence from the US in 2005. Tim makes beautiful Venetian-style glass beads using traditional techniques and, in a perfect example of creative symbiosis, Lily works them into intricate pieces of jewellery that she sells in her nearby shop, **Beaded Lily** (p139).

A right turn down via dei Velluti takes you past several restoration workshops to **Enrico Giannini**'s little *bottega* (via dei Velluti 10/r, 055 2399657). The fifth generation of a famous clan of bookbinders and paper-makers, Giannini left the big family business to go back to his artisan roots and concentrate on quality rather than quantity. In his tiny workspace, dominated by several hefty presses and an old-fashioned paper-cutting machine, he makes marbled papers, binds books and crafts beautiful leather boxes decorated with gold leaf.

Backtrack to via Toscanella and continue down, then turn right onto Sdrucciolo de' Pitti. Here, on the opposite side, you'll find the **Sarubbi brothers**' map shop (no.11/r, 340 9842320, www.sarubbibros.com). The brothers, who inherited the business from their parents, make prints of wonderful 17th- and 18th-century maps from zinc plates and then hand-paint them.

Cross over via Maggio and to your right and left are some of Florence's most exclusive **antiques dealers**; this is where to come if you want to take a Renaissance chest or a Mannerist painting back home. If your budget is rather more humble, then skip this and walk straight down via Michelozzi towards piazza Santo Spirito. Historically, leather craft is one of the artisan skills most associated with Florence and this area was once full of *botteghe* producing *articoli in pelle*. Sadly, bespoke shoemaker **Roberto Ugolini** (via Michelozzi 17r, 055 216246, www.roberto-ugolini.com) is today one of only a handful of artisans working in leather in the area. Along with his Japanese apprentices, he works in full view of the street surrounded by wooden lasts and his gorgeous men's shoes.

Once in the piazza, turn left. The names of the medieval streets around here reflect the industries once carried out in them; via delle Caldaie (straight ahead) was home to wool dyers, while the workshops in nearby borgo Tegolaio produced roof tiles (*tegole*). At via delle Caldaie 14/r, pop into **Mimmo Muratore**'s workshop. Mimmo is one of a number of younger, less traditional artisans working in the Oltrarno. The third generation of a family of ironmongers, he learned his skill from his father and grandfather, but now uses this in a more contemporary context, working alongside his American girlfriend who designs many of his pieces. He makes big, wonderfully quirky lamps and chandeliers, plus chairs, hat stands and other smaller objects, all of which make arresting window displays.

Continue up the street and turn left into via del Campuccio. On the right is **Maurizio Balloni**'s furniture painting and restoration business (no.17/r, 055 2336782). Balloni decorates cabinets, screens, lamps, boxes and vases in styles ranging from the 17th to the 19th centuries and including trompe l'oeil techniques.

Walk back towards the piazza, turn left on via Sant' Agostino and left up via Maffia. Working from their *bottega*, on the right (just past an eccentric shop selling ancient plumbing gear), **Massimo Baldini** and **Daniele Nencioni** (no.54/r, 055 212195) are *intagliatori* (woodcarvers). With the help of two apprentices, they make models for sculptures to be cast in bronze and carve intricate frames, bas-reliefs, and decorative details for furniture.

Next, head west to piazza del Carmine and then, from here, north to borgo San Frediano. This is another street characterised by traditional craft- and workshops, and a detour along any of the narrow lanes running off it will turn up more *botteghe*. Beyond the church of San Frediano di Cestello is the splendidly named 'Street of the Golden Dragon' (to the left) where, towards the top, you'll find the **Ugolini brothers**' bronze workshop (via del Drago d'Oro 25r, 055 215 343, www.bronzisti ugolini.com). Founded in 1800, this family firm still uses traditional methods of casting, engraving and polishing bronze to produce exquisite lamps and lighting fixtures and decorative home accessories such as drawer and door handles.

Back on borgo San Frediano, continue west and then take a left up via di San Giovanni. **Corniciaio Pierluigi Franceschi** (no.11, 055 220642, www.franceschicornici. com) was born in the Oltrarno and learnt his picture-framing craft from his uncle. Today, the walls of his neat, bright workshop are hung with frames of all kinds, many of them in the elaborate gilded 14th- and 15th-century Florentine style. Nowadays, his most profitable work comes from foreign customers; one of his frames even graces a Mondrian piece in the Guggenheim Museum in New York.

The circuit finishes at one of the most impressive and atmospheric workshops of the Oltrarno. Backtrack east along borgo San Frediano, turn left into via Sant' Onofrio and left into via Bartolini. The **Antico Setificio Fiorentino** (via Bartolini 4, 055 213861, www. anticosetificiofiorentino.com), now owned by the Pucci family, is housed in an old building standing in a lovely garden. Silk was introduced into Italy by Catholic missionaries working in China in 1110, and by the 14th century silk weaving was flourishing in Florence, a situation that continued for several centuries. Around the mid 17th century, a number of the city's noblest families joined forces to establish a single silk-weaving workshop in which to place their looms, garment patterns and fabric designs; in 1780, in recognition of the prestige of this factory, Grand Duke Leopoldo of Lorraine-Medici donated a number of looms that are still in use today. The *setificio* moved to its present location in 1786, and, more than 200 years later, is still producing unique hand-dyed silk fabrics, mostly used for soft furnishings. Nine skilled weavers work on six 18th-century hand looms and six semi-mechanical 19th-century looms. For safety reasons, the workshop is not normally open to the public (although you might be allowed a peek through the door), but the showroom, with its creaky old floors and heavily beamed ceiling, is in itself a dream for anyone interested in fabric and interior design. The only catch is that the majority of visitors can't actually afford to buy anything.

If the timing is right, finish the trail with lunch at simple, rustic trattoria *Sabatino* (via Pisana 2/r, 055 225955). It's located just past porta San Frediano on the right.

ITINERARIES

Perini, Mercato Centrale p46

Florence for Foodies

Florence is a food and wine lover's dream with opportunities to eat, drink and shop for gastronomic treats around every corner. This walk starts south of the river at one of the most charming of the city's many neighbourhood markets and finishes in the largest and most vibrant market, stopping off along the way at some choice foodie spots. It must be done in the morning in order to find the markets open, so start good and early.

Dominated by the iconic façade of its church, **piazza Santo Spirito** (p126) lies at the heart of the Oltrarno, and it's here that the itinerary begins. With its central fountain and stone benches shaded by leafy trees, it's one of the city's most beautiful squares, but, far from being overrun with tourists, it still belongs to the locals during the day, who come here to do their shopping, have a coffee and a gossip, buy their cigarettes and try their luck with the lottery tickets on sale at the tabacconists.

Start the day well with breakfast at **Caffè Ricchi** (p134); the pastries are nothing special, but Daniele makes one of the best cappuccinos south of the Arno. From Monday to Saturday mornings, the square is home to a handful of **market stalls**. Some sell clothes and shoes, while those nearer the church offer superb fresh produce. Just to the left of Ricchi's terrace, Marcello and Lilliana's *banco* of fruit and veg is usually crowded with local shoppers who know that their bag of waxy lemons will come with a liberal helping of Marcello's raunchy humour. Next to the church is a cluster of smaller stalls, the realm of the *contadini* (farmers), selling super-fresh, hand-picked produce, yardstick of the passing seasons; bulbous, pale-green fennel and spiny artichokes in winter, aromatic melons and peaches and a glut of the ripest tomatoes in high summer.

One of Florence's best wine shops lies one block east of the square in

Mercato Centrale p46

Procacci

ITINERARIES

borgo Tegolaio. **Millesimi** (p141) is a treasure trove of wines from all over Italy; aside from Tuscany, Piemonte is well represented and there are some interesting labels from up-and-coming wine-producing areas such as Sicily and Puglia. Shipping charges to the UK are surprisingly reasonable.

From here, walk down by the side of the church to via Santo Spirito and **Olio e Convivium** (p137), across the road to your left. This smart grocer's-cum-restaurant is a great place to stock up on edible goodies to take home. Olive oil, sourced from all over Italy, is a speciality and you can taste before you buy. Olives are harvested between October and December and new oils start arriving from February; anything before then will be the previous year's leftovers. The selection changes each year just as the quality of each region's oil varies according to climatic and other conditions, but a good year will mean up to 60 different oils to choose from. The best time to taste is early spring when, with rising temperatures, the oil clarifies and becomes more liquid.

Cross ponte Santa Trinità and walk north into via de' Tornabuoni where, on the right just beyond via Strozzi and hidden among the designer flagship stores, you'll come to **Procacci** (p74), a genuine Florentine institution and the last bastion of 'Old Florence' on this now fashion-dominated street. In spite of having been acquired quite recently by the wine-making Antinori family, Procacci has retained its wonderful old-fashioned atmosphere and is surprisingly devoid of tourists. Inside, an air of genteel elegance prevails and the decor has changed little since the late 19th century when the store opened as a luxury grocer's specialising in truffles. *The* thing to order here is a glass of Prosecco and a *panino tartufato* or five (these delectable, truffle-cream filled rolls are minute).

If it's too early for Prosecco and truffles, turn right on via Strozzi and walk across piazza della Repubblica to one of Florence's historic cafés. **Gilli** (p73) is a belle-époque beauty with a retro-grand atmosphere in which to indulge in coffee and cakes or flavoured hot chocolate.

From here, head north up via Roma to piazza San Giovanni, and then up borgo San Lorenzo. Turn left along the north flank of the church of San Lorenzo and right into stall-lined via dell' Ariento. To allow enough time for a good browse around the central market, you need to arrive by noon, so a glass of wine and a snack at **La Casa del Vino** (p99) may have to wait. But be sure to pop in to the wonderfully authentic old place at some point. Wooden cabinets stacked with wine line the room, which is virtually devoid of seating but always packed. Fans come for a great selection of reasonably priced wines from all over Italy, accompanied by delicious sandwiches and *crostini*.

A few yards further on lies the magnificent 1874 cast-iron building that houses Florence's principal produce market, the **Mercato Centrale**. The earlier in the morning you visit, the more Florentine the atmosphere will be; the locals tend to do their shopping bright and early. Once inside the central doors on via dell' Ariento, you'll immediately be assailed by the vivid sights, sounds and smells of a big, bustling working market. The **upper level** (added in 1980) is crammed with vendors selling a fabulously colourful selection of seasonal fruit and veg, salad leaves, fresh herbs, dried fruit and nuts, pulses and spices.

The **ground floor** houses deli stalls, fishmongers, butchers, poulterers and general grocers, risky territory for vegetarians and those of a delicate disposition. From the main entrance, turn right and walk along the first aisle to the **Perini** brothers' spectacular gastronomia, hung with whole *prosciutti*, strings of dried chillis and plaited garlic. Under the high glass counters are dishes of marinated vegetables, olives, toppings for *crostini*, cheeses, salamis and relishes. You may have to wait a while to be served, but there are plates laden with nibbles to get the gastric juices going. On the other side of the main entrance is **Stefano Conti**'s stall, stacked with olive oils, balsamic vinegars (aged from ten to 100 years; 100ml of the latter will set you back around €300), dried mushrooms, sun-dried tomatoes, condiments and chutneys, honeys produced on Stefano's farm, and a select choice of new season's fresh produce. Across the aisle from here is the **Baroni brothers'** deli, with the best selection of cheeses in the market, sourced from all over Italy and France.

Follow this aisle back to the main entrance and opposite is **Oreste**'s offal stall, one of the oldest in the market and still sporting its original 1920s carved wood and wrought-ironwork and its marble counter piled with tripe, *lampredotto* (cow's intestines) *zampa* (pig's trotter) and *poppa* (udder). To your left, circling the central staircases, are some of the market's best **butchers**, where you can buy anything from a vast *bistecca alla fiorentina* to a suckling pig spiked with rosemary.

The north-west corner of the ground floor is the realm of the *pescherie*, or **fishmongers**. Until a few years ago, their exotic offerings were laid out on wonderful old marble slabs, but new health and hygiene laws demanded that they be replaced by much less romantic stainless steel.

To end the walk and to prove your foodie mettle, lunch has to be a *panino con lampredotto* at **Nerbone**'s food stall (p100) on the ground floor of the market. Boiled cow's intestines sandwiched between a fresh bread roll go down a treat accompanied by a glass of the house plonk. A snip at €3.50.

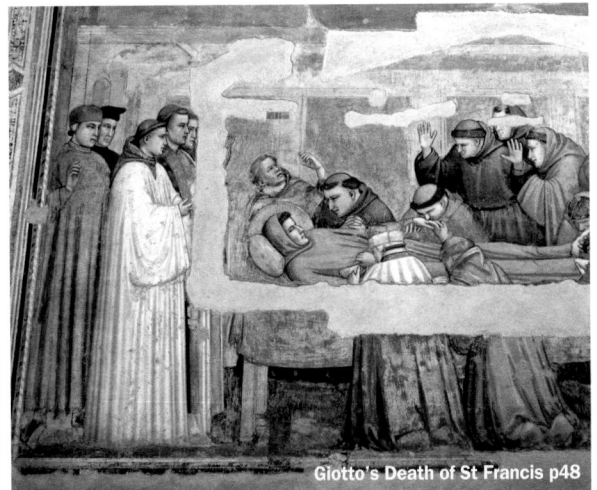
Giotto's Death of St Francis p48

Tracing the Renaissance

If you're in Florence for a short break and don't want to spend half your time queuing for the big art galleries like the Uffizi or the Accademia – or if you're here for a longer visit and wish to explore the Renaissance city beyond the walls of a museum – then this day-long itinerary could be a good bet. It will take you on a walking tour of some of the city's best frescoed chapels, providing a relaxed and organic way of learning about a crucial passage in art: the transition from medieval to Renaissance culture. Tuesday is the least suitable day to undertake the itinerary, because one of its highlights – Santa Maria del Carmine's Brancacci Chapel – is closed all day. Sundays also aren't ideal because of morning Mass.

The first step is to call the Cappella Brancacci reservation number (ideally a week in advance; 055 2768224) to book your visit – ideally to coincide with the 12pm showing of the documentary. If the 12pm slot is fully booked, the 11am or 1pm ones are also feasible. Booking is a must in the tourist high season, when you shouldn't risk simply trying your luck and arriving unannounced.

The Renaissance was the intellectual and artistic movement that flourished in Florence between the 14th and 16th centuries, when Humanist artists and scholars reinterpreted the classical heritage of Greece and Rome, rediscovering their philosophy, art, sculpture, architecture and literature.

During the medieval period, artworks had primarily been commissioned by the Catholic Church. However, from the 14th century, the wealthy families of Florence – who had become rich from the medieval cloth and banking businesses – began entrusting artists to decorate their chapels and palaces with sumptuous images. This kept the city at the forefront of the artistic and intellectual world during the 15th and 16th centuries, as artists and intellectuals mingled in the city, vying for patronage. Fresco painting (paintings done rapidly in watercolour on wet plaster) was particularly popular among artists because it was economical, and became a good way of promoting one's fame.

In the 1320s, the Bardi, a powerful banking family, commissioned **Giotto di Bondone** (1267-1337) to decorate their chapel in the Franciscan church of Santa Croce (p117), and it's here that this itinerary begins. The church opens at 9.30am (1pm on Sundays). If the route to reach Santa Croce from your hotel passes through borgo degli Albizi, north of the church, then stop off at **I Dolci di Patrizio Cosi** (p122) to savour one of the mouth-watering pastries and to fuel the day ahead.

Santa Croce is accessed through a gate to the left of the church. Buy your ticket and enter the church, parts of which are unfortunately covered in scaffolding (notably the main chapel – restoration is expected to last into 2010).

Giotto, a contemporary of Dante Alighieri, worked with his assistants here in the **Bardi** and **Peruzzi** chapels, on the east side, around 1320-28. Just as Dante abandoned Latin and wrote his *Divina Commedia* in vernacular Italian, Giotto abandoned the disembodied figures of medieval paintings and

opted for a comparatively free arrangement and accessible style. This stylistic shift incorporated greater human expression and began the interest in perspective. His Santa Croce work (technically not frescoes, but tempera murals) was whitewashed in 1714-30, but accidentally recovered after 1841-50. Although obscured by tombs and damaged by the 1966 flood, the figures in the *Death of St Francis*, in the Bardi Chapel, are set in a believable environment full of emotion. Giotto's work later influenced Masaccio's Cappella Brancacci, which we'll come to later, as well as Michelangelo, who is known to have studied the Peruzzi chapel paintings.

Take your time to look around the church, the cloisters (making sure not to miss **Brunelleschi**'s **Pazzi Chapel** in the first cloister) and the **Museo dell'Opera** (p114; the visit takes an hour on average) containing **Cimabue**'s (1240-1302) painted *Crucifix* – one of the works that was most damaged in the flood; with its ties to the previous Byzantine tradition, this work brings Giotto's naturalism into focus.

From the far western side of piazza Santa Croce, walk left along via de' Benci to the lungarno. If your Brancacci booking is for 11am and time is pressing, then cross the ponte alle Grazie and take the number D minibus from the other side, straight to piazza del Carmine (buy your ticket before boarding). If you've time to spare, however, then take the leisurely 30-minute stroll to the next destination. This involves walking beside the Arno along the *lungarni,* past the Uffizi Gallery – with its long queues that you're now avoiding – until you reach the **ponte Vecchio** (p55) flanked with gold jewellery shops; built in 1345, it's the only bridge in Florence that survived World War II.

Masaccio's Tribute Money

Cross the bridge and then turn right into borgo San Jacopo and walk the length of it. Near the corner with via Maggio – marked by a marble fountain by Bernardo Buontalenti – one of the city's oldest greengrocers (established in 1910) may tempt you to grab a piece of fruit for refreshment. Pass via Maggio and proceed ahead into via Santo Spirito, then cross via de' Serragli and continue down borgo San Frediano till the first intersection to the left, where you'll see the church of **Santa Maria del Carmine** (p132), famous for its **Cappella Brancacci**, at the far end of the square. Enter via the door on the right-hand-side.

A 40-minute documentary will tell you all you need to know about the chapel's groundbreaking frescoes started by **Masolino** and the younger **Masaccio** in 1424-28, and completed by Filippino Lippi after 1480. Once inside the chapel itself, compare the figures of Adam and Eve by Masolino (*The Fall*) and Masaccio (*The Expulsion from Paradise*) to grasp Masaccio's

innovative style. Masaccio (1401-28) was one of the first artists to apply perspective to painting and to aim at realism in art, with his character's, like Giotto's, clearly displaying emotion. In the *Tribute Money*, attributed largely to Masaccio, the artist transposed figures from the Orsanmichele (p67) to painting, depicting events from the life of St Peter. The work is a landmark example of how early Renaissance painting took its cue from sculpture, attempting to create the same sense of naturalism on a two-dimensional scale.

Before heading for the Dominican church of **Santa Maria Novella** (p87), stop for a light bite (cake and coffee or a platter of cheese and salami with a glass of house red) in the nearby, relaxed **LibreriaCafé La Cité** (p139), where you can mull over what you've learnt so far.

Then, retrace your steps down borgo San Frediano, turn left into via de' Serragli and cross the Arno. On the other side of ponte alla Carraia is piazza Goldoni. Via de' Fossi (between the gallery and the pharmacy) affords some quality window shopping for antiques and fine arts before it opens onto piazza Santa Maria Novella. The entrance to the church is on the right side of the elegant façade by Leon Battista Alberti, Florence's only finished Renaissance churchfront. Upon entering the fine late-Gothic church, lift your eyes to the overhanging Crucifix on your right and think back to Cimabue's in Santa Croce. This one is by Giotto, Cimabue's pupil. Then head to **Masaccio**'s *Trinity* fresco, opposite the entrance. Painted in 1427-28 and, like the Giottos in Santa Croce, obliterated for centuries and only rediscovered accidentally in the 1800s, this is widely acknowledged as a breakthrough in the rendering of perspective. Allegedly, Masaccio sought Brunelleschi's advice to paint the vaulted architecture, and indeed the resemblance with Santa Croce's Pazzi Chapel (which you saw earlier, and which Brunelleschi started one year after this was painted) is remarkable. Where you stand when viewing this painting is important – a distance of 6.12 metres is regarded as the point at which to appreciate the work to the full. After this, walk down the left nave to the plain chapel at the bottom, and you'll find a wooden crucifix by Brunelleschi: note the uncanny resemblance with the Christ in Masaccio's *Trinity*.

The church's **Strozzi Chapel**, frescoed in 1487-1502 by Filippino Lippi, was under restoration at the time of writing. But it's the **Tornabuoni Chapel,** behind the main altar, that holds most relevance for this itinerary. Its impressive fresco cycles by **Domenico Ghirlandaio** (1449-94) dating from 1485-90, depict the stories of the Virgin Mary (left wall) and St John the Baptist (right wall) against 15th-century Florentine

backdrops. A young Michelangelo may have worked here as an apprentice in Ghirlandaio's workshop. The striking stained glass window was also made to Ghirlandaio's design, and the central panel makes another reference to the architecture in Masaccio's *Trinity*.

Take your time to admire all the artworks in the church. When you are finished, the time should be approaching 4pm, which is when the church of **Santa Trinita** (p88), our last destination for the day, opens for the afternoon. From Santa Maria Novella, you reach it by way of via del Sole (left at the bottom of the piazza), which merges into via della Spada a few steps before via Tornabuoni. From here you head right, back towards the Arno. Santa Trinita, overlooking its eponymous piazza, lies just before the bridge. The church is unjustly ignored by tourists: you'll probably have the building all to yourself. There's no admission charge, but you'll need a few coins to operate the lighting (€0.50 every two minutes) of the recently restored **Sassetti Chapel**, **Ghirlandaio**'s other masterpiece, frescoed with the stories of St Francis in 1483, two years before he started working in Santa Maria Novella. The *Nativity* altarpiece, also by Ghirlandaio, shows the painter self-portrayed in the kneeling shepherd pointing at Baby Jesus. This chapel is considered an invaluable snapshot of Florence at the time of Lorenzo il Magnifico (1449-92), featuring as it does some of the city's most prominent Renaissance personalities.

Now turn back to page 47 and compare Ghirlandaio's bottom right scene in this chapel – the *Death of St Francis* – with Giotto's in Santa Croce. Today's tour palpably comes full circle: 160 years later, Giotto's heritage is still unmistakable.

Florence by Area

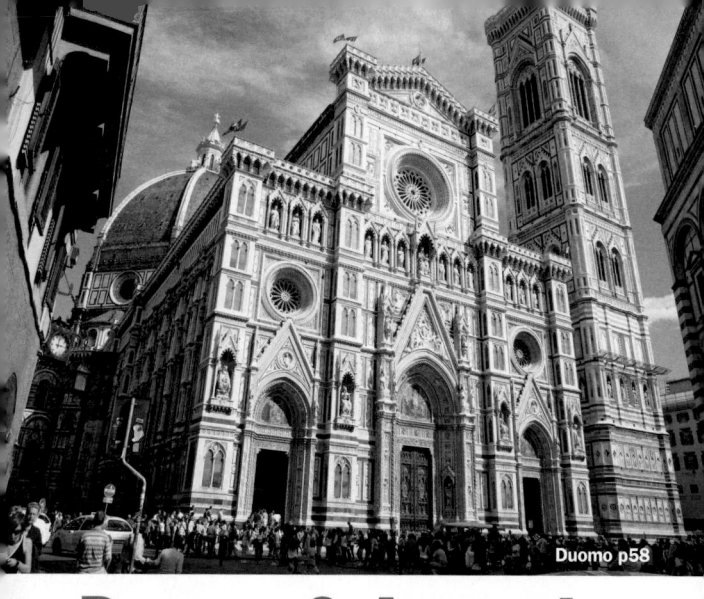

Duomo p58

Duomo & Around

Stretching from the streets just north of the Duomo to the ponte Vecchio, the compact central area of the city corresponds almost exactly to the city walls of the ninth century. As the original nucleus of Florence, it's the ideal place to start your explorations, taking in both the former administrative hub of piazza della Signoria and the religious and cultural heartland around the astounding **Duomo** – one of Europe's most recognised landmarks. The cathedral is so huge that there's no spot nearby from which you can see the whole thing. Many of the cathedral's artistic treasures, as well as the machinery used to build the magnificent structure, are now to be found in the fascinating **Museo dell'Opera del Duomo**, in the north-east side of piazza del

Duomo, while the octagonal, marble-clad **Baptistery** stands facing the Duomo's main doors, in tourist-packed **piazza San Giovanni**.

West of the Baptistery is via de' Cerretani, home to the 11th-century **Santa Maria Maggiore**, while running down from the building's south-west corner is the more upmarket via Roma, which opens into the pompous **piazza della Repubblica**, flanked by pavement cafés, and dominated at night by street artists and strollers.

South from the Duomo's façade is via de' Calzaiuoli, a heaving, pedestrianised shopping street and the main thoroughfare between the Duomo and piazza della Signoria. Here lies the main entrance to the church of **Orsanmichele**, a relic of the city's guilds that's famous for its statue-filled external niches.

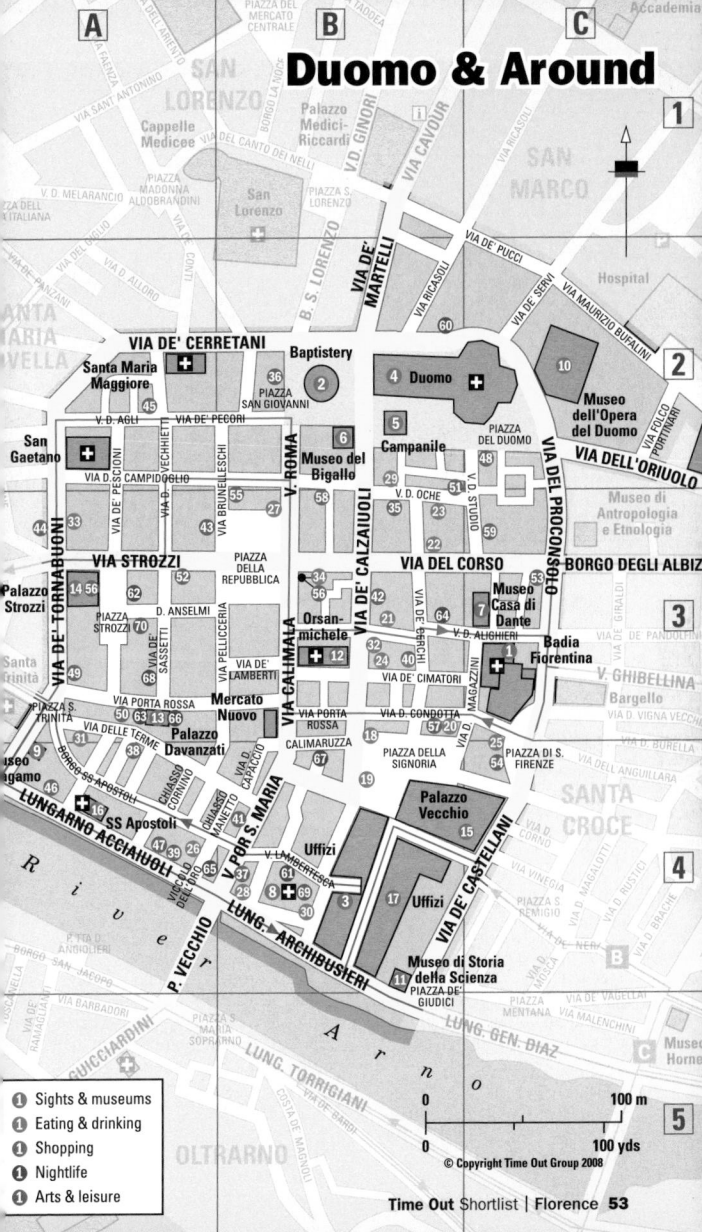

Duomo & Around

A | **B** | **C**

1 | **2** | **3** | **4** | **5**

VIA DELL'ARIENTO
PIAZZA DEL MERCATO CENTRALE
VIA TAODEA
Accademia
VIA SANT'ANTONINO
SAN LORENZO
BORGO LA NOCE
Palazzo Medici-Riccardi
VIA CAVOUR
SAN MARCO
Cappelle Medicee
VIA DEL CANTO DEI NELLI
VIA DE' GORI
PIAZZA S. LORENZO
VIA DE' MARTELLI
VIA RICASOLI
VIA DE' PUCCI
V. D. MELARANCIO
PIAZZA MADONNA ALDOBRANDINI
San Lorenzo
B. S. LORENZO
VIA DE' SERVI
VIA MAURIZIO BUFALINI
PIAZZA DELL' ITALIANA
VIA DELL' OLIO
VIA D. ALLORO
Hospital
V. D. PANZANI

VIA DE' CERRETANI
Baptistery
4 Duomo
10
Museo dell'Opera del Duomo
VIA DELL'ORIUOLO

Santa Maria Maggiore
36
PIAZZA SAN GIOVANNI
2
5
Campanile
PIAZZA DEL DUOMO
45
V. D. AGLI
VIA DE' PECORI
6
Museo del Bigallo
48
VIA FOLCO PORTINARI

San Gaetano
VECCHIETTI
VIA DE' PESCIONI
CAMPIDOGLIO
V. BRUNELLESCHI
V. ROMA
51
V. D. OCHE
23
59
Museo di Antropologia e Etnologia

33
VIA DE' PESCIONI
43
27
58
35
22
BORGO DEGLI ALBIZ
44
VIA STROZZI
PIAZZA DELLA REPUBBLICA
34
VIA DEL CORSO
VIA D. STUDIO
V. DI PANDOLFINI

Palazzo Strozzi
14 56
62
52
D. ANSELMI
56
VIA DE' CALZAIUOLI
21
64
7
Museo Casa di Dante
53
Badia Fiorentina
49
PIAZZA STROZZI
70
VIA DE' SASSETTI
VIA PELLICCERIA
Orsanmichele
32
40
V. D. ALIGHIERI
1
V. GHIBELLINA

Santa Trinita
68
VIA PORTA ROSSA
Mercato Nuovo
12
VIA DE' MARCHI
24
VIA DE' CIMATORI
Bargello
V. D. VIGNA VECCHIA
50 63 13 66
VIA DELLE TERME
Palazzo Davanzati
VIA PORTA ROSSA
CALIMARUZZA
VIA D. CONDOTTA
57 20
PIAZZA DI S. FIRENZE
V. D. BURELLA

31
BORGO SS APOSTOLI
38
CHIASSO CORNINO
CHIASSO MANETTO
13
PIAZZA DELLA SIGNORIA
54
SANTA CROCE
46
SS Apostoli
CALIMALA
19
VIA D. ANGUILLARA

16
47 39 26
V. LAMBERTESCA
61
Uffizi
Palazzo Vecchio
15
VIA DE' CASTELLANI
VIA DE' NERI

P. VECCHIO
65
V. POR S. MARIA
8 69
30
3
17 Uffizi
VIA VINEGIA
VIA D. BRACHE

LUNGARNO ACCIAIUOLI
LUNG. ARCHIBUSIERI
Museo di Storia della Scienza
11
PIAZZA DE' GIUDICI
LUNG. GEN. DIAZ
Museo Horne

River
Arno
LUNG. TORRIGIANI
COSTA DE' BARDI

OLTRARNO

- **1** Sights & museums
- **1** Eating & drinking
- **1** Shopping
- **1** Nightlife
- **1** Arts & leisure

0 ___ 100 m
0 ___ 100 yds

© Copyright Time Out Group 2008

Piazza della Signoria

Facing it is the Gothic **Madonna of the Trumpet** tabernacle.

The south-east corner of this district is home to Florence's civic showpiece square, **piazza della Signoria**. Although filled with tour groups, it's nevertheless a delightful space, and has been the focus of civic – though not necessarily civilised – activity since its creation in the late 13th century. It was here that the religious and political reformer Girolamo Savonarola lit his so-called **Bonfire of the Vanities** in 1497. The piazza is dominated by the **Palazzo Vecchio**; completed at the end of the 13th century as the seat of the Signoria (the top tier of the city's government), the building is visible from almost any point in the city, and still houses the main local government offices.

The square is also home to several very familiar sculptures, including a copy of Michelangelo's **David** (the original is in the Accademia), Giambologna's equestrian bronze of **Cosimo I**, notable for the horse cast as a single piece, and Ammannati's **Neptune** fountain, of which Michelangelo is reputed to have wailed, 'Ammannati, what beautiful marble you have ruined.' Beyond the fountain are copies of Donatello's **Marzocco** (the original of this heraldic lion is in the Bargello) and **Judith and Holofernes** (the original is in Palazzo Vecchio). Beyond *David* is **Hercules and Cacus** by Bandinelli, described by Benvenuto Cellini as a 'sack of melons'. Cellini himself is represented by a fabulous **Perseus** standing victorious in the adjacent **Loggia dei Lanzi**. Also in the loggia is Giambologna's spiralling marble **Rape of the Sabine Women**.

Leading down to the river from piazza della Signoria, the piazzale degli Uffizi is home to the world-renowned **Galleria degli Uffizi**. Head north from here and you'll

The statues at either end represent the four seasons, and were placed there in 1608 to celebrate Cosimo II's marriage to Maria of Austria.

North of **piazza Santa Trinita**, and marking the western border of the district is the designer shopping mecca of **via de' Tornabuoni**, dominated by the gargantuan stones of **Palazzo Strozzi**.

Sights & museums

Badia Fiorentina
Via Dante Alighieri (055 264402). **Open** *Cloister* 3-6pm Mon. *Church* 3-6pm Mon; 7am-6pm Tue-Sat. **Admission** donation to Eucharist. **Map** p53 C3 ❶.

A Benedictine abbey founded in the tenth century by Willa, mother of Ugo, Margrave of Tuscany, the Badia Fiorentina was the richest religious institution in medieval Florence. Willa had been deeply influenced by Romuald, a monk who travelled around Tuscany denouncing the wickedness of the clergy, flagellating himself and urging the rich to build monasteries; it was Romuald who persuaded Willa to found the Badia in 978.

Ugo, considered a visionary leader in his time, lavished money and land on what was then known as the Badia Florentia, and was eventually buried there in a Roman sarcophagus (later replaced by a tomb by Renaissance sculptor Mino da Fiesole) that's still housed in the abbey.

It was here in 1274, just across the street from his probable birthplace, that the eight-year-old Dante fell in love at first sight with Beatrice Portinari. He was devastated when her family arranged her marriage, at the age of 17, to Simone de' Bardi, and absolutely crushed when she died seven years later.

The Badia has been rebuilt many times since Dante's day, but still retains a graceful Romanesque campanile and an exquisite carved ceiling. The Chiostro degli Aranci dates from 1430 and is frescoed with scenes from the life of San Bernardo. Inside the church,

find the entrance to the **Badia Fiorentina** on via del Proconsolo, its elegant stone tower visible for the first time in years after a painfully drawn-out restoration. This is Danteland, with the **Museo Casa di Dante** and the **Chiesa di Dante** – the lovely little church where Dante's beloved Beatrice is buried – a stone's throw away.

Back at the river end of the Uffizi and to the west is the landmark **ponte Vecchio**, with its rows of gold jewellery shops, while further along, in the district's south-west corner, is the **ponte Santa Trinita**, considered by many to be the most beautiful bridge in the world. Named for Santa Trinita church directly north (p88), the bridge was first built in 1252 on the initiative of the Frescobaldi family, and then rebuilt in 1346 and again in 1567 by Ammannati. It was bombed in 1944 by retreating Germans, but reconstructed using the original stones salvaged from the Arno.

Vista esclusiva sulle più belle città d'Italia

Unique view of the most beautiful italian cities

Bernardo is celebrated once again, in a painting by Filippino Lippi. The Cappella dei Pandolfini is where writer Giovanni Boccaccio held the first public reading of the works of Dante.

Baptistery

Piazza San Giovanni (055 2302885/ www.duomofirenze.it). **Open** 12.15-6.30pm Mon-Sat; 8.30am-1pm Sun. **Admission** €3. No credit cards. **Map** p53 B2 ❷

For centuries, the likes of Brunelleschi and Alberti believed the Baptistery was converted from a Roman temple dedicated to Mars. Other scholars reckoned that the Roman site on which the octagonal church was built was the Praetorium, while still more thought its ancient origins were as a bakery. In fact, the Baptistery of St John the Baptist, patron saint of Florence, was built to an octagonal design between 1059 and 1128 as a remodelling of a sixth- or seventh-century version. In between, it functioned for a period as the cathedral for Florence (then Florentia) in place of Santa Reparata. The octagon reappears most obviously in the shape of the cathedral dome, but also on the buttresses of the Campanile, which constitute its corners. It's also the shape of the remains of the original font where children, including many of the Medici family and the poet Dante, were brought for a double baptism: both as a Christian and as a Florentine. The font near the exit that you can see today was installed in 1658, and the reliefs that decorate it are attributed to Andrea Pisano or his school.

Today, the striped octagon is best known for its gilded bronze doors. In the winter of 1400, the Calimala guild of cloth importers held a competition to find an artist to create a pair of bronze doors for the Baptistery's north entrance. Judging works by seven artists, Brunelleschi among them, they gave the commission to Ghiberti, then just 20 years old. (Brunelleschi later got revenge with superior work on the cupola but never sculpted again.) The 28 relief panels on the three-tonne, 6m-high (20ft) doors tell the story of Christ from the Annunciation to the Crucifixion; the eight lower panels show the four evangelists and four doctors of the Church. The deep pictorial space and an emphasis on figures makes many scholars believe that these doors contain the very first signs of Renaissance art.

No sooner had the north doors been installed than the Calimala commissioned Ghiberti to make another pair: the even more remarkable east doors – described by Vasari as 'undeniably perfect in every way' – took the artist and his workshop (including Michelozzo and Benozzo Gozzoli) 27 years to complete. They're known, since Michelangelo coined the phrase, as the 'Gates of Paradise' (although 'paradise' is, in fact, what the area between a baptistery and its church is called). The doors you see are copies (the originals are in the Museo dell'Opera del Duomo; p64), but the casts are good enough that it's not difficult to appreciate Ghiberti's extraordinary work, especially his fine use of the recently discovered principles of perspective.

The very first set of Baptistery doors were those on the south side, completed by Andrea Pisano in 1336, after only six years of work. The doors are composed of 28 Gothic quatrefoil-framed panels depicting scenes from the life of St John the Baptist and the eight theological and cardinal virtues. The Latin inscription on top of the door translates as 'Andrea Pisano made me in 1330'.

The Baptistery's interior is also worth visiting for the dazzling *Last Judgement* mosaic lining the vault ceiling, with the 8m-high (26ft) mosaic figure of *Christ in Judgement* dominating the apse (1225). The mosaics depicting Hell are thought to have inspired Dante's *Inferno*. The geometrically patterned marble mosaic floor showing oriental zodiac motifs was begun in 1209. Squeezed between two columns, the tomb of Antipope John XXIII (Baldassare Coscia) was designed by Donatello and his student Michelozzo in the 1420s.

FLORENCE BY AREA

Baptistery bronze doors p57

Collezione Contini-Bonacossi

Palazzo degli Uffizi, entrance on via Lambertesca (055 294883). **Open** guided group visits by appt only. **Admission** free. **Map** p53 B4 ❸

An impressive collection donated to the state by the Contini-Bonacossi family in 1974, and acquired by the Uffizi in 1998. Exhibits include renderings of the *Madonna and Child* by Duccio, Cimabue and Andrea del Castagno, and a roomful of works by artistic VIPs (like Bernini and Tintoretto). El Greco, Velázquez and Goya are numbered among the foreigners who are considered prestigious enough for the collection.

Duomo (Santa Maria del Fiore)

Piazza del Duomo (055 2302885/ www.duomofirenze.it). **Open** 10am-5pm Mon-Wed, Fri; 10am-4pm Thur; 10am-4.45pm Sat (except 1st Sat of mth, 10am-3.30pm); 1.30-4.45pm Sun. **Admission** free. **Map** p53 B2/C2 ❹

Florence's most important religious building is a truly awe-inspiring sight. It not only dominates the skyline but it represents the geographical, cultural and historical centre of the city and is the result of years of work spanning over six centuries. A hugely successful and expanding wool industry gave the Florentine population such a boost in the 13th century that several new churches had to be built; Santa Croce (p117) and Santa Maria Novella (p87) were among them, but the most important of all was Santa Maria del Fiore, or the Duomo, which replaced the small church of Santa Reparata. The project marked the first time that a guild of laymen had been entrusted with financing the city's development – traditionally, this responsibility had fallen to monks and priests. It thus marks the point at which religious architecture became a civic duty.

The building was commissioned by the Florentine Republic as an opportunity to show Florence off as the most important Tuscan city. The competition to find an architect was won by Arnolfo di Cambio, a sculptor from Pisa, and the first stones were laid on 8 September 1296 around the exterior

Piazza San Giovanni p52

of Santa Reparata. Building continued for the next 170 years with guidance and revision from three further architects, though the church was consecrated 30 years before its completion in 1436 (at which time it was the largest cathedral in Europe).

The rich exterior, in white Carrara, green Prato and red Maremma marbles, reflects the variety of time periods that work on the building covered, with a huge variation in the styles of the inlaid patterns. The visionary Francesco Talenti had sufficient confidence to enlarge the cathedral and prepare the building for Brunelleschi's inspired dome, which wasn't completed until 1436. The last significant change came in the 19th century, when Emilio de Fabris designed a neo-Gothic façade. After his death, Luigi del Moro was left to crown the façade.

After the splendid exterior, the interior looks somewhat dull, but it's actually full of fascinating peculiarities: notably, the clock on the Paolo Uccello inner façade, which marks 24 hours, operates anti-clockwise and starts its

days at sunset (it's between four and six hours fast). The clock is surrounded by the so-called Heads of the Prophets peering out from four roundels and showing the influences of Ghiberti and Donatello.

Also by Uccello is a monument to Sir John Hawkwood, painted in 1436 as a tribute to the English soldier who led Florentine troops to victory in the Battle of Cascina of 1364. The fresco has given rise to a debate about whether its perspective and the movement of the horse's right legs are wrong, or an original treatment of perspective construction, learned from Masaccio and considered by some to be visionary and even a forerunner to Cubism. Beyond Andrea del Castagno's 1456 monument to Niccolò da Tolentino, illustrating the heroic characteristics of a Renaissance man, is Domenico di Michelino's *Dante Explaining the Divine Comedy*, featuring the poet in pink and the new Duomo vying for prominence with the Mountain of Purgatory.

A couple of strides put you directly underneath the dome, the size of which

The big cover-up

Peter Paul Rubens' copy of Leonardo's Battle of Anghiari

An investigation into a long-lost Leonardo da Vinci masterpiece is under way in Florence's Palazzo Vecchio (p68) – and it's proving that real life can rival fiction when it comes to raising interest in the Renaissance master. The project is being led by biomedical engineer turned art 'diagnostician' Maurizio Seracini, who's been searching for the *Battle of Anghiari* since 1975.

The Florentine Republic commissioned both Leonardo and Michelangelo to paint two murals in the Palazzo's Hall of the Five Hundred in 1503. Michelangelo's work stopped at the preparatory stage but Leonardo is thought to have completed 15-20sq m of his mural, depicting a fierce clash of war-horses. The painting was left unfinished in 1506, but documentary evidence confirms it was still visible in 1549. Between 1563 and 1572, though, the reinstated Medici instructed Vasari to remodel the hall and paint over anything celebrating the Republic,

including Leonardo's work. Vasari complied.

Or did he? Fast-forward to 1975, and Seracini notices a green flag in Vasari's *Battle of Marciano* bearing two words: 'Cerca trova' ('Seek and you shall find'). Following this lead, Seracini then detects – through the use of laser beams and a thermo-scanner – a 3cm gap behind Vasari's work, suggesting the presence of a hidden inner wall. Might Vasari have saved the masterpiece by covering it up with another wall, and then adding the 'cerca trova' clue for posterity?

Hampered by a lack of funding, Seracini's past attempts to find the answer have been thwarted. But in autumn 2007, armed with new sponsors and more advanced technology, he began a final search for the mural, scanning the wall with medical devices, such as X-rays and thermo-scanners, to find traces of the pigments Leonardo is known to have used. He expects to have decisive answers by the end of 2008. 'Up to now', he says, 'we have not found anything that proves that the mural is not there.'

Seracini believes that the mural 'would be in the same condition now as it was then', as the wall in front would have acted as a protective layer. He also asserts that it would be possible to extract the painting without damaging whatever sits in front of it, but the issue of whether or not to do so would be out of Seracini's hands. 'It will become a political issue.'

See www.editech.com for info.

is even more breathtaking inside than out. The lantern in the centre is 90m (295ft) above you and the diameter of the inner dome is 43m (141ft) across, housing within it one of the largest frescoed surfaces in the world. Brunelleschi had intended for the inner cupola to be mosaic, to mirror the Baptistery ceiling. However, interior work began some 125 years after his death in 1572, when Cosimo de' Medici commissioned Giorgio Vasari to carry out the work; together with Don Vincenzo Borghini, who chose the iconographic subjects, they decided to fresco the surface instead.

The concentric rows of images were started by Vasari, who drew inspiration from Michelangelo's Sistine Chapel, but he died two years later before completing the project, and was succeeded by Federico Zuccari, who worked for a further five years until its completion. Zuccari had a much more flamboyant (and crude) dry-painting style, believing that the distance from which the visitor would view the cupola wasted the delicacy of Vasari's wet fresco technique. Zuccari's most crucial contribution is the rendering of Dante's vision of Hell inspired by Signorelli's frescoes in Orvieto Cathedral.

Crypt of Santa Reparata

Open 10am-5pm Mon-Wed, Fri; 10am-3.30pm Thur; 10am-4.45pm Sat (except 1st Sat of mth, 10am-3.30pm); 1.30-4.45pm Sun. **Admission** €3. No credit cards.

By the 13th century, Santa Reparata had served as the city's main church for some 900 years and desperately needed to be replaced, especially as, after a period of rapid population expansion, it had become too small to serve the needs of the community. It was decided in 1293 that a new cathedral was to be built over the top of the original church (the original date of which is unknown, but between the fifth and seventh centuries). The entrance to this is inside the Duomo itself. The intricate mosaic floor of the church was built only 30cm (12in) above the Roman remains of houses and shops,

some of which are on display in the crypt. Also here is the tomb of Brunelleschi; no trace has ever been found of those of Arnolfo di Cambio and Giotto, both also supposedly buried here.

Excavations to the building in the mid 1960s to 1970s unearthed the original crypt and medieval ruins, which are now on view for visitors.

Cupola/Dome

Open 8.30am-6.20pm Mon-Fri; 8.30am-5pm Sat (except 1st Sat of mth, 8.30am-3.20pm). **Admission** €6. No credit cards. The spectacular 37,000-tonne dome constructed with more than four million bricks is, as Alberti put it, 'a structure so immense, rising above the skies [that it is] broad enough to cover with its shadow all the peoples of Tuscany'. But the dome isn't just visually stunning: as the first octagonal dome in history to be built without a wooden supporting frame, it really is an absolutely incredible feat of engineering. Brunelleschi had dreamed of completing the cupola since childhood. He won the commission with the more experienced Lorenzo Ghiberti, riding on the back of his success with the Baptistery doors (p57). Brunelleschi made the dome support itself by building two shells, one on top of the other, and by laying the bricks in herringbone-pattern rings to integrate successive layers that could support themselves.

Just as innovative as the design were the tools used and the organisation of the work. Brunelleschi devised pulley systems to winch materials and workers up to the dome. Between the two shells of the dome, he installed a canteen so the workforce wouldn't waste time going to ground level to eat, bringing construction time down to a mere 16 years (1420-36). A separate side entrance gives access to the top of the dome (463 steps) with fantastic city views, though the climb is not recommended for the faint-hearted or those with limited mobility. In March 2007, two peregrine falcons nested and raised their young in the cathedral's cupola, while twitchers worldwide watched the hatching online via 'birdcam'.

Orsanmichele p67

Campanile

Open 8.30am-6.50pm daily.
Admission €6. No credit cards.
Map p53 B2 ❺

The cathedral's three-floor, 414-step bell tower was designed by Giotto in 1334, though his plans weren't followed faithfully. Andrea Pisano, who continued the work three years after Giotto's death, took the precaution of doubling the thickness of the walls, while Francesco Talenti, who saw the building to completion in 1359, inserted the large windows high up the tower. Inlaid, like the Duomo, with pretty pink, white and green marble, the Campanile is decorated with 16 sculptures of prophets, patriarchs and pagans (the originals are in Florence's Museo dell'Opera del Duomo; p54), bas-reliefs designed by Giotto and artfully executed by Pisano recounting the *Creation and Fall of Man* and *Redemption Through Industry*; you can make out Eve emerging from Adam's side and a drunken Noah. The steps to the top are steep and narrow, but great views await.

Museo di Bigallo

Piazza San Giovanni 1 (055 2302885).
Open 10am-2pm, 3-7pm Tue-Sun.
Admission €5. No credit cards.
Map p53 B2 ❻

The city's smallest museum is housed in a beautiful Gothic loggia built in 1358 for the Misericordia, a charitable organisation that cared for unwanted children and plague victims. The loggia was later renovated for another fraternity, the Bigallo, and the Misericordia moved to piazza del Duomo (no.19), from where it still works as a voluntary medical service. The main room has frescoes depicting the work of the two fraternities. The *Madonna della Misericordia*, a fresco of 1342 from the workshop of Bernardo Daddi, a pupil of Giotto, is the earliest known depiction of Florence, showing the Baptistery, the original Arnolfo façade to the domeless Duomo, the original Santa Reparata with its two bell towers, and an incomplete Campanile.

Museo Casa di Dante

Via Santa Margherita 1 (055 219416/ www.museocasadidante.it). **Open** 10am-6pm Tue-Sat; 10am-4pm 1st Sun

of mth; 10am-1pm, 2nd & 3rd Sun of mth. **Admission** €4. No credit cards. **Map** p53 C3 ❼

Housed in the building where Dante is thought by some to have lived, this museum, dedicated to the father of the Italian language, reopened after three years of renovation in June 2005. If you go expecting to see the poet's belongings or original works, you'll be disappointed. What the museum does offer is an extensive amount of information about the political, economic and cultural environment of Dante's time. There are miniature-model reconstructions of ancient Florence, costumed mannequins and clear illustrations of Heaven, Hell and Purgatory taken from the poet's most famous work, *The Divine Comedy*.

Museo Diocesano di Santo Stefano al Ponte

Piazza Santo Stefano 5 (055 2710732). **Open** *Summer* 4-7pm Fri. *Winter* 3.30-6.30pm Fri; also by appointment. Closed mid July-Sept. **Admission** free. **Map** p53 B4 ❽

A tiny, little-known church museum that's hidden from the tourist trail in

a square north of the ponte Vecchio. Among the religious icons and church relics are a few big surprises: a *Maestà* by Giotto, *San Giuliano* by Masolino and the *Quarate Predella* by Paolo Uccello.

Museo Ferragamo

Piazza Santa Trinita 5r (055 3360456/ 455/www.ferragamo.it). **Open** 10am-6pm Mon, Wed-Sun. **Admission** €5. **Map** p53 A4 ❾

Located down some steps from the eponymous shop and into the medieval basement (where it was moved in December 2006), this museum is as elegant and stylish as the shoes on display. In the first chamber you can see order forms signed by famous actors, including John Wayne, and wooden lasts used to design shoes for Ava Gardner and Drew Barrymore. The rest of the museum is filled with a choice selection of the company's 10,000 shoes, boasting many pairs created for the likes of Marilyn Monroe, Judy Garland and Audrey Hepburn, and, if nothing else, an opportunity for shoe fetishists to drool.

Museo dell'Opera del Duomo

Piazza del Duomo 9 (055 2302885/ www.operaduomo.firenze.it). **Open** 9am-6.50pm Mon-Sat; 9am-1pm Sun. **Admission** €6. No credit cards. **Map** p53 C2 ❿

Built on the site of the 15th-century cathedral workshop, where Michelangelo carved his famous *David*, the Museum of the Cathedral Works still contains the tools and machinery used to build the Duomo, the original wooden models of the cathedral and its cupola in various stages of development, as well as sculptures and artwork from the Duomo complex deemed too precious and vulnerable to be left to the mercy of the elements. It's one of the city's most interesting museums, though the explanatory panels can sometimes make for hard reading.

In the first rooms are Gothic sculptures from the exteriors of the Baptistery and the original but never-finished Duomo façade. There are also pieces from Santa Reparata and a collection of relics. Halfway up the stairs is the *Pietà Bandini*, a heart-rending late work by Michelangelo showing Christ slithering from the grasp of Nicodemus. The sculpture was intended as Michelangelo's tombstone; he sculpted his own features on the face of Nicodemus, showing how his obsession with the story had become too much for him to bear. In true tortured artist style, frustrated with the piece, the master smashed Christ's left arm.

The originals of Donatello's *Prophets* from the exterior of the Campanile are upstairs, notably *Habakkuk*, a work of such realism that Donatello himself is said to have gripped it and screamed, 'Speak, damn you, speak!' This room also houses two enormous and joyful *cantorie* (choir lofts). One is by Donatello, with cavorting putti; the other, by Luca della Robbia, is full of angel musicians. Beyond are bas-reliefs for the Campanile, most carved by Pisano to Giotto's designs.

Donatello was the first artist to free sculpture from its Gothic limitations: in the room to the right of the main chamber is an extreme example of the artist's unprecedented use of naturalism: an emotive wood sculpture of a dishevelled Mary Magdalene with coarse, dirty hair so realistic you can almost smell it.

Going straight back through the main chamber is a new corridor displaying the pulleys and ropes used to winch building materials (and workers) up to the inside of the dome. There's also the death mask of Brunelleschi and an 18th-century sedan chair cleverly built in a curved form so that two servants were able to carry Grand Duke Cosimo III de' Medici up the spiral steps to the top of the Dome. Back on the ground floor, under the glass roof of the courtyard, are the ten original bronze panels from the east door of the Baptistery, Ghiberti's so-called 'Gates of Paradise' (p54).

Museo di Storia della Scienza

Piazza dei Giudici 1 (055 265311/ www.imss.fi.it). **Open** *Summer* 9.30am-5pm Mon-Sat. *Winter* 9.30am-5pm Mon, Wed-Sat; 9.30am-1pm Tue; 10am-1pm 2nd Sun of mth. **Admission** €6.50. No credit cards. **Map** p53 B4 ⓫

Galileo Galilei's scientific instruments are the big draw here, but even without them, this would be one of the city's most interesting museums. Galileo's fascinatingly crafted compass and his leather-bound telescope are on display in the main room, along with a morbid reliquary in the shape of his middle right finger.

In the next rooms are a collection of prisms, optical games and armillary spheres. The second floor has an eclectic mix of machines, mechanisms and models. The display of amputation implements and models of foetuses are rather grisly. For info on events in Florence to commemorate the 400-year anniversary of Galileo's discovery, see box p32.

Palace revolution

Looming forbiddingly over its piazza, **Palazzo Strozzi** (p67) is one of the finest examples of Renaissance domestic architecture in Florence. Now municipal property, it's been used sporadically for exhibitions since the 1940s, but, in autumn 2007, the dynamic new Fondazione Strozzi – formed by a group of unusually forward-thinking local big wigs – took over the management, and big changes are afoot.

As Italy's first independent foundation that combines both public and private resources, Foundazione Strozzi was ahead of the game from the start; and its appointment of a foreign (shock horror!) museum specialist – Canadian James Bradburne – as Director General was a surprise for many used to the city's inward-looking stance. Bradburne's vision is to devise a year-round, widely varied programme of cutting-edge activities, including exhibitions, lectures and events designed to appeal to both Florentines and foreigners alike.

The building's massive doors are permanently open and people are encouraged to walk freely into the impressive internal courtyard that's open from morning till late; a café and bar, a bookshop, stone benches, plants and special lighting effects, plus a permanent exhibition on the history of the palazzo, all encourage lingering.

The main show space is on the first floor; upcoming exhibitions in 2008 include 'At the Court of the Emperors', showcasing art in Tang China, and 'Women in Power', focusing on the tapestries of Caterina and Maria de' Medici. The lower floor houses the Centre for Contemporary Culture (known as 'La Strozzina'). Bradburne describes this new space as 'an open platform for the vast array of approaches that shape contemporary culture'. It will show installations of contemporary art and explore the fields of digital art, photography, architecture and product design.

A ray of light in Florence's staid contemporary arts scene.

Uffizi Gallery p69

Orsanmichele & Museo di Orsanmichele

Via dell'Arte della Lana (055 284944/ 284715). **Open** *Church* 10am-7pm Tue-Sun. *Museum* tours 9am, 10am, 11am daily. Phone to check. Closed 1st & last Mon of mth. **Admission** free. **Map** p53 B3 ⑫

Most famous for the statues in the 14 niches that surround the building, Orsanmichele has become a relic of the extreme dedication and pride of Florentine trades, and a reminder that a competitive climate often heralds the greatest art. There's no spire and no overt religious symbols: Orsanmichele may not look much like a church, but it is – although one with a difference, melding as it does the relationship between art, religion and commerce.

In 1290, a loggia intended as a grain store was built to a design by Arnolfo di Cambio, in the garden (*orto*) of the Monastery of San Michele (hence, 'Orsanmichele'). The loggia burned down in 1304, along with a painting of the Madonna that had been said to perform miracles. When the building was reconstructed in the mid 1300s, the painting was honoured by an elaborate glass and marble tabernacle by Andrea Orcagna. This was then replaced in 1347 by Bernardo Daddi's *Coronation of the Madonna with Eight Angels*, still in place today.

During reconstruction of the building, two upper floors were added for religious services. From the outset, the council intended the building to be an advertisement for the wealth of the city's guilds, and in 1339 each guild was instructed to fill one of the loggia's 14 niches with a statue of its patron saint. Only the wool guild obliged, so in 1406, after the building's conversion into a church, the council handed the guilds a ten-year deadline.

Six years later, the wealthy Calimala cloth importers commissioned Ghiberti to create a life-size bronze of John the Baptist. It was the largest statue ever cast in Florence, and its arrival spurred the other major guilds into action. The guild of armourers was represented by

a tense *St George* by Donatello (now in the Bargello), while the Parte Guelfa guild had Donatello gild their bronze, a *St Louis of Toulouse* (later removed by the Medici in their drive to expunge all memory of the Guelphs).

All the statues in the external niches today are copies. However, the originals can be found on the first floor of the museum. On the second floor is a collection of statues of 14th-century saints and prophets in arenaria stone.

Note that the church and museum do not always stick to the official opening hours.

Palazzo Davanzati/ Museo dell'Antica Casa Fiorentina

Via Porta Rossa 13 (055 2388610/ www.polomuseale.firenze.it). **Open** 8.15am-1.50pm daily. Closed 1st, 3rd & 5th Mon, 2nd & 4th Sun of mth. **Admission** free. **Map** p53 A3 ⑬

After years of renovation, the Ancient Florentine House Museum is open again. On the first floor are the painted Sala dei Pappagalli, the Salone Madornale and the Studiolo, displaying Renaissance furniture, paintings, tapestries, an incredible 16th-century strongbox and a permanent exhibition about spinning and weaving. The building itself is a wonderful example of a 14th-century palazzo.

Palazzo Strozzi

Piazza Strozzi (Institute Gabinetto Vieusseux 055 283962/www.palazzo strozzi.org). **Open** *Library* 9am-1.30pm, 3-6pm Mon, Wed, Fri; 9am-6pm Tue, Thur. *Exhibitions* times vary. **Admission** Ground-floor courtyard free. Exhibitions vary. **Map** p53 A3 ⑭

Palazzo Strozzi is one of the most magnificent of the hundred or so palaces built in the city during the 15th century. Behind the imposing rusticated stone walls lies the Humanist Institute's Renaissance book and manuscript collection and the Centro di Cultura Contemporanea Strozzina (CCCS) – which will host contemporary art in the cellar space (see box p65).

FLORENCE BY AREA

In 1489, work began on the construction of the palazzo by order of Filippo Strozzi, whose family had been exiled from Florence in 1434 for opposing the Medici. However, the Strozzis made good use of the time, moving south and becoming bankers to the King of Naples; they had amassed a fortune by the time they returned to Florence in 1466.

When Filippo died in 1491, he left his heirs to complete the project, which eventually bankrupted them, but the palace remained in the family up until 1937 when it became the seat of an insurance company and was finally handed over to the state in 1999.

Palazzo Vecchio/ Quartieri Monumentali

Piazza della Signoria (055 2768224/ www.comune.firenze.it). **Open** 9am-7pm Mon-Wed, Fri, Sat; 9am-2pm Thur; 9am-7pm Sun. **Admission** €6. No credit cards. **Map** p53 B4 ⓯

The most important civic square in Florence is dominated by Florence's town hall; the imposing power of Palazzo Vecchio's austere and commanding walls were built to Arnolfo di Cambio's late 13th-century plans as seat to the Signoria – the city's ruling body as priors of the main guilds of the Medici. The building represented the immense strength of the city at this time.

The Medici enjoyed their own nine-year stay (1540-49) and instigated a Mannerist makeover of the interior from 1555 to 1574. However, the rustic stone exterior of the building and Arnolfo's tower, the highest in the city at 94m (308ft), remained largely intact. The tower, set just off-centre in order to incorporate a previous tower, and topped by two of the main symbols of Florence (a lion holding a lily), saw the imprisonment of Savonarola and Cosimo il Vecchio. From 1565, Palazzo Vecchio lost some of its administrative exclusivity to the Pitti Palace and the Uffizi. However, it later became the seat of the Italian government's House of Deputies from 1865 to 1871, when Florence was the first capital of the Kingdom of Italy.

The Salone dei Cinquecento (Hall of the Five Hundred), where members of the Great Council met, should have been decorated by Michelangelo and Leonardo, not the zestless scenes of victory over Siena and Pisa by Vasari that cover the walls. Leonardo abandoned the project; Michelangelo had only finished the cartoon for the *Battle of Cascine* when he was summoned to Rome by Pope Julius II. Many believe da Vinci's sketches lie beneath the Vasari mural (see box p60). Michelangelo's *Genius of Victory* statue did, however, end up here.

Off the Salone is the Studiolo di Francesco I, also decorated by Vasari, and the office where Francesco hid away to practise alchemy. From the ceiling, Bronzino's portraits of Francesco's parents, Cosimo I and Eleonora di Toledo, look down. The Quartiere di Eleonora, the apartments of the wife of Cosimo I, has two entirely frescoed chapels.

Beyond here is the garish Sala d'Udienza, with a carved ceiling dripping in gold; more subtle is the Sala dei Gigli, so named because of the gilded lilies that cover the walls. Decorated in the 15th century, it has a ceiling by Giuliano and Benedetto da Maiano, and some sublime frescoes of Roman statesmen by Ghirlandaio. Donatello's original *Judith and Holofernes*, rich in political significance, is also here. Finally, go through into the Map Room where you can inspect the gigantic 16th-century globe by Egnazio Danti and, from the same period, 53 beautifully hand-decorated maps of countries and continents.

For an insight into Palazzo Vecchio's workings, book yourself on to the Visita ai Percorsi Segreti (Secret Passageways Tour). Other tours on offer include An Invitation to Cosimo's Court (good for children) and the Tour of the Quartieri Monumentali.

Santissimi: La chiesa dei Santissimi Apostoli

Piazza del Limbo 1 (055 290642). **Open** 10.15am-noon, 4-7pm Mon-Sat; 10.15am-noon Sun. **Admission** free. **Map** p53 A4 ⓰

Uffizi olive tree p71

The design of Santissimi Apostoli is based on that of a Roman basilica. It's one of the oldest churches in Florence, retaining much of its 11th-century façade. The third chapel on the right holds an *Immaculate Conception* by Vasari; in the left aisle is an odd glazed terracotta tabernacle by Giovanni della Robbia. The church holds pieces of flint reputed to have come from Jerusalem's Holy Sepulchre, awarded to Pazzino de' Pazzi for his bravery during the Crusades. They were used on Easter Day to light the 'dove' that set off the fireworks display at the Scoppio del Carro (p33). Note that the church has a tendency to close in the afternoon without notice.

Uffizi Gallery

Palazzo degli Uffizi, Piazzale degli Uffizi 6 (055 2388651/www.polomuseale. firenze.it/english/musei/uffizi/). **Open** 8.15am-6.50pm Tue-Sun. **Admission** €6.50; €3.25 reductions. Small extra charge for special exhibitions. *Advance booking* via Firenze Musei (055 294883); booking charge €3. No credit cards. **Map** p53 B4 ⑰

Statues outside the Uffizi commemorate many of the most interesting artists and scholars in Florence's history but these pale into insignificance when you enter this stunning temple of Renaissance art. The quantity and quality of the paintings on display make this without a doubt the greatest treasure trove of Renaissance art in the world. Plans to double the gallery's display space, allowing long-hidden works to come out of storage, are finally under way, with designs by Japanese architect Arata Isozaki for a new exit wing approved in August 2007.

In the meantime the queues remain, and even booking in advance isn't foolproof: during peak times you need to reserve up to a couple of months ahead. Whether you book in advance or not, aim to arrive either when the museum opens or at lunchtime, when the tour groups are less prevalent. To see the whole collection takes a lot of time and energy: it's best to jump to the rooms in which you're most interested or, better still, to plan a return visit. Allow three hours for the unmissables.

The building was designed by Vasari in the mid 16th century as a public administration centre for Cosimo I (hence 'Uffizi', meaning

Tripe Stall, Mercato Nuovo p77

'offices'). To make way for the *pietra serena* and white plaster building, most of the 11th-century church of San Piero Scheraggio was demolished. By 1581, Francesco I had already begun turning the top floor into a new home for his art collection; a succession of Medici added to the collection, culminating in the bequest of most of the family's artworks by the last important familymember, Anna Maria, in 1743.

The chronological collection begins gloriously in **Room 2**, with three *Maestàs* by Giotto, Cimabue and Duccio painted in the 13th and early 14th centuries. **Room 3** is 14th-century Siena, evoked most exquisitely by Simone Martini's lavish gilt altarpiece *Annunciation*. Such delight in detail reached its zenith in the international Gothic movement (**Rooms 5 and 6**) and, in particular, the work of Gentile da Fabriano (1370-1427), whose *Adoration of the Magi* has been restored to its original grandeur.

It comes as something of a surprise, then, to find a strikingly contemporary *Virgin and Child with St Anne* by

Masolino and Masaccio (1401-28) in **Room 7**. Masaccio painted the *Virgin*, whose severe expression and statuesque pose make her an indubitable descendant of Giotto's *Maestà*. In the same room is the *Santa Lucia dei Magnoli* altarpiece by Domenico Veneziano (1400-61), a Venetian artist who had a remarkable skill for rendering the way light affects colour. His influence on pupil Piero della Francesca's work is clear in the younger artist's portraits of the Duke and Duchess of Urbino. Paolo Uccello (1396-1475) is represented by the *Battle of San Romano*.

Rooms 8 and **9** are dominated by Filippo Lippi and the Pollaiolo brothers, while the two most famous paintings in the Uffizi and in Italy are in **Room 10**. Botticelli's *Birth of Venus*, the epitome of Renaissance romance, depicts the birth of the goddess from a sea impregnated by the castration of Uranus. It's an allegory of the birth of beauty from the mingling of the physical world (the sea) and the spiritual (Uranus). Scholars have been squab-

In **Room 25**, the gallery makes its transition to Mannerism led by Michelangelo's Holy Family (Doni Tondo), which shows the sculptural bodies, virtuoso composition and luscious palette that characterised the new wave. Florentine works in the same room include Mariotto Albertinelli's *Visitation*. Next you'll come to the Pontormo- and Rosso Fiorentino-dominated **Room 27**; once again, Michelangelo's legacy is visible, most notably in *Moses Defends the Daughters of Jethro* by Rosso Fiorentino. The works by Titian in **Room 28** include his masterpiece *Venus of Urbino*. For more Venetian works, skip to **Rooms 31-35**, but don't miss the challenging *Madonna with the Long Neck* by Parmigianino en route in **Room 29**.

At this point it's very easy to become confused by the room numbers. Rooms 36-37 and 39-40 don't actually exist, 'room' 38 is a statue-lined area at the top of the stairwell and room 41 is a restoration laboratory. **Room 42**, also known as the Sala delle Niobe, is lined with four monumental canvases by Rubens and displays a collection of recently restored statues from the Villa Medici gardens in Rome.

Downstairs, most of the first floor is reserved for the Uffizi's temporary exhibitions, but in the middle you'll find rooms 47-51. **Room 47** is home to a particularly grisly rendering of *Judith and Holofernes* by the 17th-century Caravaggio-esque female painter Artemisia Gentileschi. Caravaggio himself is represented by his famous *Medusa*, a *Bacchus* and a *Sacrifice of Isaac*. More Caravaggio-esque artists such as Manfredi and Gherardo delle Notti employ his use of *chiaroscuro* (dramatic light contrasts) to the paintings in the final four rooms of the corridor. It's this final collection that suffered most from the last terrorist attack. At 5am on 27 May 1993, a Mafia-related car bomb exploded outside the west wing of the Uffizi (a gnarled olive tree has been placed in

bling about the true meaning of Botticelli's *Primavera*, or *Allegory of Spring*, since it was painted in 1482. Many now agree that it was intended to represent the onset of spring and to signify the triumph of Venus (centre) as true love, with the Three Graces representing her beauty and Zephyr, on the right, as lust, pursuing the nymph Chloris, who is transformed into Flora, Venus's fecundity. If you look closely at Botticelli's *Portrait of a Young Man with Medal* (1475-6), you'll see that the golden disc is not, in fact, painted but inlaid, making the portrait the only collage in the entire gallery.

In **Room 15** are several paintings by Leonardo da Vinci, including a collaboration with his master Verrocchio, *The Baptism of Christ*. The octagonal **Room 18**, known as La Tribuna, was designed to display some of the greatest masterpieces in the Medicean collection. It's dominated by portraits by Agnolo Bronzino, most strikingly that of Eleonora di Toledo. The oval **Room 24** is home to the world's biggest collection of miniatures.

Grom p76

the exact spot to remember the five people who were killed). In all, 32 paintings were damaged and three completely destroyed in the blast, which also severely hit the Sala delle Niobe. The restoration of Gherardo delle Notti's *Adoration of the Magi* is still taking place.

Note that paintings may be moved or go on loan at any time, so if you've set your heart on seeing a particular masterpiece, phone first to check it's here.

Eating & drinking

The *aperitivo* craze that took off in Florence a few years back is still going strong, and many of the venues listed in the nightlife sections of this guide offer free buffets with early evening drinks; see page 23 for more information.

Bar Perseo
Piazza della Signoria 16r (055 2398316). **Open** 7.30am-midnight Mon-Sat. Closed 3wks Nov. **Café**. **Map** p53 B3 ⑱

Even though it doesn't have the charm of the more celebrated Rivoire (below), this bar overlooks the city's most famous Renaissance square, along with its namesake – Cellini's *Perseus*, in the Loggia dei Lanzi. Inside, the centrepiece is a sculptural art deco chandelier, but most eyes are drawn to the mountains of own-made ice-cream topped with cherries, berries and chocolate curls.

Caffè Rivoire
Piazza della Signoria 5r (055 214412/www.rivoire.it). **Open** 8am-midnight Tue-Sun. Closed last 2wks Jan. **Café**. **Map** p53 B4 ⑲

Founded in 1872 as a chocolate factory, Rivoire is the most famous and best loved of all Florentine cafés. Its chocolates are divine – try the puffed rice and *gianduja* (hazlenut and almond-flavoured chocolate) – and its own-brand coffee is among the best in the city. The outside tables have views of Palazzo Vecchio and the Loggia dei Lanzi. One downside: your wallet will be hit hard for the privilege.

Cold war

Rivalry among Florence's *gelaterie* has always been strong, but the form of this rivalry has recently shifted from the amount and outlandishness of flavours offered to whose cold stuff is most 'home-made'. The signs '*produzione propro*', and '*artigianale*' are the buzzwords du jour, and parlours are going to ever greater lengths to make the authenticity grade. Ploys include making the ice-cream in full view of shoppers, shipping in fresh ingredients daily and using gourmet chocolate, organic milk, seasonal fruits and exotic spices sourced from far-flung locations.

For years, local institution **Vivoli** (p121) was regularly named as the best *gelateria* in the city. The fabulous *semi-freddi*, creamier and softer than *gelato*, wickedly rich chocolate orange and divine *riso* (rice pudding) are still right up there, but Vivoli's reputation is increasingly threatened by new contenders. Vivoli earned its ice-cream crown by being the most cited, but **Vestri** (p123) is the city's best-kept secret and locals' choice as moral winner. This chocolate shop is the best of the seasonal ice-cream vendors – shops installing corners serving a few flavours of *gelato* only in summer. The carefully chosen selection, served from metal churns, features white chocolate, wild strawberries, chocolate and peperoncino and bitter chocolate with Cointreau, sprinkled with spices, dried fruit or spoonfuls of melted chocolate. The owners of **Carabé** (p107) are Sicilian and push the envelope by bringing in fresh lemons from home to make a tangy, rustic ice-cream/sorbet cross-breed. Their crunchy *granita* is flavoured with almond milk, while the *cremolata* is made with the pulp of seasonal soft fruits. At **Gelateria dei Neri** (p119) all the ice-cream is made in the workshop behind the counter and it's one of the few parlours to serve soya ice-cream alongside the classic creamy *gelati*. For many who've found newcomer **Grom** (p76), though, the contest is all over. The place features a seasonally changing menu of flavours made on the premises and served from metal jars. Monthly specials may be delicate Mat-cha green tea or refreshing milk and fresh mint in the summer, and chunky *marrons glacés* or zingy ginger in the winter months; the year-round speciality is the sensational Crema di Grom, made with organic egg, soft cookies and Valrhona Ecuadorian chocolate.

Canova di Gustavino
Via Canova 29 (055 2399806).
Open noon-12.20am daily. **Wine bar**. Map p53 B3 ⑳

A useful address if you require a light meal or a glass of wine in the area near the Duomo, this colourful, brick-vaulted *enoteca* (property of the Lanciola wine estate near Impruneta) is an offshoot of the fancier restaurant next door; the 800-strong wine list is available in both venues. To sop it all up there's a selection of salads, *crostini*, cheeses and cold meats.

Cantinetta de' Verrazzano
Via de' Tavolini 18-20r (055 268590/ www.verrazzano.com). **Open** *Sept-June* 8am-9pm Mon-Sat. *July, Aug* 8am-4pm Mon-Sat. **Café/wine bar**. Map p53 B3 ㉑

Owned by the Castello da Verrazzano, one of the major wine estates in Chianti, the wood-panelled rooms of this 'cantinetta' are continually crowded with smartly dressed Florentines and discerning tourists. On one side are a bakery and café, on the other is a wine bar serving

(very good) estate-produced wines by the glass or bottle. Snacks include *focacce* straight from the wood oven and an unusual selection of *crostini*.

Chiaroscuro
Via del Corso 36r (055 214247).
Open 7.30am-9.30pm daily. **Café**. Map p53 B3 ㉒

Chiaroscuro's expert barmen consider themselves coffee connoisseurs, and the risk of being served a below-par brew here is practically non-existent. Coffee is also sold freshly ground by weight and there's a range of coffee makers and machines. There's usually room to sit down, even at busy lunchtimes. The buffet *aperitivo* is a safe bet.

Cocquinarius
Via delle Oche 15r (055 2302153/ www.cocquinarius.com). **Open** 9am-11pm Mon-Sat; 9am-4pm Sun. Food served from noon Mon-Sat. Closed Aug. **Café/wine bar**. Map p53 B3 ㉓

A good bet in an area largely devoid of decent places to eat, this cosy little wine bar and café tucked away behind the Duomo is great for a quiet lunch or

'Ino p76

an informal evening meal: unusually, the full menu is available between noon and 11pm. Bare brick walls and soft jazz provide the background for good pastas, carpaccio, imaginative salads and platters of cheeses and meats. The own-made cakes are divine.

I Fratellini

Via de' Cimatori 38r (no phone). **Open** 8am-8pm. No credit cards. **Wine bar**. Map p53 B3 ㉔

There used to be loads of these hole-in-the-wall *vinai* (wine merchants) in Florence; nowadays, I Fratellini, founded in 1875, is one of very few left in the city. There's nowhere to sit down: just join the locals standing in the road or squatting on the pavement for a glass of cheap and cheerful plonk or something a bit more special. Help it down with a liver-topped *crostino* or a great slab of *porchetta* (rosemary roast pork) on a hunk of bread.

Dei Frescobaldi Ristorante & Wine Bar

Vicolo de' Gondi, off via della Condotta (055 284724). **Open** 7pm-midnight

Mon; noon-midnight Tue-Sat. Closed 3wks Aug. **€€**. **Italian/wine bar**. Map p53 C3/C4 ㉕

This cosy wine bar showcases wines from the formidable Frescobaldi estates of Tuscany, Umbria, Friuli and even as far afield as Chile and California, where they collaborate with wine producer Robert Mondavi; unusually, all of the wine stocked here can be ordered by the glass. Feast on the likes of terrines, marinated anchovies, cheeses and salamis, or more substantial fare such as warm octopus salad or pumpkin and scallop risotto. You can also choose from the full menu in the smart restaurant next door (average €30).

Fusion Bar

Gallery Hotel Art, Vicolo dell'Oro 2 (055 27263). **Open** 7pm-midnight Mon-Sat; 7pm 10pm Sun. **€€€**. **Japanese/fusion**. Map p53 A4 ㉖

This East-meets-West bar and restaurant is a stylish spot for a light lunch, or an evening cocktail accompanied by nibbles or dinner. A set price (€16) help-yourself buffet is laid out at midday, featuring dishes with a fusion element. In the evening, there's a full menu of Japanese and fusion dishes. Go for one of two set menus (€35 and €50), or order à la carte from the likes of sushi, tempura and noodle dishes, tuna tartare and confit of duck with orange soy sauce. Brunch is served at weekends.

Gilli

Piazza della Repubblica 36-39r (055 213896). **Open** 8am-midnight Mon, Wed-Sun. **Café**. Map p53 B3 ㉗

With the loss in recent years of many of the city centre's most beloved shops and bars to make room for international designer flagship stores, continuing dark murmurings abound about the future of historic Gilli. Its closure would be a blow to its loyal clientele and to impressed visitors. Gilli's belle époque interior is original, its seasonally themed sweet window displays wickedly tempting and its rich, flavoured hot chocolates legendary. Outside seating year-round.

Gold/La Carrozza

Piazza Pesce 3/5r (055 2396810).
Open *Summer* 10am-midnight daily.
Winter 10.30am-7.30pm Tue, Thur-Sun. No credit cards. **Gelateria**.
Map p53 B4 ㉘

On summer nights, crowds congregate at the hatch of this classic *gelateria* in a prime position between the ponte Vecchio and the Uffizi. Specialities are exotic seasonal fruit flavours, from papaya *gelato* to lime sorbet, but the coffee flavour is also a revelation – a small cup has similar properties to a double espresso.

Grom

Via del Campanile (corner of via delle Oche) (055 216158/www.grom.it).
Open *Summer* 10.30am-midnight daily. *Winter* 10.30am-11pm daily. No credit cards. **Gelateria**. **Map** p53 B2 ㉙

See box p73.

'Ino

Via dei Georgofili 3r-7r (055 219208/www.ino-firenze.com). **Open** 11am-8pm Tue-Sun, noon-5pm Sun. €. **Sandwich bar**. Map p53 B4 ㉚

A useful address for a post Uffizi/Palazzo Vecchio gastronomic break, 'Ino is a classy, contemporary sandwich bar and deli offering panini and other goodies made with top-notch ingredients, sourced from all over Italy. Sandwiches (to eat in, perched at the counter, or take out) are made to order and filled according to seasonal availability; the price of each (from €4) includes a glass of wine. The deli is stocked with olive oils, vinegars, wines and other tempting goodies.

Oliviero

Via delle Terme 51r (055 212421).
Open 7.30pm-midnight Mon-Sat. Closed Aug. €€€. **Italian/Tuscan**. Map p53 A3 ㉛

Once a favoured haunt of Sophia Loren and Maria Callas, Francesco Altomare's restaurant still has a retro vibe in spite of a recent refit; the revolving door, wood-panelled bar and silent grand piano all hark back to *La Dolce Vita*. The food, however, is not only great but very much in keeping with today's fashion for reinterpreting traditional recipes (in this case, mainly from Tuscany and southern Italy). A glass of complimentary prosecco comes with the menu, where you'll find the likes of bay-spiked duck terrine, spinach and ricotta *gnudi* with truffles and beef fillet with Brunello-poached pears. There's an excellent cheeseboard and a fine wine list.

Perchè No!

Via dei Tavolini 19r (055 2398969/www.percheno.firenze.it). **Open** *Summer* 11am-midnight daily. *Winter* noon-7.30pm Mon, Wed-Sun. No credit cards. **Gelateria**. Map p53 B3 ㉜

This is a favourite with the locals, who have been coming here for generations. Not by chance, it is often cited as the best *gelateria* for the more traditional flavours – *crema* (vanilla), pistachio and chocolate.

Procacci

Via de' Tornabuoni 64r (055 211656).
Open 10.30am-8pm Mon-Sat. Closed Aug. **Wine bar/deli**. Map p53 A3 ㉝

One of the few traditional shops on this thoroughfare to survive the onslaught of designer names, the small wood-lined bar and shop is a favourite with nostalgic Florentines. In season (Oct-Dec), truffles (the 'white gold' variety, as well as its black cousin) arrive daily at around 10am, filling the room with their soft musty aroma (the speciality is melt-in-the-mouth truffle and butter brioche).

La Terrazza, Rinascente

Piazza della Repubblica 1 (055 219113/www.rinascente.it). **Open** 10am-9pm Mon-Sat; 10.30am-8pm Sun. **Café**. Map p53 B3 ㉞

The rooftop terrace café at this department store affords some of the most stunning views of the city; the splendour of Brunelleschi's cupola at such close quarters more than makes up for the mediocre menu and the patchy service. Come at sundown, when you can experience the city bathed in pink light.

Workshop on via dello Studio

Shopping

At the top of via Por Santa Maria is the **Mercato Nuovo**, a 16th-century loggia housing stalls selling leather and straw goods, cheap souvenirs, flowers and tripe. The market is popularly known as the Porcellino, or 'piglet', after the bronze statue of a boar. It's considered good luck to rub the boar's nose and put a coin in its mouth (the money goes to a children's charity).

For big-name designer clothes brands (Gucci, Dolce & Gabbana, Miu Miu and the like), head to **via Strozzi**, **via Tornaborni** and **via Roma**.

Café-shop **Procacci** (p76) sells great gifts, such as the chocolates in Duomo-shaped boxes.

Alessi

Via delle Oche 27r (055 214966/ www.enotecaalessi.it). **Open** 9am-1pm, 3.30-7.30pm Mon-Sat. **Map** p53 B3 ㉟
On top of the large range of wines, grappas and whiskeys, this fabulous wine cellar is piled high with cakes, biscuits and chocs. Coffee is ground on the spot.

Bologna

Piazza Duomo 13-15r (055 290545). **Open** 9.30am-7.30 Mon-Sat; 3-7.30pm Sun. **Map** p53 B2 ㊱
A weird and wonderful selection of both men's and women's styles are on display here at one of Florence's best-loved shoe stores.

Bongi

Via Por Santa Maria 82-84r (055 2398811/www.otticabongi.com). **Open** 3.30-7.30pm Mon; 10am-7.30pm Tue-Sat. **Map** p53 B4 ㊲
This is one of the best-stocked photographic shops in the city centre, offering a wide range of new and used equipment for sale, digital photo reprographics facilities, as well as print developing services.

La Bottega dell'Olio

Piazza del Limbo 2r (055 2670468). **Open** *Mar-Sept* 10am-7pm Mon-Sat. Closed 2wks Jan. *Oct-Feb* 3-7pm Mon; 10am-1pm, 2-7pm Tue-Sat. **Map** p53 A4 ㊳
La Bottega dell'Olio is the place to visit for all things olive oil, from soaps and delicacies to olive-wood breadboards and pestles and mortars.

FLORENCE BY AREA

Grazlella Jewels Sculptures

Boutique Nadine
Lungarno degli Acciaiuoli 22r (055 287851). **Open** 10am-8pm Mon-Sat; 10am-6pm Sun. **Map** p53 A4 ③⑨
See box p140.

Carte Etc
Via de' Cerchi 13r (055 268302/ www.carteetc.it). **Open** 10am-7.30pm daily. **Map** p53 B3 ④⓪
Exquisite glass and stationery, unusual postcards of Florence and handmade greetings cards.

Coccinelle
Via Por Santa Maria 49r (055 2398782/www.coccinelle.com). **Open** 10.30am-7.30pm daily. **Map** p53 B4 ④①
Smart, contemporary leather bags in seasonal colours, crafted in smooth durable leather.

COIN
Via de' Calzaiuoli 56r (055 280531/ www.coin.it). **Open** *Jan-Mar* 10am-7.30pm Mon-Sat; *Apr-Dec* 10am-8pm Mon-Sat; 11am-8pm Sun. **Map** p53 B3 ④②

Furnishings are the strong point of this mid-range store, with bright contemporary homeware and regular consignments of Far Eastern furnishings. COIN also stocks fashion, shoes, accessories and gifts.

Edison
Piazza della Repubblica 27r (055 213110/www.libreriaedison.it). **Open** 9am-midnight Mon-Sat; 10am-midnight Sun. **Map** p53 A3 ④③
This multi-storey superstore sells books, maps, magazines, calendars and CDs. The travel section includes lots of guides in English. Internet terminals, a café and a lecture area are further attractions.

Erboristeria Inglese
Via Tornabuoni 19 (055 210628/ www.officinadetornabuoni.it). **Open** 3.30-8pm Mon; 10am-8pm Tue-Sat. Closed 2wks Aug. **Map** p53 A3 ④④
From a 15th-century palazzo, the very knowledgeable Donatella sells handmade gifts, perfumes and candles from Diptyque, herbal remedies and Dr Hauschka toiletries and cosmetics. She

FLORENCE BY AREA

Flower Market, Mercato Nuovo p77

can also recommend alternative medicine practictioners. There's no main shop window so look for the raised entrance set off the street.

Gerard Loft

Via dei Pecori 36r (055 282491/ www.gerardloft.com). **Open** 2.30-7.30pm Mon; 10am-7.30pm Tue-Sat. **Map** p53 A2 ❹❺

Hip clothing with men's and women's lines by the likes of Marc Jacobs, Chloé and Helmut Lang.

Graziella Jewels Sculptures

Lungarno degli Acciaiuoli 74r (055 211498/www.gruppograziella.it). **Open** 10am-7pm daily. **Map** p53 A4 ❹❻

This shop is so stunning that it out-shines even its sumptuous jewellery. The spiralling silver, silver gilt and gold chunky swirl rings and flower bracelets encrusted with tiny diamonds and semi-precious stones are shown in glass 'safes' set into black walls, while a gold resin bench inset with fibre optics ripples down the middle of the room.

Lungarno Details

Lungarno degli Acciaiuoli (055 287367/ www.labotteghina.com). **Open** 10.30am-1.30pm, 3.30-7.30pm Mon-Fri; 10.30am-1.30pm Sat. **Map** p53 A4 ❹❼

So many guests of the Lungarno Suites above (p167) asked where they could find items from their hotel apartments that this shop was opened. On sale are furniture, framed photos, food gifts and beautifully packaged candles and toiletries by Sicilian company Ortigia.

Mandragora ArtStore

Piazza del Duomo 50r (055 292559/ www.mandragora.it). **Open** 10am-7.30pm Mon-Sat; 10.30am-6.30pm Sun. **Map** p53 C2 ❹❽

Decent reproductions by local artists of famous Florentine works of art, on furnishings, scarves, bags and ornaments, plus great books, cards and prints.

L'Olfattorio

Via de' Tornabuoni 6 (055 286925). **Open** 10.30am-7.30pm Tue-Sat. **Map** p53 A3 ❹❾

Sensory overload is inevitable in this stunning new perfumery. A decorated stone passageway leads into the main shop, where the cloudy onyx perfume bar holds 200 scents and a full moon gold leaf sculpture is lit by big bang chandeliers. Perfume and make-up consultations are free, with Diptyque and L'Artisan Parfumeur among the brands. A back room with black lacquered walls is a powder compact museum, with hundreds of examples from the late 1800s onwards.

Otisope

Via Porta Rossa 13r (055 2396717). **Open** 2-8pm Mon; 10am-1pm, 2-7.30pm Tue-Sat; 11am-7.30pm Sun. **Map** p53 A3 ⑤⓪

Fantastic, wearable styles for men and women all at €59. There are ranges of mocassins in various colours, simple pumps and courts, and the odd find from Hobbs. The outlet at piazza N Sauro 17r stocks previous seasons' stock for even less.

Paperback Exchange

Via dell Oche 4r (055 293460/www. papex.it). **Open** 9am-7.30pm Mon-Fri; 10am-7.30pm Sat. Closed 2wks Aug. **Map** p53 B2 ⑤①

This old favourite stocks thousands of new and used English-language fiction and non-fiction titles, specialising in art, art history and Italian culture. The noticeboard has information about literary events, courses, accommodation and language lessons. Second-hand books can be traded.

Patrizia Pepe

Via Strozzi 1r (055 2645056/www. patriziapepe.com). **Open** Call for details. **Map** p53 A3 ⑤②

Local-girl-done-good Patrizia Pepe has made a name for herself creating a sassy clothing brand that's expanded worldwide, and this new flagship store opposite Dolce & Gabbana puts her on the map as a design force to be reckoned with. Expect to find little black dresses with a twist, beautifully cut jackets and suits, chiffon shirts and the odd flash of bright colour, especially in the clubbing gear line. There are also men's and junior ranges.

Peppe Peluso

Via del Corso 5-6r (055 268283). **Open** 2-8pm Mon; 10am-8pm Tue-Sat; 11am-7.30pm Sun. **Map** p53 C3 ⑤③

A pair of shoes or boots from the vast (men's and women's) ranges here may or may not last the season, but at these bargain prices, who cares? The branch opposite (No.6r) has even cheaper footwear.

Al Portico

Piazza San Firenze 1 (055 213716/ www.semialportico.it). **Open** 8.30am-7.30pm Mon-Sat; 10am-1pm Sun. **Map** p53 C4 ⑤④

Al Portico is an extraordinary shop in the Renaissance courtyard of a magnificent palazzo, selling seeds for Italian vegetables and flowers, and with trees, fountains and plants on display. The owner is happy to show customers round, even if they don't want to buy. **Other location** Piazza della Signoria 36 (055 2608658).

Ricordi

Via Brunelleschi 8r (055 214104). **Open** 9.30am-7.30pm Mon-Sat; 3-7.30pm last Sun of mth. **Map** p53 B3 ⑤⑤

Ricordi has the best choice of DVDs and CDs in town, with original-language films and classical, jazz, rock and dance sections. Ricordi also sells instruments, sheet music and scores.

La Rinascente

Piazza della Repubblica 1 (055 219113/ www.rinascente.it). **Open** 10am-9pm Mon-Sat; 10.30am-8pm Sun. **Map** p53 B3 ⑤⑥

This classic department store has casual and designer clothes, the most extensive cosmetics and perfume department in the city, a decent lingerie section and smart bedding supplies. The rooftop café, La Terrazza, reached via the top floor, has fantastic views (p76).

Romeo

Via della Condotta 43r (055 210350). **Open** 10am-7.30pm Mon-Sat. **Map** p53 B3 ⑤⑦

The interior of this lovely stationery shop is filled to the ceiling with Spalding's

Caruso Jazz Café

full range, Aurora pens and Giorgio Fedon's smart coloured leather bags.

Sandro P 2
Via dei Tosinghi 7r (055 215063).
Open 3-7.30pm Mon; 10am-1pm, 3.30-7.30pm Tue-Sat. **Map** p53 B3 ⓝ
One of Florence's hippest men's and unisex clothing shops, with the latest from New York and London.

Zecchi
Via dello Studio 19r (055 211470/ www.zecchi.com). **Open** 8.30am-12.30pm, 3.30-7.30pm Mon-Fri; 8.30am-12.30pm Sat. Closed 3wks Aug. **Map** p53 C3 ⓝ
Zecchi is the best shop in town for art supplies, selling everything from pencils to gold leaf.

Nightlife

Astor Caffè
Piazza del Duomo 20r (055 284305). **Open** noon-2am daily. **Map** p53 B2 ⓝ
This huge, lively jazz bar draws an enthusiastic young crowd. The central skylight, soft red lighting and flash chrome-and-glass bar are a clean back-drop for the regular art and photography exhibitions, while internet points provide distraction from the busy socialising of the main bar – where you can sip cocktails or enjoy an *aperitivo* or a full dinner. There's jazz in the downstairs bar some evenings.

Caruso Jazz Café
Via Lambertesca 14-16r (055 281940/ www.carusojazzcafe.com). **Open** 9.30am-3:30pm, 6pm-midnight Mon-Sat. **Map** p53 B4 ⓝ
This cavernous bar, with its huge papier mâché sculptures of Florentine landmarks and cherubs, is a magnet for talented jazz musicians, including many famed Italians. Every Thursday and Friday, jazz echoes around the much-loved watering hole's brick vaults in a buzzy yet easygoing atmosphere. Simple lunch and tea menus are available, as are four computers offering internet access.

Colle Bereto
Piazza Strozzi 5r (055 283156/ www.collebereto.com). **Open** *Summer* 8am-midnight Mon-Sat. *Winter* 8am-9pm Mon-Sat. Food from noon. **Map** p53 A3 ⓝ

Perhaps because of its roots as a wine producer, this spin-off bar is one of the more grown-up of the central hangouts. Rivalling Noir (p93 and box p92) in popularity and location, it's packed with designer-clad model types till late, from Thursdays to Saturdays. Upstairs is the Attico, the VIP privé for which you have to book a table to enter, while the ludicrously luxurious covered terrace overlooking Palazzo Strozzi is often booked for private parties for fashion launches.

Loonees

Via Porta Rossa 15r (055 212249/ www.loonees.it). **Open** 8pm-3am Tue-Sun. Closed Aug. **Admission** free. No credit cards. **Map** p53 A3 63

A dark, sweaty underground hole, Loonees is popular with a young crowd from the international universities, as well as random punters and locals on the pull. There's a relaxed atmosphere, partly due to the very loud live music (reggae- and rock-covers to Italian pop and blues), which leaves you with little to do but take advantage of the free shot with every pint. The two-for-one happy hour is from 8pm to 10pm.

Mayday Lounge Café

Via Alighieri 16r (055 2381290/ www.maydayclub.it). **Open** 8pm-2am Mon-Sat. Closed 2wks Aug. **Admission** free, membership required (free). No credit cards. **Map** p53 B3 64

This wacky joint with odd art installations and hundreds of old Marconi radios hanging from the ceilings has earned itself something of a cult following. Somewhere between a beatnik refuge and something from *Lost in Translation*, Mayday is dark and edgy. There's a wildly diverse programme of events, with the only constant being a jazzy basis to the sounds.

Sky Lounge, Bar Continentale

Hotel Continentale, Vicolo dell'Oro 6r (055 27262/www.lungarnohotels.com). **Open** *Mar-Oct* 2.30-11.30pm daily. **Map** p53 A4 65

In-the-know Florentines mix with hotel guests at sundown for aperitifs at the Hotel Continentale's swanky rooftop bar. The sides are lined with smart biscuit-coloured upholstered benches, and cocktails are served with crudités

popular among tourists and young locals of both sexes. Music is mostly techno.

Yab
Via Sassetti 5r (055 215160).
Open 9pm-4am Mon, Tue, Thur-Sat.
Closed June-Sept. **Admission** free
(€15 drinks minimum-spend Fri, Sat).
Map p53 A3 **68**
Some refer to this large, trendy city-centre locale as a disco; others, a 'glamour club'. You Are Beautiful – popularly known as Yab – has existed since the late 1970s, and plays up to any narcissist tendencies by its liberal use of mirrors, flattering lighting and on-tap female-focused compliments from the stalwarts. The sound system has the mammoth dancefloor shimmying with dancers. Monday hip hop nights are an institution, while Thursdays is deep house; the place is packed on Saturdays.

Arts & leisure

The historic **Teatro Niccolini**, on via Ricasoli, has recently been bought by a publishing entrepreneur. Closed since 1995, it should come back to life in late 2009 as a state-of-the-art cultural centre.

Chiesa di Santo Stefano al Ponte
Piazza Santo Stefano 5 (tourist office 055 290832). **Map** p53 B4 **69**
Located north-east of the ponte Vecchio, this large, deconsecrated church hosts regular concerts. See also p63.

Odeon Original Sound
Piazza Strozzi 2 (055 295051/ 295331/www.cinehall.it). **Open** times vary. Closed Aug. **Tickets** €7.20.
No credit cards. **Map** p53 A3 **70**
Mondays, Tuesdays and Thursdays are big draws for English-speakers at this stunning art nouveau cinema. Films on current release in English are screened, sometimes with Italian subtitles. There's a discount of up to 40% with a club card for eight films from a programme of 13 (€36); alternatively, use the voucher from the previous Sunday's *La Repubblica* for 30% off.

and mini brioches. The main attraction though is the 360-degree bird's-eye view of the city. The bar is open in 'fine weather'; while officially closed in winter, it may be open or closed for a few weeks longer depending on the weather.

Slowly
Via Porta Rossa 63r (055 2645354).
Open 7pm-2am Mon-Sat. **Map**
p53 A3 **66**
The ultimate chillout Bohemian-chic bar, Slowly is softly lit by candles in mosaic lanterns, with big soft sofas in alcoves, laid-back staff and mellow Buddha Bar sounds when the DJ gets stuck in. Even the inevitable crowds of pretty young things can't break the nice and easy spell. The restaurant overlooking the bar serves imaginative global cuisine.

Tabasco Disco Gay
Piazza Santa Cecilia 3r (055 213000/ www.tabascogay.it). **Open** 10pm-6am Tue-Sun. **Admission** €13 Tue-Fri; €15 Sat. **Map** p53 B4 **67**
Founded more than 35 years ago, Tabasco was Florence's first gay club, and has stood the test of time, remaining

Church of Santa Maria Novella p87

Santa Maria Novella

Many visitors initially think of this part of the city in functional terms – it is, after all, where coaches and trains arrive, and where most car-hire firms can be found. However, there's another, more tranquil and cultured side to Santa Maria Novella. Artistic treasures to be found here include the exquisite **church of Santa Maria Novella** and the **Alinari Photography museum**; and the nearly completed restoration work on **piazza Santa Maria Novella**, with its Giambologna statues, is set to increase the district's cultural cachet further.

To the north-west of the piazza is traffic-heavy via della Scala, home to the famous **Officina Profumo-Farmaceutica di Santa Maria Novella**, while a little south of the piazza, the triangle formed by via de' Fossi,

via della Spada and via della Vigna Nuova is a friendly, lively area cluttered with antiques emporia, designer clothes shops, cafés and *trattorie*. In the centre of the triangle are fine **Palazzo Rucellai** (not open to the public, but its Colosseum-inspired frontage can still be enjoyed), the **Capella Rucellai**, and the modern art museum, **Museo Marino Marini**.

At the end of via de' Fossi, next to the Arno, is **piazza Goldoni**, from which lungarno Vespucci and the elegant borgo Ognissanti lead off, opening out into **piazza Ognissanti**, a square flanked by swanky hotels and topped by the church of **Ognissanti** – the cloister of which houses the **Cenacolo di Ognissanti**. A little further along from here lies the mammoth park of **Parco delle Cascine**.

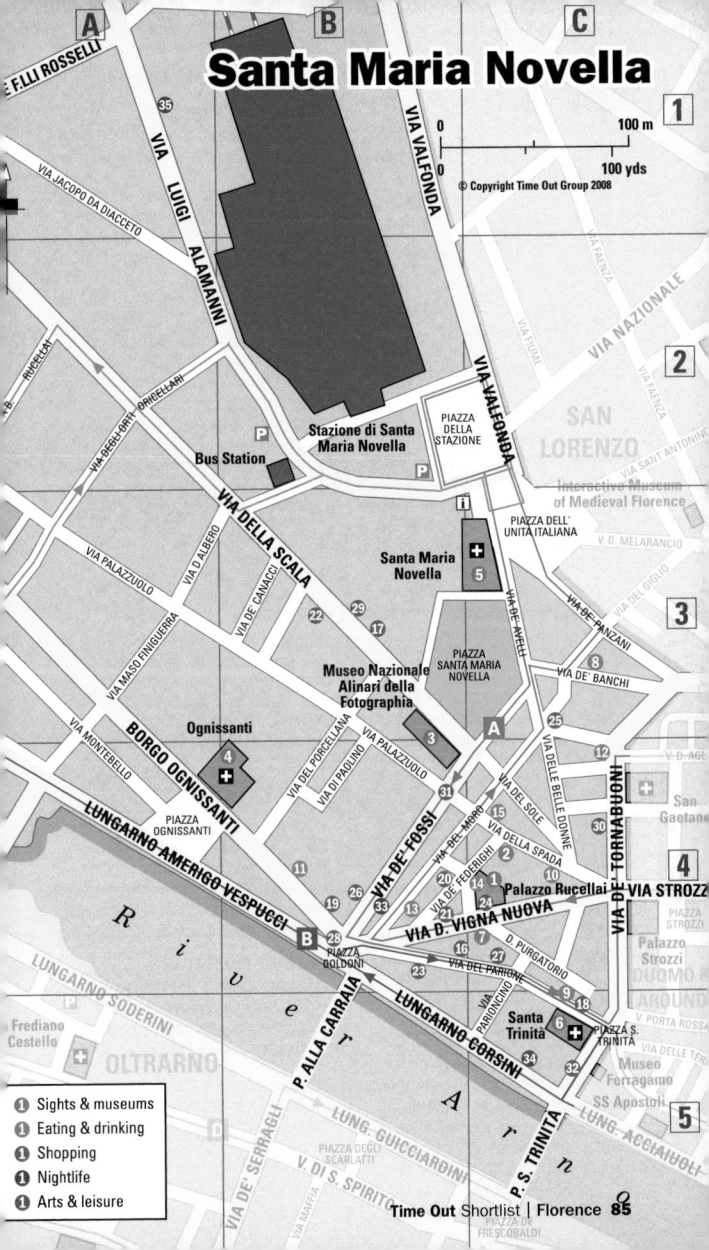

Santa Maria Novella

100 m

100 yds

© Copyright Time Out Group 2008

A VIA F.LLI ROSSELLI

VIA JACOPO DA DIACCETO

VIA LUIGI ALAMANNI

B VIA VALFONDA

VIA NAZIONALE

VIA FAENZA

SAN LORENZO

VIA DEGLI ORTI ORICELLARI

VIA RUCELLAI

P Bus Station

Stazione di Santa Maria Novella

PIAZZA DELLA STAZIONE

VIA VALFONDA

P

VIA FIUME

VIA SANT'ANTONINO

Interactive Museum of Medieval Florence

VIA PALAZZUOLO

VIA DELLA SCALA

VIA DI ALBERO

VIA DE CANACCI

PIAZZA DELL' UNITÀ ITALIANA

Santa Maria Novella **5** ✚

V. D. MELARANCIO

VIA DEL GIGLIO

VIA DE' PANZANI

VIA MASO FINIGUERRA

22 29 17

PIAZZA SANTA MARIA NOVELLA

Museo Nazionale Alinari della Fotografia

8

VIA DE' BANCHI

VIA MONTEBELLO

BORGO OGNISSANTI

Ognissanti **4** ✚

VIA DE' PORCELLANA

VIA DI PAOLINO

VIA PALAZZUOLO

3

A

31

VIA DELLE BELLE DONNE

25

VIA DE' SOLE

12

V. D. AGLI

San Gaetano

PIAZZA OGNISSANTI

LUNGARNO AMERIGO VESPUCCI

11

VIA DE' FOSSI

VIA DEL MORO

VIA DELLA SPADA

2

10

VIA DE' TORNABUONI

30

VIA STROZZI

PIAZZA STROZZI

Palazzo Strozzi

DUOMO & AROUND

26

19

63

VIA DE' FEDERIGHI

20 **14** 21

13

27

24

Palazzo Rucellai

VIA D. VIGNA NUOVA

7

D. PURGATORIO

River

B

28

PIAZZA GOLDONI

P. ALLA CARRAIA

16

23

VIA DEL PARIONE

LUNGARNO CORSINI

PARIONCINO

9 18

Santa Trinita **6** ✚

PIAZZA S. TRINITA

V. PORTA ROSSA

VIA DELLE TERME

Museo Ferragamo

SS Apostoli

LUNGARNO SODERINI

Frediano Cestello

✚

OLTRARNO

VIA DE' SERRAGLI

Arno

34

32

P. S. TRINITA

LUNG. GUICCIARDINI

PIAZZA DEGLI SCARLATTI

V. DI S. SPIRITO

VIA MAFFIA

V. DI SERRAGLI

LUNG. ACCIAIUOLI

PIAZZA DE' FRESCOBALDI

Sights & museums
Eating & drinking
Shopping
Nightlife
Arts & leisure

Time Out Shortlist | Florence **85**

Photo opportunity

A major step in piazza Santa Maria's recent and badly needed regeneration was taken in October 2006 with the opening on the southern side of the piazza of the new **Alinari National Museum of Photography** (below, right) in the restored 15th-century Loggia di San Paolo. The museum heralds a fresh era for the piazza, and has been popular with locals and tourists alike.

The Florentine Alinari brothers were among the pioneers of photography, opening the world's first photographic firm in 1852. Their legacy includes some four million pictures, many of which serve as evidence of historical events, including the floods of 1966. The museum periodically rotates its displays to allow at least a glimpse of such immense archives, but it also recounts the history of Italian and world photography from the earliest prototypes to modern digital devices. Displays include video screens, camera obscuras and a vast collectors' dream of cameras. Reconstructions of many photographs using plastic and textiles, and explanatory panels written in braille, make it possible for the museum to be appreciated by blind visitors.

The museum also has two rooms for temporary exhibitions, where half a dozen events are held throughout the year. The 2008 programme ranges from Italian authors like Oscar-winning director Giuseppe Tornatore, to international names such as John Phillips.

Sights & museums

Cappella Rucellai

Via della Spada (055 216912). **Open** 10am-noon Mon-Sat. **Admission** free. **Map** p85 C4 ❶

It's not so much a case of blink and you'll miss this tiny chapel; more that if you oversleep or linger over breakfast, you'll find it's already closed for the day. Once part of the church of San Pancrazio (now Museo Marino Marini; below), the chapel retains the church's charming bell tower and contains tombs of members of the family of 15th-century wool magnate Giovanni Rucellai. It's worth a visit to see Alberti's *Temple of the Santo Sepolcro*, commissioned by Giovanni in 1467 in an attempt to ensure his own salvation.

Museo Marino Marini

Piazza San Pancrazio (055 219432/ www.museo marinomarini.it). **Open** *Summer* 10am-5pm Mon, Wed-Fri. *Winter* 10am-5pm Mon, Wed-Sat. Closed Aug. **Admission** €4. No credit cards. **Map** p85 C4 ❷

The original Albertian church on this site, San Pancrazio, was redesigned to accommodate the works of prolific sculptor and painter Marino Marini (1901-80). It's now a huge, modern exhibition space filled predominantly with sculptures on the theme of horse and rider; the central exhibit is the 6m (20ft) *Composizione Equestre*. The second floor houses a series of other bronze and polychrome plaster pieces, including the hypnotic *Nuotatore* (Swimmer), and some fabulous colourful paintings and sculptures of dancers and jugglers created during the early 1950s.

Museo Nazionale Alinari della Fotografia

Piazza Santa Maria Novella 14a (055 216310/www.alinarifondazione. it). **Open** 9.30am-7.30pm Mon, Tue, Thur, Fri, Sun; 9.30am-11.30pm Sat. **Admission** €9; €7.50 each for 2 or more visitors, children, and visitors during happy hour (last hour before closing). **Map** p85 B3/B4 ❸ See box, left.

Ognissanti

Borgo Ognissanti 42 (055 2398700).
Open 9am-12.30pm, 4-7.30pm daily.
Admission free. **Map** p85 A4/B4 ➍
The church of Ognissanti (All Saints)
was founded in the 13th century by the
Umiliati, a group of monks from
Lombardy. The monks introduced the
prosperous wool trade to Florence; without them, perhaps, there would have
been no Florentine Renaissance. The
Umiliati were so rich by the 14th century that they commissioned Giotto to
paint the *Maestà* for their high altar; 50
years later, they got Giovanni da Milano
to create a flashier altarpiece. Both are
now in the Uffizi. Ognissanti was also
the parish church of the Vespucci, a
family of merchants that included 15th-
century navigator Amerigo, who sailed
to the Venezuelan coast in 1499 – and
had two continents named after him.

The church has been rebuilt numerous times and is now visited mainly for
paintings by Ghirlandaio, including *St
Jerome* and the *Madonna della
Misericordia*. To see Ghirlandaio's
masterful *Last Supper* you have to go
outside and through the next door. The
Chapel of St Peter of Alcantara houses
the tomb of Botticelli, marked with his
family name of Filipepi.

Cenacolo di Ognissanti

Open *Last Supper* 9am-noon Mon, Tue,
Sat. **Admission** free.
The Ognissanti's beautiful cloister,
accessed via a separate entrance on
borgo Ognissanti, is painted with frescoes illustrating the life of St Francis.
The cloister's main point of interest,
however, is Ghirlandaio's most famous
Last Supper, dated 1480, housed in the
refectory. There's also a museum of
Franciscan bits and bobs.

Santa Maria Novella

*Piazza Santa Maria Novella (055
2645184/219257/www.smn.it).* **Open**
9am-5pm daily. **Admission** €2.50.
No credit cards. **Map** p85 C3 ➎
Called Novella (New) because it was
built on the site of the ninth-century
Santa Maria delle Vigne, the church
dominates its eponymous piazza, with

its pièce de résistance, the magnificent
Alberti façade. In 1465, the architect
incorporated the Romanesque lower
storey into a refined Renaissance
scheme, adding the triangular tympa-
num and the scrolls that mask the side
nave exteriors in an exercise of con-
summate classical harmony. The interior, however, was designed by the
order's monks and is fittingly severe.

The church houses the *Crocifisso* by
Giotto, a simple wooden crucifix. It was
returned to the church in 2001 after a
12-year restoration and placed in the
centre of the basilica where the
Dominicans had positioned it in 1290.

Until Vasari had them whitewashed in
the mid 16th century, the church walls
were covered with frescoes. Fortunately,
Masaccio's *Trinità* of 1427 on the left
nave remains, a triumph of trompe l'œil.

In 1485, the Dominicans allowed
Ghirlandaio to cover the walls of the
Cappella Tornabuoni, behind the altarpiece, with scenes from the life of John
the Baptist, featuring lavish contemporary Florentine interiors and a supporting cast from the Tornabuoni family all
wearing beautiful clothes – effectively
making the work part-advertisement,
as the family were cloth merchants. At
about the same time, Filippino Lippi
was at work next door in the Cappella
di Filippo Strozzi, painting scenes from
the life of St Philip. A wooden crucifix
by Brunelleschi, the envy of Donatello,
is to the left of the altarpiece.

To compare Masaccio's easeful use of
perspective with the contorted struggles
of Paolo Uccello, visit the Chiostro
Verde (green cloister) to the left of the
church (via a separate entrance).
Uccello's lunettes can be considered
either visionary experiments of modern
art or a complete perspective mess,
depending on your tolerance of artistic
licence. Off the Chiostro you'll find the
Cappellone (or Cappella) degli Spagnoli,
named for the Spanish wife of Cosimo I,
Eleonora di Toledo, and decorated with
vibrant scenes by Andrea di Bonaiuto.
Look out for the odd-looking cupola
on the Duomo fresco: it's the artist's

own design for the dome, ultimately rejected in favour of Brunelleschi's plan.

Santa Trinita

Piazza Santa Trinita (055 216912).
Open 8am-noon, 4-6pm Mon-Sat; 4-6pm Sun. **Admission** free.
Map p85 C5 **6**

This plain church, the entrance of which is in piazza Santa Trinita (p55), was built in the 13th century over the ruins of two earlier churches belonging to the Vallombrosans, an order founded in 1038 by San Giovanni Gualberto Visdomini, who spent much of his life attempting to persuade pious aristocrats to surrender their wealth and live a life of austerity. The order became extremely wealthy and powerful, reaching a peak in the 16th and 17th centuries. Santa Trinita's façade was made at the end of the 16th century by Bernardo Buontalenti (who created the Boboli Gardens' Grotta Grande) but the church is well worth a visit for the Cappella Sassetti alone, which was luminously frescoed by Ghirlandaio in 1486 with scenes from the life of St Francis.

Eating & drinking

Amerini

Via della Vigna Nuova 63r (055 284941). **Open** 8.30am-8.30pm Mon-Sat. Closed 2wks Aug. **Café**. **Map** p85 C4 **7**

Smart but cosy, Amerini is such a lunchtime favourite that you're sometimes asked to endure the classic café faux pas of unknown companions being seated at your small table. Choose from sandwiches such as grilled vegetables with brie, or order a bowl of fresh pasta. Breakfast time and afternoons are more relaxing, so you can sample luscious lemon tart relatively undisturbed.

Bar Galli

Via de' Banchi 14r (055 213776).
Open noon-3.30pm Mon-Sat. Japanese food served 12.30-3pm & 7-10.30pm Tue-Sat. **€**. **Japanese/sandwich bar**. **Map** p85 C3 **8**

The tourist-worn strip between the station and the Duomo is a gastronomic

desert, but salvation is at hand in the form of this busy bar, which, alongside the usual pastries, panini and (above average) hot dishes, offers a menu of delicious Japanese fare. The setting in the bar's back room is spartan and the choice is limited to such homely dishes as ramen noodles and soups with the odd additional rice dish (the evening menu is a bit more elaborate), but it's very good and it's cheap.

Caffè Florian

Via del Parione 28r (055 284291/ www.caffeflorian.com). **Open** 9am-8pm daily. **Café**. **Map** p85 C5 **9**

The Venice icon recently opened this pretty, genteel sister café in a small backstreet off via de' Tornabuoni. Tisanes and coffees are served with dainty petite fours that look too good to eat, and the savouries are exquisite morsels with truffle or delicious cheeses.

Caffè Megara

Via della Spada 15-17r (055 211837).
Open 8am-2am daily (lunch noon-3pm). **Café**. **Map** p85 C4 **10**

Always full at lunchtimes with tourists and loyal regulars who know the great menu has daily specials. Pasta dishes are always a safe bet and the *bruschette* are enormous. Megara gets even busier when big matches are on. Smooth jazzy sounds play out in the evenings and in summer a hatch serves *aperitivo* snacks to the tables outside.

Caffè San Carlo

Borgo Ognissanti 32-34r (055 216879/ www.caffesancarlo.com). **Open** 7.30am-midnight Mon-Sat. **Café**. **Map** p85 B4 **11**

Pre-lunch and dinner aperitifs are the big draws in this stylish and lively bar. In good weather, the French windows are opened up, wine barrels are used as serving tables and the canopied outside area becomes a miniature socialising hub.

Cantinetta Antinori

Piazza degli Antinori 3 (055 2359827).
Open 12.30-2.30pm, 7-10.30pm Mon-Sat. Closed 3wks Aug. **€€€**. **Florentine/ wine bar**. **Map** p85 C4 **12**

Heaven scent

Florence's legendary pharmacy is in vogue once again.

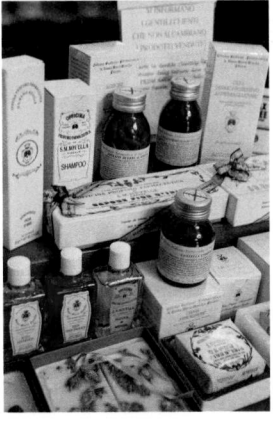

A beautiful 13th-century frescoed chapel in Santa Maria Novella is home to one of the world's oldest herbal pharmacies – now a global brand. The **Officina Profumo-Farmaceutica di Santa Maria Novella** (p91) was officially founded in 1612 by Fra' Angiolo Marchissi, though its origins date back as far as 1221, to the time of the Dominican friars.

As you reach the entrance, the scent of the *antica farmacia*'s potpourri fills the air, a mix of locally grown flowers and herbs, macerated in terracotta jars. A domed marble passageway leads to the main hall, which was turned into the shop in 1848. It's lined with mahogany and glass cabinets, and filled with the pharmacy's signature soaps, delicate glass bottles of pure oils and perfume essences, and scented paper.

Through a gilded archway is the apothecary, a grand antechamber decorated with Medici portraits, where herbal concoctions are still weighed up on brass scales. A back room dotted with ancient apothecary tools is where jams, sweets and soaps are packaged in lovely cream vellum boxes.

The pharmacy's serenity and beauty is in stark contrast to the bloodthirsty nature of some of its past patrons. The pharmacy must have its roots in the gentler side of Florence's torture-loving Dominican monks. Perfumes – including the original Eau de Cologne – were also created here for the notorious Caterina de' Medici. And more recently, the olfactory powers of Thomas Harris's Hannibal the cannibal led him to the Officina Profumo-Farmaceutica when it came to choosing a scent for his paramour.

But it's the contemporary boom for luxury natural products that has transformed the *farmacia* from local icon into internationally coveted brand with branches in London, New York and Tokyo. The original lavender-smelling salts, 'anti-hysteria' Acqua di Santa Maria Novella, 14th-century Acqua di Rose and powder produced from the ground rhizomes of irises are practically unchanged formulas, and appeal to the increased demand for natural products. Other renowned items include orange-blossom water and pomegranate perfume.

However, with globalisation comes the march of modernity: you can now find parabens in the rose cream and tan-prolonging shower gel alongside the medieval ladies' fave: skin-whitening powder.

Well-heeled tourists rub shoulders with business types and ladies who lunch at this classic restaurant/wine bar, open since 1965. It occupies an elegantly vaulted ground-floor room of the 15th-century Palazzo Antinori, the historic home of one of Tuscany's foremost wine-producing families. Waiters in white jackets and black bow ties bring out textbook versions of Florentine classics, such as *pappa al pomodoro*, *salsicce e fagioli* (sausage and beans), tripe and fillet steak. Very civilised, if a little expensive.

Garga
Via del Moro 48r (055 2398898).
Open 7.30-10.30pm Tue-Sun. **€€€€**.
Italian. **Map** p85 B4 ⑬
Bohemian in everything but its prices, this *trattoria* is perennially popular, particularly among well-heeled visitors. Owner Giuliano Gargani (who has been known to regale customers with operatic arias) presides over his colourful kingdom with its quirky decor, while chatty staff serve up well-executed pastas, meats and fish dishes. The vibe may not be particularly Tuscan, but the cooking is undeniably good.

I Latini
Via dei Palchetti 6r (055 210916).
Open 12.30-2.30pm, 7.30-10.30pm Tue-Sun. Closed last wk Dec & 1st wk Jan.
€€€. **Florentine**. **Map** p85 C4 ⑭
You'll inevitably have to queue (no bookings are taken after 8pm) and once inside, it'll be noisy and you'll probably be sharing a table, but that's all part of the fun at this rustic eatery, run by the Latini family since 1950. Vegetarians should keep well away: the thing here is the meat, great hunks of it. Skip the mediocre pasta dishes and go for soups and *secondi*. If you order *arrosto misto*, a vast platter of roast meats will arrive at the table defying all but the most prodigious appetites.

Rosticceria della Spada
Via della Spada 62r (055 218757/ www.laspadaitalia.com). **Open** noon-3pm, 6-10.30pm daily. **€**. **Rosticceria**. **Map** p85 C4 ⑮

This centrally located *rosticceria* has been selling delicious dishes to take-away for a good many years, but now you can also eat in, and plenty do. The menu is more or less the same whether you sit in or take away, but you'll pay about 50% less if you do the latter. There are good pastas (try the lasagne), roast meats and vegetables and a truly delicious *melanzane alla parmigiana*.

Shopping

A Cozzi
Via del Parione 37r (055 294968).
Open 3.30-7.30pm Mon; 10am-1pm, 3.30-7.30pm Tue-Sat. **Map** p85 B4 ⑯
A bookbinder's workshop and show-room with a wonderful selection of books with swirled-coloured paper covers, and some bound in leather.

Antica Orologeria Nuti
Via della Scala 10r (055 294594).
Open 4-7pm Mon; 9am-12.30pm, 4-7pm Tue-Sat. Closed Aug. **Map** p85 B3 ⑰
Fabulous antique and reproduction art deco and art nouveau jewellery, plus an eclectic collection of lantern, long-case, bracket and mantel clocks.

Il Bisonte
Via del Parione 31r (055 215722/ www.ilbisonte.net). **Open** 9.30am-7pm Mon-Sat. **Map** p85 C5 ⑱
A renowned, long-established outlet for top-tier soft leather bags and accessories and rugged cases.

BM American British Bookstore
Borgo Ognissanti 4r (055 294575/ www.bmbookshop.com). **Open** 9.30am-7.30pm Mon-Sat. **Map** p85 B4 ⑲
This tiny independent has a good collection of books in English, many with Italian and Florentine themes. Some used books and a range of new and collectable children's titles are stocked, as well as an odd array of gifts. Specialists in Italian traditions and folklore.

Bottega della Frutta
Via de' Federighi 31r (055 2398590).
Open 8am-7.30pm Mon, Tue,

Thur-Sat; 8am-1.30pm Wed. Closed Aug. **Map** p85 B4 **⑳**
Alongside fruit and veg, this charming shop sells wines, vintage balsamic vinegars, truffle-scented oils and speciality sweets. Be prepared to queue.

BP Studio
Via della Vigna Nuova 15r (055 213243/www.bpstudio.it). **Open** 3-7pm Mon; 10am-2pm, 3-7pm Tue-Sat. **Map** p85 B4 **㉑**
Delicate knitwear, rosebud-edged chiffon skirts and mohair stoles from young designers are shown at this upmarket but youthful store.

Dolceforte
Via della Scala 21 (055 219116/ www.dolceforte.it). **Open** 10am-1pm, 3.30-8pm Mon-Sat. **Map** p85 B3 **㉒**
Connoisseur chocolates, plus novelty treats like chocolate Duomos. In hot months, melting stock is replaced with jams, sugared almond flowers and jars of *gianduja*, a chocolate hazelnut spread.

Elio Ferrano
Via del Parione 47r (055 290425/ www.elioferraro.com). **Open** 9.30am-7.30pm Mon-Sat. **Map** p85 B4 **㉓**
See box p140.

Emilio Cavallini
Via della Vigna Nuova 24r (055 2382789/www.emiliocavallini.com). **Open** 3-7pm Mon; 10am-7pm Tue-Sat. Closed 2wks Aug. **Map** p85 C4 **㉔**
Cavallini's trademark wacky tights are stocked here, plus lines of black and white clothing, and lingerie with Warhol Marilyn and motif prints.

Franco Maria Ricci/ Babele
Via delle Belle Donne 41r (055 283312). **Open** 3.30-7.30pm Mon; 10am-1pm, 3.30-7.30pm Tue-Sat. **Map** p85 C3 **㉕**
A delightful art bookshop and arts and crafts gallery stocking limited editions and handmade stationery.

G Veneziano
Via de' Fossi 53r (055 287925). **Open** 3-7pm Mon; 9am-1pm, 3-7pm Tue-Sat. Closed Aug. **Map** p85 B4 **㉖**

A friendly, smart shop selling Venetian glass jewellery, bottle-stoppers and plates, funky printed crockery, flower-embroidered cushions and tablecloths and a quirky Barbapapa range of gifts.

Mariano Alimentari
Via del Parione 19r (055 214067). **Open** 8am-3pm, 5-7.30pm Mon-Fri; 8am-3pm Sat. Closed 3wks Aug. **Map** p85 C4 **㉗**
This tiny, rustic food shop-cum-sandwich bar offers focaccia filled with marinated aubergines and oil-preserved pecorino, and an array of delicacies. Have a coffee at the bar or in the vaulted wine cellar.

Münstermann
Piazza Goldoni 2r (055 210660/www.munstermann.it). **Open** 9am-1pm, 4-8pm Mon-Fri. **Map** p85 B4 **㉘**
This charming shell-shaped corner icon was opened in 1897, a stone's throw from the ponte Vecchio, and still has its original shop fittings. It stocks pharmaceutical and herbal medicines, toiletries, silver pillboxes, hair accessories and bathroom oddities. Its own-brand products (body lotions, hand creams, shampoos, fragrances) use high-quality, natural ingredients.

Officina Profumo-Farmaceutica di Santa Maria Novella
Via della Scala 16 (055 216276/ www.smnovella.it). **Open** 9.30am-7.30pm Mon-Sat; 10.30am-6.30pm Sun. Closed Sun Feb & Nov, 2wks Aug. **Map** p85 B3 **㉙**
See box p89.

Parenti
Via de' Tornabuoni 93r (055 214438/ www.parentifirenze.it). **Open** 3-7pm Mon; 9am-1pm, 3-7pm Tue-Sat. Closed Aug. **Map** p85 C4 **㉚**
A slightly daunting-looking emporium with Baccarat rings, art deco pieces and 1950s Tiffany jewellery.

Il Rifugio
Piazza Ottaviani 3r (055 294736/ www.rifugiosport.it). **Open** 9.30am-7.30pm Mon-Sat. **Map** p85 B4 **㉛**

The new black

Noir (p93) is the most desired of the city's central nightspots, and heaving most nights of the year. But the riverside bar is also the chameleon of Florentine nightlife, and was known as Capocaccia until it woke up to its most-recent incarnation in December 2006.

The bar started life in 1996 as a franchise (the sister bars are in Monte Carlo and Geneva), bought by Luigi Grassi, an Italian with an eye for design and a serious case of wanderlust. Capocaccia was an immediate hit. It was the kind of place you could take a maiden aunt for lunch and a wild cousin for a night out. The decor was relaxed-chic, and after dark, hurricane lamps appeared, the bar was transformed into a DJ's console and the beautiful people flocked to see and be seen in the hippest of nightspots.

Then, in 2001, things really started happening. Capocaccia was closed for 'redecoration', and when the new bar was unveiled, the walls were scarlet and denim-blue and industrial wall-lamps hung in place of mini-chandeliers. Luigi, it seems, had been inspired while on holiday across the pond.

Next came his trips to exotic climes and, in 2004, Capocaccia was dotted with decapé tables and zebra-print pouffes. In 2005, Luigi came back from London keen to pay homage to the Sanderson Hotel, and billowing white curtains adorned every door and window.

Though Capocaccia's popularity continued to grow, the parent group apparently wasn't amused by Luigi's overhauls. When, in 2006, he created the 'Maldives look', with turquoise tables, bamboo, wall shells and sand on the floor of the frescoed saloon, things came to a head and Luigi ended up buying the bar outright.

This led to the new name of Noir and to the most dramatic yet of the new skins. Black walls and velvet capitonée seating were inspired by Paris's Hotel Costes, the lights by a Marrakech souk and the glass bar by designs for the Red Sea's El Gouna Sheraton. The new get-up works best in the evening for the legendary *aperitivo*.

Luigi is rumoured to be plotting his next trip abroad, destination unknown. But by the time this guide has been printed, Noir's decor may be completely different.

Vast selections of sporting equipment and accessories, as well as trainers and sports clothing. Staff are helpful. **Other locations** Piazza della Stazione 1 (055 289328).

Save the Queen Circus
Via de' Tornabuoni 49r (055 213231/ www.savethequeen.com). **Open** 10am-7pm Mon-Sat, last Sun of mth. **Map** p85 C5 ㉜
A fantasy space for kids and adults. The displays can be anything from rocking horses hanging from the ceilings to kooky dancing mannequins flaunting the whimsical (in everything but price) women's line of couture dresses.

Nightlife

Art Bar
Via del Moro 4r (055 287661). **Open** 7pm-1am Mon-Thur; 7pm-2am Fri, Sat. Closed 3wks Aug. No credit cards. **Map** p85 B4 ㉝
Battered French horns hanging from the ceiling and sepia photos of jazz musicians lend a beatnik air to this popular bar. The ambience is cosy but animated, with student types holed up in the brick cellar sipping potent piña coladas. During happy hour (7-9pm), drinks cost €5; on Mondays and Wednesdays, the happy 'hour' lasts all night.

Noir
Lungarno Corsini 12-14r (055 210751/ www.noirfirenze.com). **Open** noon-2am daily. **Map** p85 C5 ㉞
See box p92.

Sintetika
Via Luigi Alamanni, 4 (333 3591575/ www.sintetikalive.it). Bus 2, 14. **Open** 11.30pm-4am. Days vary, call for info. **Tickets** €8 membership. No credit cards. **Map** p85 A1 ㉟
With a rapidly increasing number of local rock bands sprouting up, and no dedicated venue in which to house them, Sintetika stepped up to accept the challenge. This is one of few clubs in Florence that plays only live music. Though the bar is fairly basic, the prices will be a welcome relief from the main

city bars. It can be tricky to find: look for a crowd loitering outside a garage door.

Arts & leisure

Teatro del Maggio Musicale Fiorentino
Corso Italia 16 (055 2779350/box office 055 213535/www.maggiofiorentino. com). **Open** Phone bookings 8am-8pm Mon-Fri; 8am-3pm Sat. Box office 10am-4.30pm Tue-Fri; 10am-1pm Sat; 1hr before performance. **Map** p85 A3 ㊱
Despite deep-seated financial worries (due to gargantuan overheads and a reduction in state funding), there has been an attempt over the past year or so to revamp and modernise this theatre's rather stuffy image. Principal conductor Zubin Mehta hit 70 in 2007, but he's showing no signs of retiring. When on form, the Teatro del Maggio's resident orchestra and chorus are on a level with La Scala in Milan. However, lack of funds means that big-name conductors and soloists are often padded out with mediocre unknowns. While few risks are taken in terms of repertoire, the highlight of recent years has been the fabulous 2007/08 staging of Wagner's marathon Ring Cycle. The theatre is also home to Florence's mainstream ballet group MaggioDanza.

The performing year is divided into three parts: January to March is concert season, with performances on Fridays, Saturdays and Sundays; October to December is opera and ballet season; and the Maggio Musicale Fiorentino festival (p33) runs for two months from late April/early May. The last offers a mix of opera, ballet and recital programmes, culminating in a free open-air concert and dance extravaganza in piazza della Signoria.

The building itself, built in 1882 and renovated in 1957, is architecturally unexciting. Of the 2,000-odd seats, the best acoustics are to be had in the second gallery (they are also the cheapest), but if you want to strut your stuff alongside the designer outfits of *Firenze per bene*, you need to fork out for an opening night in the stalls or one of the *palchi* (boxes).

FLORENCE BY AREA

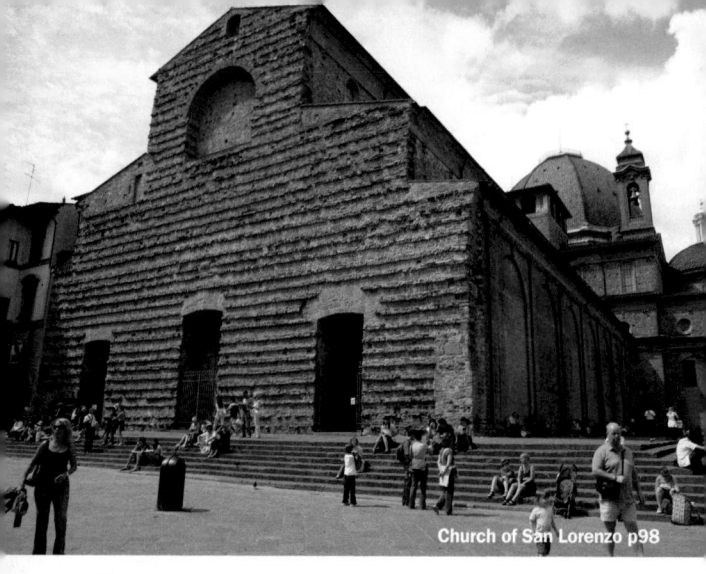
Church of San Lorenzo p98

San Lorenzo

The district of San Lorenzo is marked out by the frenetic activity of the huge **Mercato Centrale** – still an active part of the local community, as well as a draw for tourists. But the market isn't the only foodie-orientated attraction here; the area is also home to a number of homely and quintessentially Florentine eateries and wine bars.

The market constitutes the hub of the area, and spreads its tentacles over a wide swathe of *piazze* that snake north from the **church of San Lorenzo** – known for its incongruously unfinished façade. The street stalls around here sell cheap clothes, mediocre leather goods and tacky souvenirs.

North-east from **piazza San Lorenzo** (to the east of the church), on via Cavour, lie the **Palazzo Medici Riccardi**, with its lovely frescoed chapel, the tacky gimmick that is the new **Serial Killer & Death Penalty Museum** (51r, 055 210188, www.serialkiller museum.com) and the **Chiostro dello Scalzo**. Further out is the Benedictine refectory of **Cenacolo di Sant'Apollonia**.

Head south from the piazza for the fashionable shops in borgo San Lorenzo. North-west you'll find the spectacular **Cappelle Medicee** and, beyond that, the **Interactive Museum of Medieval Florence** (via Faenza 13r, 055 282432, www. oscuromedioevo.com) – another naff money-spinner. Further up via Faenza lies the **Cenacolo di Fuligno**, while north-east from here is **piazza dell'Indipendenza**, with its grand *palazzi*. Past the square are the pleasant gardens of the otherwise unspectacular (albeit massive) **Fortezza da**

San Lorenzo

Basso, a relic of Alessandro de' Medici's reign, now used for trade fairs and industry exhibitions.

Sights & museums

Cappelle Medicee

Piazza di Madonna degli Aldobrandini 6 (055 2388602). **Open** 8.15am-4.20pm Tue-Sat, 1st, 3rd, 5th Mon & 2nd, 4th Sun of mth. **Admission** €6. No credit cards. **Map** p95 B2 ❶
The spectacular Medici mausoleum is the most splendid and fascinating part of the basilica of San Lorenzo. Up the curling stairs at the back of the entrance chamber is the grand Cappella dei Principi (Chapel of the Princes), which was constructed from hunks of porphyry and ancient Roman marbles hauled into the city by Turkish slaves, and houses six sarcophagi of the Medici grand dukes. The floor plan of the Cappella dei Principi was based on that of Florence's Baptistery and, possibly,

that of the Holy Sepulchre in Jerusalem. It had been hoped that the tombs would be joined by that purporting to be of Christ, but the authorities in Jerusalem refused to sell it. This mausoleum was commissioned in 1602 but, amazingly, the beautifully intricate inlay of marble and precious stones wasn't fully completed by the workers of the Opificio delle Pietre Dure (p105) until an external pavement was finished in 1962, at which point the Medici dynasty had been over for 220 years.

Although it's closed to the public, the discovery of the crypt in 1994 caused much excitement, especially the sensational unearthing of a stone under the chapel's altar that concealed its entrance. The exhumation of 49 Medici bodies ensued and enabled scientists to determine in what manner many of them died. It was originally thought that Francesco I de' Medici and his mistress Bianca Cappella, who died within hours of each other, had suffered from

Cappelle Medicee p95

symbolising the 'sun' of salvation. The Sagrestia Nuova was finished by Giorgio Vasari, Michelangelo himself having been hauled off to Rome to finish the Sistine Chapel. The great man was furious at having to leave the city, but he'd worked long enough on the project to leave it as one of his masterpieces.

Cenacolo del Conservatorio di Fuligno

Via Faenza 42 (055 286982).
Open 9am-noon & by appointment Tue, Thur, Sat. **Admission** free.
Map p95 A1 ❷
The harmonious fresco on the refectory wall of the ex-convent of St Onofrio was discovered in 1845, and was at first thought to be the work of Raphael. In fact, it is one of the best of Perugino's works: a *Last Supper* from about 1490. In the background is a representation of the *Oration of the Garden* in the characteristically Umbrian landscape, a giveaway of the Perugian-born painter's roots.

Cenacolo di Sant'Apollonia

Via XXVII Aprile 1 (055 23885).
Open 8.30am-1.50pm Tue-Sat, 1st, 3rd, 5th Mon & 2nd, 4th Sun of mth.
Admission free. **Map** p95 C1 ❸
The works in this Benedictine refectory, such as the frescoes of the *Passion of Christ*, were covered over during the Baroque period and only came to light in the late 19th century. The most important is Andrea del Castagno's *Last Supper*.

Chiostro dello Scalzo

Via Cavour 69 (055 2388604).
Open 9am-1pm Mon; by appointment only other days. **Admission** free.
Map p95 C1 ❹
The 'Cloister of the Barefoot', so called because the monk holding the cross in the re-enactments of the *Passion of Christ* traditionally went shoeless, is frescoed with the *chiaroscuro* episodes from the life of St John the Baptist by Andrea del Sarto. Built to a design by Sangallo around a double courtyard with Corinthian columns, it's a must-see epitome of delicacy and understatement.

malaria: it's now been proven that they had in fact been the victims of acute arsenic poisoning – probably at the hand of Francesco's jealous brother Ferdinando.

Out of the Cappella dei Principi, a passage to your left leads to Michelangelo's Sagrestia Nuova (New Sacristy). This chamber, begun in 1520, makes a stark contrast to the excesses of the Cappella dei Principi. It's dominated by the tombs of Lorenzo il Magnifico's relatives: grandson Lorenzo, Duke of Urbino, and son Giuliano, Duke of Nemours who grew up alongside Michelangelo. The tombs were designed by the artist with the allegorical figures of Night and Day, and, opposite, Dawn and Dusk reclining on top; their gaze directs the visitor's eyes to a sculpture of a Madonna and child on a facing wall. Also here, under the sacristy, is the incomplete tomb of Lorenzo il Magnifico and his brother Giuliano. The chapel's coffered dome was designed to contribute to Michelangelo's allegory within the tomb of the inevitability of death,

Finishing the façade

Projection of the 'virtual façade'

In 2007, a 'virtual façade' showing Michelangelo's original design for the façade of **San Lorenzo church** was projected on to the famously bare-fronted building, causing much excitement. Now, the team who produced it is hoping to stage an even more impressive display: a temporary life-size construction of the façade in fabric or plastic.

Michelangelo had never tried his hand at designing buildings when, in 1516, Pope Leo X – a Medici – decided to have a grand façade erected for his family church of San Lorenzo. Competition to win the job of architect for the project was fierce. Michelangelo was initially only meant to provide the sculptures. Yet he began sketching his own designs, and against all odds, in 1518, he was formally commissioned the whole project.

His unorthodox plans concealed the three naves behind a classical marble front, decorated with freestanding statues. A wooden model of the project (minus its miniature wax statues) is on display in Casa Buonarroti (p113). The artist threw himself body and soul into the task, supervising every step, and arranging the opening of new marble quarries.

However, to Michelangelo's deep frustration, the Pope decided to call off the commission in 1520.

Several other ideas for the unfinished façade were submitted over the centuries, but none were ever carried out. Then, in 1998, Professor Morolli of Florence University found, in a marble warehouse near Pietrasanta, three huge columns that might pertain to the set quarried by Michelangelo for his façade. We know that one such marble column had already been shipped up the Arno and was later interred in the square beside the church. If this was dug up, we could find out if they all belonged to Michelangelo's planned façade.

The discovery triggered the production of computer-generated models of Michelangelo's design – resulting in the 'virtual façade'. Whether or not this will eventually lead to a permanent façade for San Lorenzo will ultimately be up to the Florentines – a conservative bunch who seem to be perfectly contented with its rustic front. The planned material version would at least bring Michelangelo's plan to fruition, if only temporarily.

The tourist board (p187) should be able to give project updates.

La Casa del Vino

Palazzo Medici Riccardi

Via Cavour 1 (055 2760340/www. palazzo-medici.it). **Open** 9am-7pm Mon, Tue, Thur-Sun. **Admission** €5. No credit cards. **Map** p95 C2 ⑤

In true Medici fashion, the family's 15th-century Renaissance palace is strategically placed. The Medici bought a string of adjacent houses on via Larga (now via Cavour) in the mid 14th century when it was a fairly broad road in a residential area – but still close to the Duomo, and merely a few steps from their church, San Lorenzo (below). They ensured not only that their home (until they moved into Palazzo Vecchio in 1540) was in a position of power but that it would subtly intimidate any opposition with its strongbox-like appearance. Not wishing to appear too ostentatious, however, Cosimo il Vecchio rejected Brunelleschi's design as too extravagant and plumped for one by Michelozzo. Michelozzo designed a façade with a heavily rusticated lower storey in the style of many military buildings, a smoother and more refined first storey and a yet more restrained second storey.

The building was expanded and revamped in the 1600s by the Riccardi, its new owners, but retains Michelozzo's charming chapel. Almost entirely covered with frescoes by Benozzo Gozzoli, a student of Fra Angelico, the chapel features a vivid *Journey of the Magi* – actually a portrait of 15th-century Medici. In another room is Fra Filippo Lippi's winsome *Madonna and Child*. Don't miss the new interactive technology on the ground floor (in what was once the chamber of Lorenzo the Magnificent).

San Lorenzo

Piazza San Lorenzo (055 2645184). **Open** 10am-5.30pm Mon-Sat. *Summer* 10am-5.30pm Mon-Sat; 1.30-5.30pm Sun. **Admission** €2.50. No credit cards. **Map** p95 B2 ⑥

Built on the site of Florence's cathedral from the end of the fourth to the ninth century – and thus occupying the spot of Florence's oldest church – San Lorenzo's sheer size more than compensates for its very plain exterior. It was built between 1419 and 1469 to a design by Brunelleschi (largely completed by Manetti, his erstwhile assistant, who made several design alterations), and was the first church to which the architect applied his theory of rational proportion. It sprawls, heavy and imposing, between piazza San Lorenzo and piazza di Madonna degli Aldobrandini.

Despite the fortune spent on the place, the façade was never finished, hence the digestive biscuit-like bricks. In 1518, the Medici pope Leo X commissioned Michelangelo to design a façade – the models are in the Casa Buonarroti (p113) – and ordained that the marble should be quarried at Pietrasanta. Michelangelo disagreed, preferring Carrara marble. In the end, it didn't matter: the scheme was cancelled in 1520. Recently, there has been great excitement about this absent façade: a column built for the project was discovered buried in the piazza and others – that some now believe were destined for San Lorenzo – were found in Pietrasanta. The basilica hosted six nights of a projected 'virtual façade' in March 2007 (see box p97).

A couple of artworks in the church merit a closer look. Savonarola snarled his tales of sin and doom from Donatello's bronze pulpits, but the reliefs are also powerful: you can almost hear the crowds scream in the *Deposition*. On the north wall is a *Martyrdom of St Lawrence* by Mannerist painter par excellence Bronzino. In the second chapel on the right is another Mannerist work, a *Marriage of the Virgin* by Rosso Fiorentino, while the north transept holds an *Annunciation* by Filippo Lippi, with a clarity of line and depth of perspective that make it perfect for this interior.

Opening off the north transept is the Sagrestia Vecchia (Old Sacristy): another Brunelleschi design, it has a dome segmented like a tangerine and proportions based on cubes and spheres, along with a fabulous painted *tondo* by Donatello. The doors, also by Donatello, feature martyrs and apostles.

Reached via the door to the left of the façade, Michelangelo's architectural classic, the Biblioteca Mediceo-Laurenziana (Laurentian Library), was built to house the Medici's large library. It still contains priceless volumes, papyri, codices and documents, though not all of them are on permanent display. The entrance corridor has a stunning red and cream inlaid mosaic floor, while the library itself displays Michelangelo's predilection for the

human form over any classical architectural norms. However, it's in the vestibule leading into the reading room that the true masterpiece is to be found. The original three-sweep stairwell in pietra serena was a groundbreaking design, the first example of the expressive Mannerist style in architecture and one of the most elegant staircases ever built.

Eating & drinking

BZF (Bizzeffe)

Via Panicale 61r (055 2741009/www. bzf.it). **Open** 4pm-midnight Tue-Sun. Closed June-Aug. **Café**. **Map** p95 B1 **7**

A stunning 13th-century convent with an intellectual spirit. The bar is adjoined to the bookshop, internet terminal and an art space. As well as hosting jazz gigs and serving grown-up brunches, BZF organises regular lectures and debates. A range of coffees and teas from around the world is served, and there's a strong food menu: try the divine pumpkin soup, cheeseboards or American-style sweets. Sunday brunch has accompanying jazz sounds and traditional roasts.

La Casa del Vino

Via dell'Ariento 16r (055 215609/ www.casadelvino.it). **Open** 9.30am-5.30pm Mon-Fri, 10am-3.30pm Sat. Closed Aug. **Wine bar**. **Map** p95 B2 **8**

The only seating at this crowded, authentic wine bar, hidden behind the stalls of the San Lorenzo market, is on benches backed up against the wine cabinets. No matter: punters continue to pile in for a glass of good wine and some delicious panini and *crostini*. Bottles for all budgets sit on lovely old carved wood shelves that line the room; you'll find fairly priced wines from all over Italy, plus labels from further afield and plenty of choice by the glass.

Da Mario

Via Rosina 2r (055 218550). **Open** noon-3.30pm Mon-Sat. Closed 3wks Aug. **€**. No credit cards. **Florentine**. **Map** p95 B1 **9**

Be prepared to queue for a table at this tiny, cramped eaterie, in which four generations of the Colsi family have reigned.

San Lorenzo street market p94

Your fellow lunchers will include stall-holders, businessmen, students and tourists, an egalitarian mix all drawn by the excellent Florentine home cooking and cheap prices: try the earthy *zuppa di fagioli e cavolo nero* (bean and black cabbage soup), a terrific *bollito misto* (mixed boiled meats) served with a biting salsa verde and the excellent *bistecca*.

Nannini Coffee Shop

Borgo San Lorenzo 7r (055 212680).
Open 7.30am-7.30pm Mon-Fri, Sun; 7.30am-8.30pm Sat. **Café**. **Map** p95 B2 ⑩
Perennially bustling, Nannini is perfect for coffee and panforte (a sticky Sienese cake made with dried fruits and nuts) after a visit to the nearby central market. Sweets from Siena are the bar's speciality, including *cantuccini* (almond biscuits) and ricciarelli (choc-covered marzipan petits fours).

Nerbone

Mercato Centrale (055 219949).
Open 7am-2pm Mon-Sat. Closed Aug.
€. Florentine/food stall. No credit cards. **Map** p95 B1 ⑪
This food stall/*trattoria*, located on the ground floor of the covered central

market and dating back to 1872, is a good place to find local colour. It's packed from breakfast time with market workers: even if you can't face a *lampredotto* (cow's intestine) sarnie and a glass of rough red plonk at 7am, the locals can, and it only costs them €3.50. Plates of simple pasta and soups (from €4) offer alternatives at lunchtime.

Da Sergio

Piazza San Lorenzo 8r (055 281941).
Open noon-3pm Mon-Sat. Closed Aug.
€€. Florentine. **Map** p95 B2 ⑫
Hidden away behind the market stalls, this family-run eaterie opened in the early 1900s selling just wine and olive oil. Today, it oozes old-fashioned Florentine atmosphere and makes a less frantic alternative to Da Mario (p99) as a place to sample genuine home cooking. Begin with *minestrone, ribollita* or *minestra di farro* (spelt soup) before moving on to a roast or *bistecca alla fiorentina*. There's tripe on Mondays and Thursdays and fresh fish on Tuesdays and Fridays.

Zanobini

Via Sant'Antonino 47r (055 2396850).
Open 8am-2pm, 3-8pm Mon-Sat.
Wine bar. **Map** p95 B1 ⑬

FLORENCE BY AREA

This no-frills stand-up *vineria* has bags of atmosphere. It's usually full of locals propping up the bar, many looking as if they've been there since opening time. The shelves are filled with interesting, well-priced bottles; don't neglect the back room, with its fine selection of *digestivi* and whiskies. A good place for a quick slurp (there's nothing to eat) on your way to the market.

Shopping

For information on the stalls of **Mercato Centrale**, see page 46 of our Florence for Foodies chapter.

Alberti
Borgo San Lorenzo 45-49r (055 294271). **Open** 3.30-7.30pm Mon; 9am-7.30pm Tue-Sat. **Map** p95 B2 ⑭
The oldest record shop in the city has a vast selection of pop, dance, jazz and indie CD recordings, some vinyl, a variety of DVDs and a great selection of portable DVD and CD players.

Alinari
Largo Alinari 15 (055 2395232/ www.alinari.it). **Open** 9am-1pm, 2-6pm Mon-Fri; 10am-1pm, 2-6pm Sat. Closed 3wks Aug. **Map** p95 A1 ⑮
One of the world's first and most famous photographic firms, established in 1852. Photography books and exhibition catalogues are stocked; prints can be ordered from its archives. See also p86 and box p86.

La Botteghina del Ceramista
Via Guelfa 5r (055 287367). **Open** 10am-1.30pm, 3.30-7.30pm Mon-Fri; 10am-1.30pm Sat. Closed 2wks Aug. **Map** p95 C1 ⑯
Superb hand-painted ceramics in intricate designs and vivid colours.

Hito Estetica
Via de' Ginori 21 (055 284424). **Open** 9am-7.30pm Mon-Fri; 9am-7pm Sat. **Map** p95 C1 ⑰
A range of natural treatments and pampering for men and women, including Ayurvedic techniques.

L'Olandese Volante
Via San Gallo 44r (055 473240). **Open** 10am-1pm, 3.30-8pm Mon-Sat. Closed 3wks Aug. **Map** p95 C1 ⑱
Northern European specialities, including Dutch cheeses with cumin, mustard seeds or herbs, smoked herrings, and gourmet chocs.

Nightlife

During the trade shows in Fortezza da Basso, the watering hole of choice is the café/bar **Porfirio Rubirosa** on viale Strozzi (nos.18-20, 055 490965). Locals also flock here at weekends, when a deluge of motors often creates traffic mayhem.

Bar 85
Via Guelfa 85r (055 216050/ www.bar85.eu). **Open** 5pm-3am Mon-Thur; 5pm-6am Fri, Sat. **Admission** €6; membership free. **Map** p95 B1 ⑲
A new bar in Florence with a 'leather' vibe, geared to a mature crowd and popular with the gay community.

Maracana Casa di Samba
Via Faenza 4 (055 210298/www. maracana.it). **Open** *Restaurant* 8.30-11.30pm Tue-Sun. *Club* midnight-4am Tue-Sun. Closed June-Aug. **Admission** €10-€20. **Map** p95 B2 ⑳
Give this place a wide berth if you can't stomach the sight of middle-aged suits drooling over Brazilian booties – after the restaurant stops serving its South American fare, all decorum is shed. The main dancefloor is surrounded by poseur platforms; balconies assure views of cleavages and bald patches.

Arts & leisure

Teatrino del Gallo
Via San Gallo 25-27r (055 2658324/ www.teatrinodelgallo.it). **Open** see website for show times. Closed 3wks in Aug. **Tickets** €5 children; €7 adults. **Map** p95 C1 ㉑
The lemon house and garden of the Libri Liberi bookshop host a regular afternoon programme of puppet and theatre shows for kids aged three to 13.

Santissima Annunziata p106

San Marco

Most visitors to Florence head to the district of San Marco for the museums – a diverse array of structures containing fascinating displays of weird and wonderful things. From prehistoric gems to flying machines and Renaissance masterpieces (not to mention a certain statue), each collection vies for the attention of the visiting hordes. However, San Marco is far from just a tourist centre: head to the nigh-on perfect porticoed square of **Santissima Annunziata** – with its equestrian statue of **Grand Duke Ferdinando I** by Giambologna – and it'll become apparent that the area thrives on the crowds of students from nearby university faculties, and that it's still an active centre of religious worship.

On the eastern side of the square is the **Spedale degli Innocenti**; designed by Filippo Brunelleschi, it marks the advent of Renaissance town planning. But when it comes to landmark attractions, San Marco has all the other central-outer districts trumped, housing as it does Michelangelo's **David** in the **Galleria dell'Accademia**.

Just past the Accademia, at the end of via Ricasoli, is **piazza di San Marco**, home to both the eponymous church and the **Museo di San Marco**, filled with works by Fra Angelico. Gem-lovers, meanwhile, should continue onto via Giorgio La Pira, where, to the west of the **Giardino de' Semplici**, lies the minerals section of the **Museo di Storia**

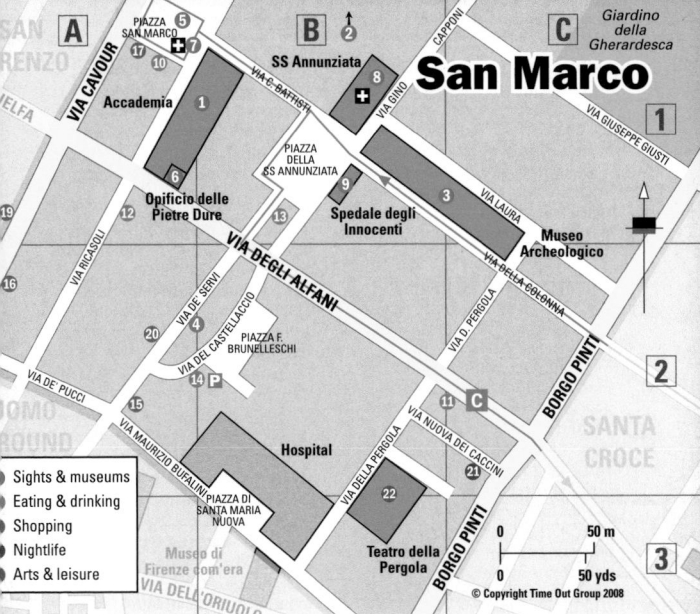

Legend:
- Sights & museums
- Eating & drinking
- Shopping
- Nightlife
- Arts & leisure

Naturale (no.4, 055 265111), packed full of strange and lovely stones.

Despite all the cultural action, though, there's a paucity of decent eating, drinking and nightlife venues here, but there is the **Focacceria Pugi** – renowned for selling the best *schiacciata con l'uva* (flat bread with grapes) and – bordering Santa Croce – the lively **Jazz Club**.

Sights & museums

Galleria dell'Accademia

Via Ricasoli 58-60 (055 2388609).
Open 8.15am-6.50pm Tue-Sun.
Admission €10, €13 with reservation.
No credit cards. **Map** p103 A1/B1 ❶
Although the Accademia contains a huge number of magnificent works, the queue snaking around the corner is for one reason above all: Michelangelo's monumental *David* (1501-04), still gleaming from a 2003 €400,000 clean-up – his first bath in 130 years.

David started life as a political icon portraying strength and resolve, to encourage Florentines to support their fledgling constitution. However, having carved it from a 5m-high (16ft) slab of marble, Michelangelo undoubtedly considered it a monument to his genius. He intended it to stand high up on the Duomo, and so gave *David* a top-heavy shape so that it would look its best from the beholder's viewpoint (notice the slightly oversize head and hands). However, in 1873, when the statue was moved from piazza della Signoria (where a copy still stands) following acts of vandalism, the authorities decided to keep the plinth low so visitors could witness its curves close-up; hence it's a little out of proportion.

Other Michelangelo works line the walls of the *David* salon; among them are his *Slaves*, masterly but unfinished sculptures struggling to escape from marble prisons. They were intended for Pope Julius II's tomb, a project

Michelangelo was forced to abandon in order to paint the Sistine Chapel ceiling in Rome. On the right of *David* is the unfinished *Pietà Palestrina*, often attributed to Michelangelo.

The gallery also houses a mixed bag of late Gothic and Renaissance paintings on the ground floor, and a fabulous collection of musical instruments from the Conservatory of Luigi Cherubini.

Giardino dei Semplici

Via Micheli 3 (055 2757402). **Open** 9am-1pm Mon, Tue, Thur, Fri, Sun; 9am-5pm Sat. **Admission** €4. No credit cards. **Map** p103 B1 ❷

Florence's botanical gardens were planted by landscape gardener 'Il Tribolo' in 1545 for Cosimo I to cultivate and research exotic plants. Essential oils were extracted, perfumes distilled and cures and antidotes sought for various ailments and poisons. The garden's species of plants (including a large collection of azaleas) and trees is increasing every year, and lovely strolls can be had along the large and small avenues.

Museo Archeologico

Via Gino Capponi 1, piazza della SS Annunziata (055 23575/www.comune. fi.it/soggetti/sat). **Open** 2-7pm Mon; 8.30am-7pm Tue, Thur; 8.30am-2pm Wed, Fri-Sun. **Admission** €4. No credit cards. **Map** p103 B1 ❸

It's easy to come to Florence and get completely submerged in the Renaissance but the archaeological museum, housed in Palazzo della Crocetta, explains what happened before the Golden Age. The recently renovated museum now boasts an impressive entrance hall, an enormous temporary exhibition space and a new Etruscan money display. Guided tours run every 45 minutes from 9am. Elsewhere you'll find jewellery, funerary sculpture, urns and bronzes dating from the fifth century BC, as well as the fabulous Chimera, a mythical beast that's part lion, part goat and part snake. Also present is the first-century BC Etruscan bronze Orator. The first rooms house Egyptian artefacts (including sarcophagi complete with creepy shrivelled bodies) from prehistoric eras through to the Copta period (310 AD). Outside is a beautiful garden lined with Etruscan tombs and monuments (only open on Saturdays).

Museo Leonardo da Vinci

Via de' Servi 66-68r (055 282966). **Open** 10am-7pm daily. **Admission** €6. **Map** p103 A2 ❹

The painter, sculptor, musician, engineer, inventor, scientist and all-round genius Leonardo da Vinci justly has a museum to himself. The museum offers an attractive, interactive insight into the machines that featured in da Vinci's codes. Several of his most extraordinary inventions have been built from studies taken from his drawings: flying machines, a hydraulic saw, a printing machine and even a massive tank measuring 5.3m by 3m (17ft by 10ft) and weighing 2 tonnes. Most of the exhibits can be touched, moved and even dangled from, making the place immensely popular with kids.

Museo di San Marco

Piazza San Marco 1 (055 2388608). **Open** 8.15am-1.40pm Tue-Fri, 1st, 3rd & 5th Mon of mth; 8.15am-6.40pm Sat; 8.15am-7pm 2nd & 4th Sun of mth. **Admission** €4. No credit cards. **Map** p103 A1 ❺

The Museo di San Marco is not only a fascinating coming-together of religion and history, but a wonderful place to rest and take in the general splendour. Housed in the monastery where he lived, the museum is largely dedicated to the ethereal paintings of Fra Angelico (aka Beato Angelico), one of the most important spiritual artists of the 15th century, who would never lift a brush without a prayer and who wept whenever he painted a crucifixion. You're greeted on the first floor by one of the most famous images in Christendom, an other-worldly *Annunciation*, but the images Fra Angelico and his assistants frescoed on the walls of the monks' white vaulted cells are almost as impressive.

Queue outside the Galleria dell'Accademia p103

Particularly outstanding is the lyrical *Noli Me Tangere*, which depicts Christ appearing to Mary Magdalene in a field of flowers, and the surreal *Mocking of Christ*, in which Christ's torturers are represented simply by relevant fragments of their anatomy (a hand holding a whip, a face spitting).

The cell that was later occupied by Fra Girolamo Savonarola is adorned with portraits of the rabid reformer by Fra Bartolomeo. You can also see his black wool cloak and his cilith, which was tied around the thigh to cause constant pain in reminder of the suffering of Christ. Near the cells reserved specially for Cosimo de' Medici is the beautiful library designed by his favourite architect, Michelozzo, in 1441.

On the ground floor, in the Ospizio dei Pellegrini (pilgrims' hospice), are more works by Fra Angelico. The *Tabernacle of the Madonna dei Linaiuoli*, his first commission from 1433 for the guild of linen makers, is here: painted on wood carved by Ghiberti, it contains some of his best-known images, the polichrome musical angels. Also here are a superb *Deposition* and a *Last Judgement*. The small refectory is dominated by a Ghirlandaio *Last Supper* (1479-80).

Opificio delle Pietre Dure

Via degli Alfani 78 (055 265111). **Open** 8.15am-1.45pm Mon-Wed, Fri, Sat; 8.15am-7pm Thur. **Admission** €2. No credit cards. **Map** p103 A1 **6**

Pietra dura is the craft of inlaying gems or semi-precious stones in intricate mosaics and you'll see fine examples in all the grandest palaces and most expensive shops of Florence. The Opificio (workshop) was founded by Grand Duke Ferdinando I in 1588; it's now an important restoration centre, but also provides a fascinating insight into this typically Florentine art, with its mezzanine exhibitions of tools and stones, and its displays of the methods used for the cutting and polishing of the stones through to the inlaying and mosaic techniques.

San Marco

Piazza San Marco (055 287628). **Open** 8.30am-noon, 4-6pm Mon-Sat; 4-6pm Sun. **Admission** free. **Map** p103 A1 **7**

The amount of money lavished by the Medici family on San Lorenzo (p97) is

FLORENCE BY AREA

Opificio delle Pietre Dure p105

nothing compared with that spent on the church and convent of San Marco. After Cosimo il Vecchio returned from exile in 1434 and organised the transfer of the monastery of San Marco from the Silvestrine monks to the Dominicans from Fiesole, he went on to fund the renovation of the decaying church and convent by Michelozzo. Cosimo also founded a public library that greatly influenced Florentine humanists; meetings of the Humanist Academy were held in the gardens. Ironically, later in the 15th century, San Marco became the base of religious fundamentalist Fra Girolamo Savonarola, who burned countless humanist treasures in his notorious Bonfire of the Vanities.

Inside the church you can see Giambologna's 16th-century nave with side chapels. He completed the Cappella di Sant'Antonino in 1589 where you can now, creepily, see the whole dried body of the saint.

The altarpiece *Madonna and Child* (1440s) is by Fra Angelico, whose other more famous works can be seen in the Museo di San Marco next door (p104).

Santissima Annunziata

Piazza della SS Annunziata (055 266181). **Open** 7am-12.30pm, 4-6.30pm daily. **Admission** free. **Map** p103 B1 ⑧

Despite Brunelleschi's perfectionist ambitions for the square it crowns, Santissima Annunziata – the church of the Servite order – is a place of popular worship rather than pewfect proportion. Highlights include a frescoed Baroque ceiling and an opulent shrine built around a miraculous *Madonna*, purportedly painted by a monk in 1252 and, as the story goes, finished overnight by angels. Surrounding the icon are flowers, silver lamps and pewter body parts, ex votos left in the hope that the Madonna will cure the dicky heart or gammy leg of loved ones.

Michelozzo was the directing architect and built the Villani and Madonna chapels, and the oratory on the left side of the church. In 1453, after almost ten years of work and not much progress, directorship was handed to Antonio Manetti. When Manetti ran into financial difficulty, the governing

pieces include an unsurprising concentration of Madonna and Bambino pieces, including a Botticelli and a vivid Luca della Robbia. The high point, however, is Ghirlandaio's *Adoration of the Magi*, commissioned for the high altar of the hospital's church.

Eating & drinking

L'Accademia

Piazza San Marco 7r (055 217343/ www.ristoranteaccademia.it). **Open** noon-3pm, 7-11pm daily. €€. **Italian/ pizzeria**. **Map** p103 A1 ⑩

Sure, it's geared towards tourists, but nonetheless, L'Accademia is a useful spot in an area where there aren't many good eating choices. It's best to stick to the reliable staples on the menu, such as pasta with mixed seafood. The pizzas are a decent choice too. The wine list is surprisingly comprehensive, prices are reasonable and the Iacovitti brothers are cheerful hosts.

Caffellatte

Via degli Alfani 39r (055 2478878). **Open** 8am-midnight Tue-Sat; 9am-midnight Sun. No credit cards. **Café**. **Map** p103 C2 ⑪

The lattes in this small café, done out with rustic wooden tables, are among the best in Florence. But if they're too dull for you, the *cappuccione* comes piping hot in a giant bowl with honey and Turkish cinnamon. The pastries are made in the café's organic bakery.

Carabé

Via Ricasoli 60r (055 289476). **Open** *Summer* 9am-1am daily. *Winter* 9am-8pm daily. Closed mid Dec-mid Jan. No credit cards. **Gelateria**. **Map** p103 A1 ⑫

See box p73.

Robiglio

Via de' Servi 112r (055 214501/ www.robiglio.it). **Open** 7.30am-7.30pm Mon-Sat. Closed 3wks Aug. **Café**. **Map** p103 B1 ⑬

The sublime hot chocolate here is so thick that the spoon stands up in it, and the delicious pastries are a Florentine

priests ceded the venture to the Gonzaga family. In 1477, Leon Batisti completed the church with slight modifications. The atrium was frescoed the following century by Pontormo, Rosso Fiorentino and, most strikingly, Andrea del Sarto, whose *Birth of the Virgin* is set within the walls of a Renaissance palazzo with cherubs perched on a mantelpiece.

Spedale degli Innocenti

Piazza della SS Annunziata (055 2037308/www.istitutodeglinnocenti.it). **Open** 8.30am-7pm Mon-Sat; 8.30am-2pm Sun. **Admission** €4. No credit cards. **Map** p103 B1 ⑨

This collection is housed in the recreation room of Brunelleschi's foundling hospital. Opened in 1445, the building marks the advent of Renaissance town planning. (Brunelleschi had designed it to fit into his greater plan for a perfectly symmetrical piazza – to be modern Europe's first – but died before realising his dream.) The collection inside received a substantial blow in 1853, when several important works were auctioned off (for a relative pittance) to raise money for the hospital. The remaining

Teatro della Pergola

institution. Robiglio's sister café located on via Tosinghi (no.11r, 055 215013) has outside tables in summer.

Zona 15
Via del Castellaccio 53-55r (055 211678/ www.zona15wine.it). **Open** 11am-3am Mon-Fri; 6pm-3am Sat, Sun. **Café**. **Map** p103 A2/B2 ⑭
Looking something like a futuristic American wine diner, this decidedly hip café-cum-wine bar's leather and chrome stools hug a massive central spotlit bar area. Walls are clad in oyster mosaics and crowned by dramatic vaulted ceilings. The *aperitivo* tapas menu, based on Basque recipes, is available daily from 6pm, while the decent wine menu offers around 200 different options.

Shopping

Bartolini
Via de' Servi 30r (055 211895/www. dinobartolini.it). **Open** 3.30-7.30pm Mon; 10am-1pm, 3.30-7.30pm Tue-Sat. Closed 2wks Aug. **Map** p103 A2 ⑮
This charming kitchen shop has extensive selections of cutlery and crockery, plus accessories ranging from garlic mincers to kitchen sinks.

Feltrinelli International
Via Cavour 12-20r (055 219524/ www.feltrinelli.it). **Open** 9am-7.30pm Mon-Sat. **Map** p103 A2 ⑯
This modern bookshop has strong art, photography and comic-book sections, plus a huge range of titles in English and language-teaching books and videos.

Focacceria Pugi
Piazza San Marco 10 (055 280981/ www.focacceria-pugi.it). **Open** 7.45am-8pm Mon-Sat. **Map** p103 A1 ⑰
An institution since 1924, this bakery is famed for its *schiacciata* – a delicious flat bread with olive oil or grapes.

Frette
Via de' Martelli 23r (055 211369/ www.frette.com). **Open** 3-7pm Mon; 10am-7pm Tue-Sat. Closed 3wks Aug. **Map** p103 A2 ⑱
The full range of bedding, towels and *robes so* beloved of boutique hotels.

Il Papiro
Via Cavour 55r (055 215262/www. ilpapiro.it). **Open** 9am-7.30pm Mon-Sat; 10am-6pm Sun. **Map** p103 A1 ⑲
A chain of olde-worlde shops with bright paper desk accessories, photo frames, playing cards and more.

Sugar e Spice
Via dei Servi 43r (055 290263). **Open** 10am-7.30pm Mon-Fri. Closed Aug. No credit cards. **Map** p103 A2 ⑳
Own-made, American-style sweets and cakes, including muffins.

Nightlife

Jazz Club
Via Nuova de' Caccini 3 (055 2479700/ www.jazzclubfirenze.com). **Open** 9pm-2am Mon-Fri; 9pm-3am Sat. Closed July, Aug. **Tickets** €8.50 membership. No credit cards. **Map** p103 C2 ㉑
One of the few places in Florence where you can hear live jazz almost nightly, this hard-to-find club is worth searching out. From Tuesday to Saturday, it hosts an array of popular local jazz bands, and it's also welcomed notable international acts such as jazz musician/actor Peter Weller. Every Monday there's a live jam session where you can hop on stage with the house band accompanying.

Arts & leisure

Teatro della Pergola
Via della Pergola 18-32 (055 2264316/ www.pergola.firenze.it). **Season** Oct-Apr. **Map** p103 B2/B3 ㉒
Inaugurated in 1661, the exquisite, intimate Pergola is one of Italy's oldest theatres. Richly decorated and with three layers of boxes, it's ideal for chamber music and small-scale operas. The excellent series of chamber music concerts promoted by the Amici della Musica is held here, while the Teatro del Maggio also occasionally uses it for opera during the Maggio festival (p33). Shakespeare, Pirandello and Goldoni feature regularly in the programme of ancient and modern dramatic works shown.

Church of Santa Croce p117

Santa Croce

The largest of Florence's medieval parochial areas has, like much of the centre, a heady air of history and learning – it encompasses the impressive church with which it shares its name, the national library, the city's synagogue and several fascinating museums. But it's not hard to have fun here too, with some of the best ice-cream in the city, a lively market, excellent shopping and two world-class restaurants, **Cibrèo** and **Enoteca Pinchiorri**; and in terms of new openings and a general feeling of buzziness, Santa Croce is now beginning to rival the Oltrarno for the title of Florence's most exciting neighbourhood.

Central **piazza Santa Croce** is a natural meeting spot, and home to the imposing Gothic church and attached **Museo dell'Opera di Santa Croce** and **Cappella dei Pazzi**. Lining the square is a mix of shops and restaurants with outside tables. On the south side is the frescoed sepia façade of **Palazzo d'Antella**: decorated in 1620, it now houses smart apartments. Outside the church is Enrico Pazzi's 1865 statue of Dante. But it's not always so relaxing: the sui/homicidal team sport of **calcio storico** is played here every June (although it was suspended in 2006 and 2007) and from the end of November there's a vibrant **Christmas market**.

South-west from the piazza, via de' Benci is dotted with crafts shops and bohemian restaurants running down towards the Arno to the **ponte alle Grazie**. The bridge was blown up just before the Germans' retreat at the end of

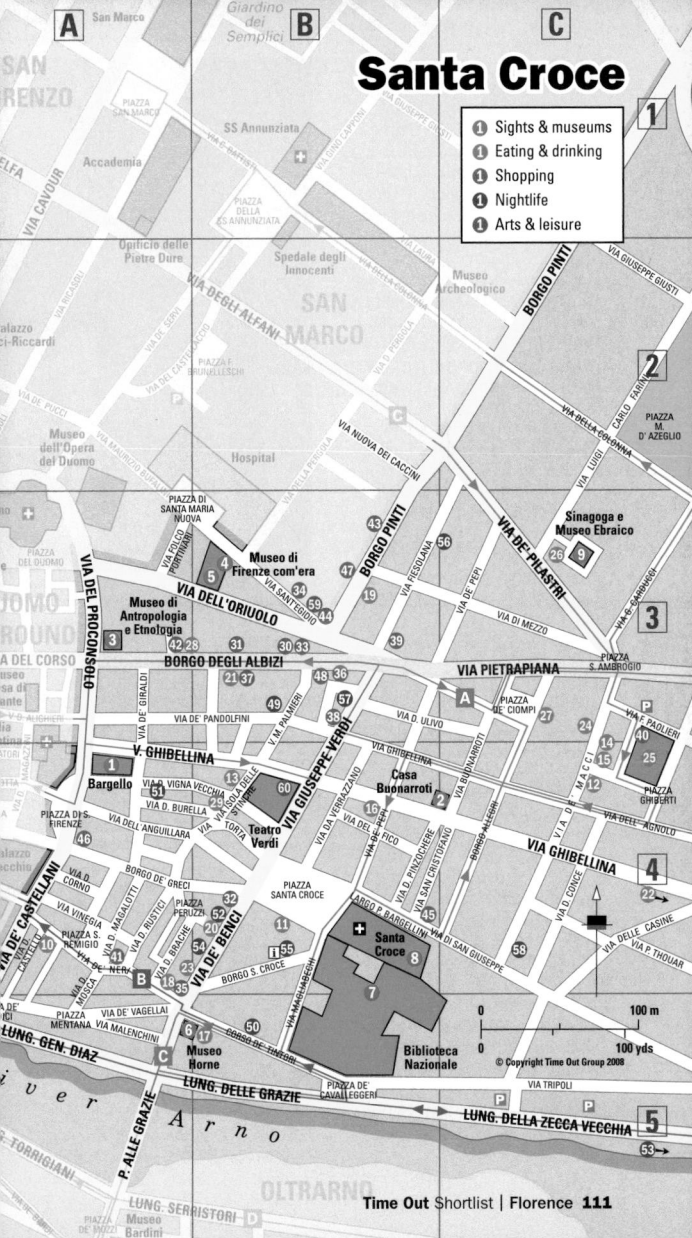

Santa Croce

- **1** Sights & museums
- **1** Eating & drinking
- **1** Shopping
- **1** Nightlife
- **1** Arts & leisure

World War II and was rebuilt in 1957. Heading east from here, you'll come across piazza de' Cavalleggeri, dominated by the **Biblioteca Nazionale**. Built to house the three million books and two million documents that were held in the Uffizi until 1935, the library has two towers with statues of Dante and Galileo.

Until recently, the area that lies north of the church of Santa Croce, stretching up past **Casa Buonarroti** in via Ghibellina to **piazza de' Ciompi**, was the rough-and-ready home to gangs of bored Florentine youths. Increasingly yuppified, it now yields trendy *trattorie* and wine bars. Piazza de' Ciompi was named after the dyers' and wool workers' revolt of 1378, and is taken over by an antiques market during the week and a huge flea market on the last Sunday of the month. It's dominated by the **Loggia del Pesce**, built by Vasari in 1568 for the Mercato Vecchio, previously in piazza della Repubblica. It was taken apart in the 19th century and re-erected here.

Further east is **piazza Ghiberti**, home of the fruit and vegetable market of Sant'Ambrogio, the world-famous **Cibrèo** restaurant and the shops, bars, *pizzerie* and restaurants of borgo La Croce.

The **Sinagoga & Museo di Arte e Storia Ebraica** lies in northern Santa Croce, just south of the elegant piazza d'Azeglio. To the west of here is borgo Pinti – watch out for the hard-to-find entrance to the church of **Santa Maria Maddalena dei Pazzi** (no.58). The **Museo di Antropologia e Etnologia**, meanwhile, can be found in the north-west corner of the district; south of here, piazza San Firenze houses the sculpture-packed **Bargello**.

Sights & museums

Bargello

Via del Proconsolo 4 (055 2388606/ www.sbas.firenze.it/bargello). **Open** 8.15am-1.50pm Tue-Sat, 1st, 3rd & 5th Mon of mth, 2nd & 4th Sun of mth. **Admission** €4. No credit cards. **Map** p111 A4 ❶

This imposing, fortified structure has had so many different purposes over the years that although it's now most famous for containing Florence's main set of sculptures, the building itself and its history are equally fascinating. The Bargello started life as the Palazzo del Popolo in 1250 and soon became the mainstay of the chief magistrate, or *podestà*. The bodies of executed criminals were displayed in the courtyard during the 14th century; in the 15th century, law courts, prisons and torture chambers were set up inside. The Medici made it the seat of the *bargello* (chief of police) in the 16th century.

Officially the Museo Nazionale del Bargello, the museum opened in 1865 to celebrate Florence becoming the

Bargello

capital of Italy, and now holds the city's most eclectic and prestigious collection of sculpture, with treasures ranging from prime pieces – among the most famous works are Michelangelo's *Drunken Bacchus and Brutus* (the only bust he ever sculpted) and Giambologna's fleet-footed *Mercury* – to Scandinavian chess sets and Egyptian ivories. The Salone Donatello contains the artist's two triumphant Davids (the more famous of which is undergoing on-site restoration until the end of 2008; see box p115) and a tense *St George*, the original sculpture that once stood outside the Orsanmichele. Also fascinating are the two bronze panels of the *Sacrifice of Isaac*, sculpted by Brunelleschi and Lorenzo Ghiberti for a competition to design the north doors of the Duomo Baptistery. Back out on the grand loggia you can see Giambologna's bronze birds that used to spout water in a Medici grotto. On this floor you can also find the little frescoed Magdalen Chapel, which contains the oldest confirmed portrait

of Dante Alighieri, painted by Giotto. The easily missable second floor has a fascinating selection of small bronze statues and Andrea del Verrocchio's *Lady with a Posy* (1474), which may have been carved with his student Leonardo da Vinci.

Casa Buonarroti

Via Ghibellina 70 (055 241752/www. casabuonarroti.it). **Open** 9.30am-2pm Mon, Wed-Sun. **Admission** €6.50. No credit cards. **Map** p111 B4/C4 ❷

In 1612, Michelangelo Buonarroti the Younger took the decision to create a building in order to honour the memory of his more famous great-uncle. Even though Michelangelo (1475-1564) never actually lived here, this 17th-century house, owned by his descendants until 1858, has a collection of memorabilia that gives an insight into Florence's most famous artistic son. On the walls are scenes from the painter's life, while the pieces collated by the artist's great-nephew Filippo include a wooden model for the façade of San Lorenzo (see box p97) and two important original works: a bas-relief *Madonna of the Stairs* breastfeeding at the foot of a flight of stairs, and an unfinished *Battle of the Centaurs*.

Museo di Antropologia e Etnologia

Via del Proconsolo 12 (055 2396449). **Open** 9am-1pm Mon-Fri, Sun; 9am-5pm Sat. **Admission** €4. No credit cards. **Map** p111 A3 ❸

Among the eclectic mix of global artefacts on display are a collection of Peruvian mummies, an Ostyak harp from Lapland in the shape of a swan, an engraved trumpet made from an elephant tusk from the Congo and Ecuadorian shrunken heads alongside a specially designed skull-beating club.

Museo Fiorentino di Preistoria

Via Sant'Egidio 21 (055 295159/ www.museofiorentinopreistoria.it). **Open** 9.30am-12.30pm Mon, Wed, Fri, Sat; 9.30am-4.30pm Tue, Thur; guided tours by appointment. **Admission** €3. No credit cards. **Map** p111 B3 ❹

Florence's Museum of Prehistory traces humanity's development from the Paleolithic to the Bronze Age, but – as most evidence is found in caves – it has to content itself with various displays of photographs and illustrations. The first floor follows hominid physical changes, and also examines Italy's prehistoric art. The second floor includes a fascinating collection of stone implements.

Museo di Firenze com'era

Via dell'Oriuolo 24 (055 2616545). **Open** 9am-1.30pm Mon-Wed; 9am-6.30pm Sat. **Admission** €2.70. No credit cards. **Map** p111 B3 ❺

This charmingly named museum ('Florence As It Was') traces the city's development through collections of maps, paintings and archaeological discoveries. There are rooms devoted to Giuseppe Poggi's plans from the 1860s to modernise Florence by creating Parisian-style boulevards; the famous lunettes of the Medici villas painted in 1599 by Flemish artist

Giusto Utens; and the history of the region from 200 million years ago to Roman times. New exhibits include a model of 'Florentia' that shows how the city may have been in Roman times.

Museo Horne

Via de' Benci 6 (055 244661/www. museohorne.it). **Open** 9am-1pm Mon-Sat. **Admission** €5. No credit cards. **Map** p111 A5/B5 ❻

The 15th-century Palazzo Corsi-Alberti was purchased in the 1800s by English architect and art historian Herbert Percy Horne, who restored it to its Renaissance splendour. When he died in 1916, he left his palazzo and vast collection to the state. Objects range from ceramics and Florentine coins to a coffee grinder and a pair of spectacles. Upstairs is a damaged wooden panel from a triptych attributed to Masaccio; but the pride of the collection is a gold-black *Santo Stefano* by Giotto.

Museo dell'Opera di Santa Croce & Cappella dei Pazzi

Piazza Santa Croce 16 (055 2466105/ www.operadisantacroce.it). **Open** 9.30am-5.30pm Mon-Sat; 1-5.30pm Sun. **Admission** €4 (incl museum & chapel). No credit cards. **Map** p111 B4 ❼

Brunelleschi's geometric tour de force, the Cappella dei Pazzi, was planned in the 1430s and completed almost 40 years later. The chapel is based on a central square, topped by a cupola flanked by two barrel-vaulted bays. The pure lines of the interior are decorated with Luca della Robbia's painted ceramic roundels of the 12 apostles and the four evangelists. The chapel opens on to the cloisters of Santa Croce (p117).

Across the courtyard is a small museum of church treasures; the collection includes Donatello's pious bronze *St Louis of Toulouse* from Orsanmichele. The backbone of the collection is in the former refectory, with Giotto's godson Taddeo Gaddi's imposing yet poetic *Tree of Life* above his *Last Supper* (unfortunately, in very bad condition).

Florence's other David

Donatello's bronze is undergoing a momentous restoration.

For the whole of 2008, visitors to the Bargello Museum (p112) will be treated to an unprecedented experience: witnessing a world-class artwork being painstakingly restored steps away from them, in the very room where it's permanently on display.

Donatello's near-life-size bronze *David* currently lies surrounded by state-of-the-art appliances on an 'operating table' in the middle of the Donatello Room on the first floor of the museum. Volunteers provide information to visitors, while an expert restorer works within a fenced enclosure.

Though not as universally celebrated as Michelangelo's imposing marble on the same subject (in the Accademia; p103), Donatello's *David* (thought to date from just before his departure for Padua in 1443) is both the artist's finest accomplishment and a watershed in art history, being the first full-relief nude figure since Roman times, and the first large-scale, free-standing sculpture of the Renaissance.

The restoration started in June 2007 and is being funded by the Department of Civil Protection, which offered up €200,000 to mark the 40th anniversary of the tragic 1966 flood. Ironically, Donatello's *David* was not among the many artworks that suffered the flood, as it was standing safely above the raging waters in its lofty hall. But it's thanks to the experience gained from cleaning bronze works that *did* suffer (like Ghiberti's panels for the Gates of Paradise) that experts finally felt confident enough to proceed with this sensitive restoration.

David has never been restored before. 'Beautifying' coats of glaze were applied in the 18th and 19th centuries, but these only managed to trap more dirt and obliterate the gold-leaf decoration, traces of which are now emerging. At the time that this guide went to press, about a quarter of the statue had undergone the first cleaning, done by softening the excess layers with special solvents and then removing them with tiny scalpels.

Sinagoga & Museo di Arte e Storia Ebraica

In equally poor condition is Cimabue's *Crucifixion*, which hung in the basilica until it was damaged in the flood of 1966. There's also a small permanent exhibition of the woodcuts and engravings of the modern artist Pietro Parigi. Access to the museum and chapel is through Santa Croce (below).

Santa Croce

Piazza Santa Croce 16 (055 2466105).
Open 9.30am-5.30pm Mon-Sat; 1-5.30pm Sun. **Admission** €5 (incl museum & chapel). No credit cards. **Map** p111 B4 ❽

The richest medieval church in the city, Santa Croce has a great deal to offer, even to visitors long tired of church-hopping. The Museo dell'Opera di Santa Croce is housed here, along with the delightful chapter house known as the Cappella dei Pazzi (for both, see p114) and two beautiful cloistered courtyards, not to mention the church itself, which is crammed with illustrious tombs and cenotaphs. The coloured marble façade is impressive, but at first sight the interior seems big and gloomy, with overbearing marble tombs clogging the walls. Not all of them contain bodies: Dante's, for example, is simply a memorial to the poet, who is buried in Ravenna.

In the niche alongside Dante's is the tomb of Michelangelo, by Vasari. The artist had insisted on burial here, as he wanted 'a view towards the cupola of the Duomo for all eternity', and had worked on his obsession, the *Pietà* (now in the Museo dell'Opera del Duomo) to adorn his tomb. At the top of the left aisle is Galileo's tomb, created by Foggini more than a century after the astronomer's death, when the Church finally permitted him a Christian burial.

It's something of a paradox that while the church is filled with the tombs of the great and the grand, it formerly belonged to the Franciscans, the most unworldly of the religious orders. They founded it in 1228, ten years after arriving in the city. A recently established order, they were supposed to make their living through manual work, preaching and begging. At the time, the area was a slum, home to the city's dyers and wool workers, and Franciscan preaching, with its message that all men were equal, had a huge impact on the poor folk who lived there. But the Franciscans vow of poverty slowly eroded. By the late 13th century, the old church was felt to be inadequate and a new building was planned: intended to be one of the largest in Christendom, it was designed by Arnolfo di Cambio, architect of the Duomo and Palazzo Vecchio, who himself laid the first stone on 3 May 1294.

The church underwent various stages of restoration and modification, with one of Vasari's infamous remodernisations robbing it of some frescoes by Giotto's school in favour of heavy classical altars. Fortunately, he left the main chapels intact, though subsequent makeovers completely destroyed the decorations of the Cappella Tosinghi-Spinelli. Among the remaining gems are the fabulous stained-glass windows at the east end by Agnolo Gaddi, the marble tomb of Leonardo Bruni and the Cavalcanti tabernacle.

At the eastern end, the Bardi and Peruzzi chapels, completely frescoed by Giotto, are masterpieces (and covered further in our itinerary that starts on page 47). The condition of the frescoes, rediscovered in the mid 19th century, is not brilliant, however – a result of Giotto painting on dry instead of wet plaster. The most striking of the two chapels is the Bardi, with scenes from the life of St Francis in virtual monotone, the figures just stylised enough to make them otherworldly yet individual enough to make them human.

Don't miss the leather school (Scuola del Cuoio; p123) behind the church (accessible from via San Giuseppe).

Sinagoga & Museo di Arte e Storia Ebraica

Via Farini 4 (055 2346654).
Open Apr, May, Sept, Oct 10am-1pm, 2-5pm Mon-Thur, Sun; 10am-1pm Fri. June-Aug 10am-6pm Mon-Thur, Sun;

10am-2pm Fri. Oct-Mar 10am-4pm
Mon-Thur, Sun; 10am-2pm Fri.
Admission €4. No credit cards.
Map p111 C3 **9**

Built in 1870, following the demolition
of the ghetto, this synagogue is an
extraordinarily ornate mix of Moorish,
Byzantine and Eastern influences, with
its walls and ceilings covered in polychrome arabesques. The Museum of
Jewish Art and History, which was
extended up on to a second floor in
March 2007, holds a collection tracing
the history of Jews in Florence, from
their supposed arrival as Roman slaves
to their official introduction into the
city as money-lenders in 1430.

Eating & drinking

For the *gelateria* **Vestri**, see p123.

All'Antico Vinaio

Via de' Neri 65r (no phone). **Open**
8am-8pm Tue-Sat; 8am-1pm Sun. Closed
Aug. **Wine bar**. **Map** p111 A4 **10**

This small neighbourhood *vineria* is
often packed with locals – especially in
the evening, when there's time to mull
over the day's proceedings with a *got-
tino* (a stubby glass) of wine and a delicious artichoke-topped *crostino*. Food
comes from the *rosticceria* over the
road: soups and hearty pasta in winter
and rice salads and carpaccio in summer. The panini are also good. A good
place to soak up some atmosphere.

Boccadama

*Piazza Santa Croce 25-26r (055
243640).* **Open** *Summer* 8.30am-11pm
daily. *Winter* 8.30am-3pm Mon; 8.30am-
11pm Tue-Sun. **€€**. **Tuscan**. Map
p111 B4 **11**

This inviting restaurant and wine bar
is open all day: visit for breakfast or
coffee, a light lunch or a more creative
full dinner (like beetroot-flavoured
pasta with duck and black olive sauce).
Wine by the glass is rather limited for
a place that stocks over 400 labels.
Nevertheless, thanks to its location,
Boccadama is swamped with tourists
(particularly for lunch) in the summer,
when the terrace comes into its own.

Caffè Cibrèo

*Via Andrea del Verrocchio 5r (055
2345853).* **Open** 8am-1am Tue-Sat
(lunch 1-2.30pm). Closed 2wks Aug. No
credit cards. **Café**. Map p111 C4 **12**

This delightful café has exquisite
carved wood ceilings, antique furniture, a candlelit mosaic and outside
tables, and also a knack for making
everything it presents look beautiful.
As you'd expect from an outpost of
Cibrèo (below), the savoury dishes are
both inventive and refined, but the
desserts, like the cheesecake with bitter orange sauce, are also amazing.

Caffè Italiano

*Via Isola delle Stinche 13r (055
289020/www.caffeitaliano.it).* **Open**
12.30-2.30pm, 7.30pm-11am Tue-Sun.
Closed 3wks Aug. **€**. **Pizzeria**.
Map p111 B4 **13**

There's almost no choice – marinara,
margherita or Napoli – and just four
bare tables, but the pizzas at this
annexe to the upmarket Osteria del
Caffè Italiano are authentic and delicious, their light and puffy bases
topped with San Marzano tomatoes
and proper mozzarella *di bufala*. After
10.30pm, the overflow is seated at the
elegant restaurant.

Cibreino

Via de' Macci 122r (055 2341100).
Open 12.50-2.30pm, 7-11.15pm Tue-
Sat. Closed Aug. **€€**. No credit cards.
Tuscan. Map p111 C3/C4 **14**

If your budget won't stretch to Cibrèo
(below), nip next door to its *trattoria*
sibling. You can't book (prepare to
queue), the atmosphere is rustic and
often overcrowded, there are no complimentary extras and the menu has a little less choice. But the food is the same
excellent standard, the bill will be less
than a third of what you would pay in
the parent restaurant, and you get the
added extra of witnessing weak-stom-
ached experience-hunters blanch when
a chicken's head arrives on their plate.

Cibrèo

*Via Andrea del Verrocchio 8r
(055 2341100).* **Open** 12.50-2.30pm,

7-11.15pm Tue-Sat. Closed Aug.
€€€€. **Tuscan**. p111 C4 ⑮
Cibrèo is a Florentine institution. The
dishes at the flagship of Fabio Picchi's
little gastronomic empire (that includes
Cibreìno and Caffè Cibréo, p118) are a
modern interpretation of traditional
cucina povera (poor-man's food), with
prime ingredients and intense flavours.
There's no menu (and no pasta or coffee), but a chummy waiter will sit at
your table to take you through the
options. A series of delicious *antipasti*
arrives automatically with a glass of
wine to be followed by some of the best
cooking – many think *the* best – to be
found in Florence. The place provokes
extreme opinions, however, with others
claiming it's overrated and overpriced.
Superb wine list.

Enoteca Pinchiorri
*Via Ghibellina 87 (055 242757/www.
enotecapinchiorri.com).* **Open** 7.30-
10pm Tue; 12.30-2pm, 7.30-10pm Thur-
Sat. Closed Aug. €€€€. **Tuscan/
Modern Italian**. Map p111 B4 ⑯
Generally acknowledged to be one of
Italy's great temples to gastronomic
excellence, Enoteca Pinchiorri won back
its third Michelin star in 2004. You can
choose à la carte, but there are several
set menus, each involving eight or nine
tiny but superbly executed courses.
Then there's the stellar cellar. Wherever
you eat – inside the palazzo or in the jas-
mine-scented courtyard – it all looks
fabulous; the old-fashioned service is
elegant and prices are very high. Men
are required to wear jackets.

Del Fagioli
Corso de' Tintori 47r (055 244285).
Open noon-2pm, 7pm-10.30pm Mon-
Sat. €€. **Florentine**. Map p111 B5 ⑰
Opened by Luigi 'Gigi' Zucchini just
after the flood in 1966, this is one of
those unpretentious time-worn places
where little has changed over the years.
It offers genuine Florentine traditional
cooking and such standards as *ribollita, pappa al pomodoro, bollito misto con
salsa verde* (mixed boiled meats served
with a bright green parsley sauce). Gigi
is still cooking and his *involtini* (thin

rolls of beef stuffed with cheese, ham
and artichokes) are delicious. There's
warm apple cake to finish.

Gelateria dei Neri
Via de' Neri 22r (055 210034). **Open**
Summer 11am-midnight daily. *Winter*
11am-midnight daily. No credit cards.
Gelateria. Map p111 A4 ⑱
See box p73.

La Giostra
*Borgo Pinti 12r (055 241341/www.
ristorantelagiostra.com).* **Open**
1-2.30pm, 7.30pm-midnight Mon-Fri;
7.30pm-midnight Sat, Sun. €€€€.
Italian. Map p111 B3 ⑲
La Giostra is run with eccentric charm
by Principe Dimitri Kunz d'Asburgo
Loreno and his twin sons. Walls are
covered with pics of visiting celebs, the
place is full of tourists and prices are
high – but the food is very good, verg-
ing on excellent. It's well known for its
primi. Portions for all courses are huge,
but if you happen to have room for
dessert, try the gooey *Sachertorte*. The
wine list features big names.

Kome
*Via de' Benci 41r (055 2008009/
www.komefirenze.it).* **Open** noon-3pm,
7pm-midnight Tue-Sun. €€-€€€.
Japanese. Map p111 B4 ⑳
Boasting Florence's first *kalten* (conv-
eyer belt) and Italy's only *yakiniku* (barbecue), the 'Grain of Rice' is making
waves both for its Japanese and Asian
specialities and its stunning decor.
Downstairs, perch on green bar stools
under a gold ceiling to select good sushi,
sashimi and nighiri from the belt. On the
upper floor, a gas barbecue is set into
each table. If you choose one of the set
menus, a series of hors d'oeuvres and
a soup arrive, followed by raw fish/
chicken/beef that you cook yourself.

La Loggia degli Albizi
Borgo degli Albizi 39r (055 2479574).
Open 7.30am-8.30pm Mon-Sat. Closed
Aug. **Café**. Map p111 B3 ㉑
Offering some of the best pastries and
cakes in town, La Loggia degli Albizi
is the perfect stop-off after some hard

Ora d'Aria

shopping. Be sure to try the *torta della nonna* (consisting of crumbly pastry filled with baked pâtisserie cream).

Ora d'Aria
Via Ghibellina 3/Cr (055 2001699/ www.oradariaristorante.com).
Open 7.30-11.30pm Mon-Sat. €€€.
Modern Italian. Map p111 C4 ㉒
This minimalist restaurant at the eastern end of via Ghibellina is quietly but confidently making waves among local foodies. Marco Stabile's menus, featuring fish, seafood and meat and Mediterranean flavours, are based on the freshest of seasonal ingredients, and there are several tasting menus, which range between 'traditions' and 'innovations'. With an excellent and fairly-priced wine list, this is arguably the best-value gourmet dining experience to be had in Florence.

Osteria de' Benci
Via de' Benci 13r (055 2344923).
Open 1-2.45pm, 7.30-10.45pm Mon-Sat.
€€. **Tuscan**. Map p111 A4 ㉓

There's a great atmosphere at this lively *trattoria*, complementing the impressive size and flavour of its meat. You'll pay about €20 for a Chianina fillet, but it'll be worth it – it's vast, cooked over an open fire and served *al sangue* (rare). Local specialities like *ribollita* and *trippa alla fiorentina* are also good, while pasta dishes are creative and desserts strong. Service can be brusque, but such popularity can only be a good sign.

Il Pizzaiuolo
Via de' Macci 113r (055 241171).
Open 12.30-3pm, 7.30pm-12.30am Mon-Sat. Closed Aug. €. **Pizzeria/ Neapolitan**. Map p111 C3 ㉔
Il Pizzaiuolo is not a celebrated as it once was, following a change of ownership, but the place still turns out more-than-decent Neapolitan pizzas. For an authentic taste of Naples, try the *salsiccia e friarelli* topping – sausage and a kind of bitter greens. Pasta dishes are also delicious. Finish off with a *babà al rhum* (rum-flavoured Neapolitan dessert). Booking is a must.

with a full view of the open kitchen. The cooking has palpable Middle Eastern and North African influences, resulting in dishes like falafel and other typical mezedes, fish or vegetable couscous, and fish *brik* (deep-fried flaky pastry parcels) served with a Tunisian salad, along with pastas and salads.

La Vie en Rose

Borgo Allegri 68r (055 2346943/ www.lver.it). **Open** 7-11pm Mon-Sat. **€€. Italian/French**. Map p111 C3 ㉗
After several changes of identity over the past few years, this cute little restaurant has been grounded by the new, young French owner's good-value Italo-French food. Opt for a set menu (€22 and €32) or choose from the short *carta*; we were impressed by a mint-spiked courgette and ricotta *tortino* (pastry-less flan) and a tart, summery lemon cream. This is officially a *circolo*, or club, so you have to take out (free) membership the first time you go.

I Visacci

Borgo degli Albizi 80r (055 2001956). **Open** 10.30am-2.30am Mon-Sat. **Café**. Map p111 A3 ㉘
Cosy up in one of the padded alcove seats in this cutesy bar, decked out in multicoloured stripes. The best cappuccinos in the city are served, and mellow music helps to lull you into a long stay. The lunchtime menu hits the right notes: cheap hot *crostoni*, salads, omelettes and cold meat plates. The place hots up come night-time, with salsa beats, steaming coffee and liqueur concoctions.

Vivoli

Via Isola delle Stinche 7r (055 292334/ www.vivoli.it). **Open** Summer 7.30am-midnight Tue-Sun. Winter 7.30am-9pm Tue-Sun. Closed mid Aug. No credit cards. **Gelateria**. Map p111 B4 ㉙
See box p73.

Da Rocco

Inside Sant' Ambrogio market, piazza Ghiberti (no phone). **Open** noon-2pm, 7-10pm Mon-Sat. **€. Snacks/fast food**. Map p111 C4 ㉕
The bustling Sant'Ambrogio market is a much more local affair than its larger San Lorenzo counterpart, and Rocco's glorified food kiosk is where many of the neighbourhood shoppers end up for a quick lunch. Located right in the middle of the covered part of the market, it serves up cheap and cheerful versions of rustic classics such as *pappa al pomodoro*, *spezzatino* (a kind of beef stew) and tripe salad. Pastas cost €2.50 and mains are only €3.10.

Ruth's

Via Farini 2A (055 2480888). **Open** 12.30-2.30pm, 7.30-10.30pm Mon-Thur; 12.30-2.30pm Fri. **€€. Vegetarian/fish**. Map p111 C3 ㉖
Located beside the city's synagogue, Ruth's serves great-value kosher vegetarian food and fish dishes. The dining area is pleasant, modern and bright

Shopping

A Piedi Nudi nel Parco

Borgo degli Albizi 46r (055 2340768). **Open** noon-8pm Mon; 10am-8pm Tue-Sat. Map p111 B3 ㉚

These sister shops take their name from the 1960s film *Barefoot in the Park*, but the style of clothing is more neo-1970s, with beautifully cut, long, fluid and asymmetrical styles with a decorative twist, in understated colours and high-quality fabrics.

Borgo degli Albizi 48 Rosso

Borgo degli Albizi 48r (055 2347598/ www.borgoalbizi.com). **Open** 3.30-7.30pm Mon; 10am-1pm, 3.30-7.30pm Tue-Sat. **Map** p111 B3 ③①
Opulent chandeliers and glass peardrop lamps made with antique or new crystals. You can also order items to your own design.

La Bottega dei Cristalli

Via de' Benci 51r (055 2344891/ www.labottegadeicristalli.com). **Open** 10am-7.30pm daily. Closed mid Jan-mid Feb. **Map** p111 B4 ③②
A lovely range of Murano and Tuscan-made glass plates, picture frames, lamps and chandeliers, and tiny glass 'sweets' and bottles.

Cartoleria Ecologica La Tartaruga

Borgo degli Albizi 60r (055 2340845). **Open** 1.30-7.30pm Mon; 9.30am-7.30pm Tue-Sat. **Map** p111 B3 ③③
Unusual stationery, toys and gifts made of recycled paper, wood and papier mâché.

Casa della Cornice

Via Sant'Egidio 26r (055 2480222). **Open** 9am-1pm, 3-7.30pm Mon-Fri; 9.30am-1pm Sat. No credit cards. **Map** p111 B3 ③④
A huge catalogue of traditional and contemporary picture frames in silver and gold leaf.

Data Records

Via de' Neri 15r (055 287592/ www.superecords.com). **Open** 3.30-7.30pm Mon; 10am-1pm, 3.30-7.30pm Tue-Sat. Closed 2wks Aug. **Map** p111 A4/A5 ③⑤
The staff at Data are true music buffs with a local reputation for being able to find the unfindable. Home to over

80,000 titles, new and used, with an emphasis on psychedelia, blues, R&B, jazz and soundtracks.

I Dolci di Patrizio Cosi

Borgo degli Albizi 11r (055 2480367). **Open** 8.30am-7.30pm Tue-Sat; 9am-1pm Sun. Closed Aug. No credit cards. **Map** p111 B3 ③⑥
A huge range of sweet treats on offer. Delicious hot doughnuts (*bomboloni caldi*) are served at 5pm.

Ethic

Borgo degli Albizi 37r (055 2344413). **Open** 3-8pm Mon; 10am-8pm Tue-Sat. **Map** p111 B3 ③⑦
A unique clothing store with items at low to mid-range prices as well as a cutting-edge selection of CDs and a homewear section with curtains, cushions and accessories.

Il Guardaroba

Via Giuseppe Verdi 28r (055 2478250). **Open** 3.30-7.30pm Mon; 9.30am-7.30pm Tue-Sat. **Map** p111 B3 ③⑧
Il Guardaroba deals in designer end-of-lines and past seasons' stock with good deals to be had.

Libreria delle Donne

Via Fiesolana 2B (055 240384). **Open** 3.30-7.30pm Mon; 9.30am-1pm, 3.30-7.30pm Tue-Fri. Closed Aug. **Map** p111 B3 ③⑨
A good reference point for women in Florence, not just for its books but also for the useful noticeboard that has details on local activities.

Lisa Corti Home Textiles Emporium

Piazza Ghiberti 33r (055 2001860/ www.lisacorti.com). **Open** 3.30-7.30pm Mon; 10am-7.30pm Tue-Sat; 11am-1.30pm, 2.30-7pm Sun. **Map** p111 C3 ④⓪
Brightly coloured cushions, bedspreads, quilts and curtains, in silks and cottons and with an oriental feel. Designer Lisa Corti has also created a small range of furniture and pottery, and has a clothing and accessories store in the Oltrarno (p141).

McRae Books

Via de' Neri 32r (055 2382456/ www.mcraebooks.com). Open 9am-7.30pm daily. **Map** p111 A4 ④

This excellent bookstore specialises in English titles, from travel guides and maps to novels, art history, cookery and current affairs titles. There's also a small range of CDs, DVDs and used books.

Maestri di Fabbrica

Borgo degli Albizi 68r (055 242321/ www.maestridifabbrica.it). Open 3.30-7.30pm Mon; 10am-7.30pm Tue-Sat. **Map** p111 A3 ④

A sprawling, frescoed space stocking gifts, fashion and homeware, the common denominator being their hand-made Tuscan provenance. Knives from the Mugello, glassware from Vinci, locally made jewellery and painted ceramic tiles are some of the highlights.

Maison Dumitru

Borgo Pinti 25r (055 7189417). Open 9.30am-7pm Mon-Sat. **Map** p111 B3 ④

See box p140.

Sbigoli Terrecotte

Via Sant'Egidio 4r (055 2479713/www. sbigoliterrecotte.it). Open 9am-1pm, 3-7.30pm Mon-Sat. **Map** p111 B3 ④

Handmade Tuscan ceramics and terracotta in traditional designs are the order of the day here.

Scuola del Cuoio

Via San Giuseppe 5r (055 244533/ www.leatherschool.com). Open 9.30am-6pm Mon-Sat; 10am-6pm Sun. **Map** p111 B4 ④

At this leather school in the cloisters of Santa Croce (p117), you can watch the craftsmen making bags and accessories. The prices add further appeal.

Signum

Borgo de' Greci 40r (055 280621/ www.signumfirenze.it). Open 9am-7.30pm Mon-Sat; 10am-7pm Sun. **Map** p111 A4 ④

This delightful shop stocks an appealingly wide range of gifts, among them miniature models of shop windows and bookcases, as well as Murano glass inkwells and pens.

Soqquadro

Borgo Pinti 13r (055 2347502). Open 4-7.30pm Mon; 11am-1pm, 4-7.30pm Tue-Sun. Hours may vary. No credit cards. **Map** p111 B3 ④

See box p140.

Vestri

Borgo degli Albizi 11r (055 2340374/ www.vestri.it). Open Summer 10am-8pm daily. *Winter* 10am-8pm daily. Closed Aug. **Map** p111 B3 ④

Handmade chocolates with chilli pepper, cinnamon and more prosaic fillings, as well as a full range of pralines and bars. The upmarket shop is beautifully designed to evoke a luxurious experience all-round, and it's an excellent bet for gifts for sweet-toothed friends. Flavoured hot chocolates are served in winter, with rich ice-creams the speciality in summer (see box p58).

Nightlife

Café-bar **I Visacci** (p121) hots up come night-time with Latin beats and eccentric regulars.

Doris

Via de' Pandolfini 26r (055 2466775/ www.dorisfirenze.it). Open Bar 7-10pm Tue-Sun. *Club* 11.30pm-4am Tue-Sun. **Admission** €10. **Map** p111 B3 ④

This venue has old-timers recounting nostalgic tales of the down 'n' dirty dancefloor of the 1990s, after it recently reopened as the sweet as cherry pie-sounding Doris. The three rooms have been brought up-to-date with a design makeover of white sofas and pendant lamps, and there's a two-tier opening system to accommodate the *aperitivo* craze early evening before the club night kicks in. The management has also managed to wangle a smokers' corner.

ExMud

Corso de' Tintori 4 (055 2638583/ www.exmud.it). Open 11.30pm-4am Tue-Sun. **Admission** €10. **Map** p111 B5 ⑤

Newly reopened ExMud has been welcomed back with open arms. A warren

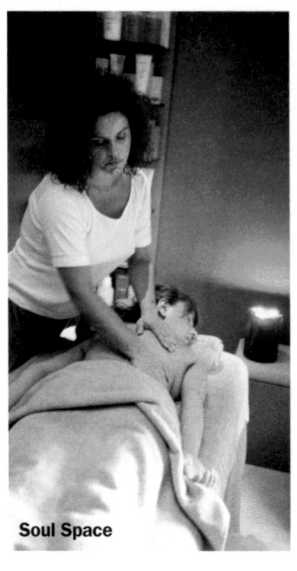

Soul Space

of passageways and rooms in a stone basement, this is, on a good night, everything a great underground nightclub should be. Expect hot, sweaty and rocking fun, with a young, cosmopolitan crowd boogying to international DJs spinning house, garage, drum 'n' bass or liquid funk. Hit a bad night, on the other hand, and you'll be listening to hardcore Italian electronica played to empty dancefloors.

Full-Up

Via della Vigna Vecchia 23r (055 293006). **Open** 11pm-4am Tue-Sat. Closed June-Sept. **Admission** free. **Map** p111 A4 **51**

Friendly staff from the defunct Dolce Zucchero have set up residence in this long-running club, bringing new ideas and pepping up the proceedings. The best night to go is Thursday, when the team from Yab (p82) is enlisted to re-run its legendary hip hop night, Smoove. Saturday is an altogether more commercial affair. The club's flash VIP privé is unusual in that

it often really does have celebrities (albeit minor ones) quaffing bubbly at its eight tables.

Kikuya English Pub

Via de' Benci 43r (055 2344879/ www.kikuyapub.it). **Open** 6pm-2am daily. **Map** p111 B4 **52**

Here's a taste of British pub culture, with Guinness and John Bull English Ale, live footie on plasma screens and Tex-Mex cuisine. Allusions to authenticity stop there, though: Brazilian barmaids mix the drinks with panache and Kikuya's claim to fame is that it was voted one of the best pubs in Italy by *Playboy* magazine. There's free Wi-Fi for anyone who cares to risk a pint down their laptop – this pub packs 'em in, especially during happy hour, from 7pm to 10pm.

Lido

Lungarno Pecori Giraldi 1r (055 2342726). **Open** 12.30pm-2am Tue-Sat; 1pm-2am Sun. *Lunch served* 1-3pm daily. Closed Jan, Feb. **Admission** free. No credit cards. **Map** p111 C5 **53**

Santa Croce

Large glass doors open from this bar to a garden that extends to the riverbank, making it a good bet for summer nights, when queues inevitably form. The music is a thumping mix of drum 'n' bass, R&B and the like, though the dancefloor is entirely taken up by the queue for the bar. Fridays is stomping deep house.

Moyo
Via de' Benci 23r (055 2479738). **Open** 6pm-2am daily. **Admission** free. **Map** p111 B4 54

Being the first to have wireless internet in Florence is just one claim to fame for this buzzing bar. The cool wood decor and outdoor seating make for a welcoming year-round environment, and being on the edge of the no-drive zone means that parking is only a five-minute walk away. Come *aperitivo* time, it's packed out with hip Florentines.

Piccolo Caffè
Borgo Santa Croce 23 (055 2001057/ www.piccolofirenze.com). **Open** 6.30pm-2.30am daily. **Admission** free. **Map** p111 B4 55

Attracting a very mixed crowd from the gay and lesbian community, the Piccolo gets especially packed on Fridays and Saturdays. Check out the frequent art exhibitions and live shows.

Rex Café
Via Fiesolana 25r (055 2480331/www. rexcafe.it). **Open** 6pm-2.30am daily. Closed June-Aug. **Map** p111 B3/C3 56

With more of a club than a bar vibe, Rex is king of the east of the city, filling up with loyal subjects who sashay to the sounds of the session DJs playing bassy beats and jungle rhythms. Gaudí-esque mosaics decorate the central bar, wrought-iron lamps shed a soft light while a luscious red antechamber creates welcome seclusion for more intimate gatherings. Tapas are served during the *aperitivo* happy hour (5-9.30pm), and the cocktails are especially good.

Twice
Via Giuseppe Verdi 57r (055 0517374/ www.twiceclub.com). **Open** Bar

7.30-11pm Tue-Sun. *Club* 11pm-3am Tue-Sun. Closed mid May-Sept. **Admission** free. **Map** p111 B3 57

The main news at the latest incarnation of this long-running venue is the division of the night into early-evening wine bar and club (hence the name). The gimmicks don't stop there and while the wine bar's a safe stop-off for an *aperitivo*, the themed club nights become a tad tedious. Hip hop and R&B Thursdays shed the tack.

YAG B@R
Via de' Macci 8r (055 2469022/www. yagbar.com). **Open** 8pm-3am daily. **Admission** free. **Map** p111 C4 58

This spacious, futuristic gay dance bar draws a young crowd of both genders, often here as a first stop on the club-hopping route. Current tunes dominate, and internet access and video games are also to hand.

Arts & leisure

Soul Space
Via Sant'Egidio 12r (055 2001794/ www.soulspace.it). **Open** 10am-7pm Mon-Sat. **Map** p111 B3 59

A luxurious new spa with pool, garden, real hammam, relaxation room with a fireplace, and a range of spa treatments including hot stone therapies.

Teatro Verdi
Via Ghibellina 99 (055 212320/ www.teatroverdifirenze.it). **Season** Sept-June. **Map** p111 B4 60

This theatre – the city's largest – was extensively revamped in 2004 for its 150th anniversary. A wood floor was added in the auditorium and new designer red velvet seats were installed (although they're extremely uncomfortable, with less legroom than a Ryanair flight). Teatro Verdi is the home of the dynamic Orchestra della Toscana, which gives two or three concerts a month here. It also hosts all the top-notch light theatrical comedies, musicals and dance shows whose more lavish sets and elaborate choreography would not fit in any of the smaller venues in town.

FLORENCE BY AREA

Piazza Santa Spirito

Oltrarno

Spanning the width of the city centre along the southern banks of the Arno and extending down to Porta Romana in an oblique triangle is the Oltrarno (literally, 'beyond the Arno'). This eclectic area is a beguiling, contradictory world of ornate *palazzi* with splendid gardens, church squares and tumbledown artisan workshops.

To the west are the salt-of-the-earth parishes of San Frediano and Santo Spirito. **San Frediano** is dominated by piazza del Carmine, a social hub by night and home to the church of **Santa Maria del Carmine** and the **Brancacci Chapel**. This area still very much belongs to the locals.

Santo Spirito's piazza Santo Spirito is the heart of its bohemian neighbourhood, bustling with the comings and goings of locals.

A morning market is held in the square from Monday to Saturday, with a flea market on the second Sunday of every month and an organic food market every third Sunday. In winter, this is a lively but low-key space, but on summer evenings the square's bars and restaurants and the steps of the church of **Santo Spirito** are packed to the gills.

Between Santo Spirito and a maze of narrow streets to the east is the grand **via Maggio**, with its fabulous antiques shops and massive stone crests. At its river end the street meets borgo San Jacopo, with its mix of medieval towers, hip clothes shops and 1960s monstrosities built to replace houses bombed in the war. San Jacopo leads east to the southern end of the **ponte Vecchio**. Heading south-west down from the bridge is via de' Guicciardini, with its expensive paper, crafts and jewellery shops (as well as tourist tat) and the small church of **Santa Felicita**. Passing the grandeur of the Medici's **Palazzo Pitti**, it ends in a square dominated by Palazzo Guidi, housing **Casa Guidi**, former home of Robert Browning and Elizabeth Barrett Browning. Here via Maggio and via de' Guicciardini join to become via Romana, a long thoroughfare that leads to **Porta Romana**, lined with picture framers and antiques shops and home to the gory **La Specola** museum and the second entrance to **Boboli Gardens**.

South-east of the ponte Vecchio are the *costas* (meaning 'ribs'). These pretty, narrow lanes snake steeply uphill towards the **Forte di Belvedere**, now used for summertime cultural events and film screenings following a recent restoration. Halfway up costa San Giorgio is one of the two entrances to the spectacular, newly opened **Giardino Bardini**, while the other is in via de' Bardi, a quiet street running uphill behind the riverbank, which leads into lungarno Serristori and the **Casa Museo Rodolfo Siviero**. Behind lies the parish of **San Niccolò**, a sleepy area with a village feel until the evening, when the wine bars and *osterie* along via de' Renai open up, overlooking the riverside piazza Demidoff. Note that the nearby **Museo Bardini** (piazza de' Mozzi 1, 055 2342427) is undergoing a torturous restoration that should end in 2009 with the birth of the **Galleria Corsi**.

Sights & museums

After a long period of restoration, the 16th-century **Forte di Belvedere** (p143) at the top of the Boboli Gardens is now open once again, and used mainly for exhibitions and cultural events.

Casa Guidi
Piazza San Felice 8 (UK number 01628 825925). **Open** *Apr-Nov* 3-6pm Mon, Wed, Fri. **Admission** by donation. **Map** p128 B3 ❶
English poets Robert Browning and Elizabeth Barrett Browning came to Florence in April 1847 after a clandestine marriage, and for 14 years an apartment in this house was their home. Now owned by the Landmark Trust and partly rented out as a holiday home, key rooms of the apartment where they lived and wrote are open for visits during certain months.

Casa Museo Rodolfo Siviero
Lungarno Serristori 1-3 (055 2345219/guided tours 055 293007). **Open** 9.30am-12.30pm Mon; 3.30-6.30pm Sat. **Admission** free. **Map** p129 D3 ❷
This was previously the house of government minister Rodolfo Siviero, dubbed the 'James Bond of art' for his efforts to prevent the Nazis plundering Italian masters. The pieces he saved were returned to their owners but Siviero left his own private collection to the Regione Toscana on condition that it would be open to the public. Among the 500 pieces on display are paintings and sculptures by friends of Siviero including de Chirico, Annigoni and da Messina.

Cenacolo di Santo Spirito
Piazza Santo Spirito 29 (055 287043). **Open** 9am-2pm Tue-Sun. **Admission** €2.20. No credit cards. **Map** p128 B2 ❸
Orcagna's 14th-century fresco *The Last Supper*, housed in a former Augustinian refectory, was butchered by an 18th-century architect commissioned to build some doors into it. Only the fringes of the fresco remain, though there's a more complete (albeit heavily restored) *Crucifixion* above it. The small Museo della Fondazione Romano here houses an eclectic collection of sculptures given to the state in 1946 on the death of sailor Salvatore Romano.

Oltrarno

Giardino Bardini

*Via de' Bardi 1r, costa San Giorgio 2
(055 290112).* **Open** *Nov-Feb* 8.15am-
4.30pm daily. *Mar* 8.15am-5.30pm daily.
Apr, May, Sept, Oct 8.15am-6.30pm
daily. *June-Aug* 8.15am-7.30pm daily.
Closed last Mon of the mth. **Admission**
€9 (incl Museo degli Argenti, Museo
del Costume, Museo delle Porcellane
& Giardino di Boboli). No credit cards.
Map p129 D3 ❹

Created in the 1200s by the Mozzi family, this intriguing garden has just been
opened after five years of restoration. It's
divided into three areas: the Baroque
steps, leading to a terrace with amazing
views; the English wood, a shady haven
of evergreens; and the farm park, with a
dwarf orchard, rhododendron collection
and 'tunnel' of wisteria and hydrangea.

Giardini di Boboli

*Piazza Pitti 1, via Romana (055
2651816/2651838).* **Open** *Jan-Feb,
Nov-Dec* 8.15am-4.30pm daily. *Mar*
8.15am-5.30pm daily. *Apr, May, Sept*
8.15am-6.30pm daily. *June-Aug, Oct*
8.15am-7.30pm daily. Closed 1st &
last Mon of mth. **Admission** €7
(incl Museo degli Argenti, Museo del
Costume, Museo delle Porcellane &
Giardino Bardini). No credit cards.
Map p128 B3/C3 ❺

Part of Palazzo Pitti (p129), Boboli is
the best loved of the few green spaces
in the city centre, and despite the
entrance fee is a popular oasis. Far to
the left of the entrance is a fountain
showing Cosimo I's obese dwarf as a
nude Bacchus, heralding the walkway
that leads to Buontalenti's grotto with

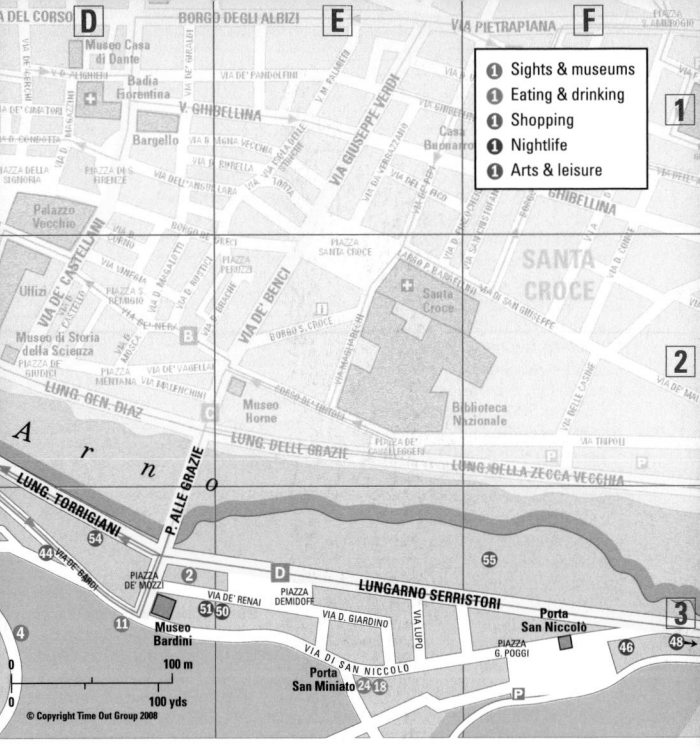

Bandinelli's statues of Ceres and Apollo, casts of Michelangelo's *Slaves* and a second grotto adorned with frescoes of classic Greek and Roman myths and encrusted with shells. The ramps take you to the amphitheatre. At the top of the hill is the Museo delle Porcellane (p132), entered through the Giardino dei Cavalieri.

Palazzo Pitti

Piazza Pitti 1, via Romana (055 2654321/www.palazzopitti.it). **Open** 8.15am-6.50pm Tue-Sun. **Admission** €7. **Map** p128 B3 ❻
The Pitti Palace was built in 1457 for Luca Pitti, a Medici rival, supposedly to a design by Brunelleschi that had been rejected by Cosimo il Vecchio as too grandiose. However, it also

proved too grandiose for the Pitti, who, gallingly, were forced to sell to the Medici. Its ornate, opulent rooms now hold the vast Medici collections plus later additions in the museums detailed below. The Palazzo's Giardini di Boboli (p128) is one of the city's best-loved green spaces.

Galleria d'Arte Moderna

055 2388616. **Open** 8.15am-1.50pm (last entry 1.15pm) Tue-Sat, 2nd, 4th Mon of mth & 1st, 3rd, 5th Sun of mth. **Admission** €7 (incl all Palazzo Pitti museums). No credit cards.
The 30 rooms on the second floor of the Pitti were royal apartments until 1920; today they're given over to Florence's Modern Art museum. The collection covers neoclassical to early 20th-century art, with highlights including

Sand in the city

Florence isn't known for being quick to act on new-fangled trends – at least not these days. But when it comes to a helping hand for the euphemistic and de rigueur *tintarella*, or 'little suntan', it's a different story.

Hot on the heels of the successes of city beaches in London, Paris and Milan, summer 2007 saw the opening of **Florence Beach** (p143), on a raised stretch of riverbank south of the Arno, just ten minutes' walk from the city centre.

Aside from the small detail of not being able to go for so much as a paddle (the Arno is off-limits for bathing), the beach has everything any self-respecting beach bum could ask for: sand, sun loungers, parasols, beach volley and a children's play area. The Florentine summer can be suffocating, and the beach is equipped with showers, a wooden gazebo, a cooling zone and watermelon and ice-cream vendors to help beat the heat.

The popularity of this mini Forte dei Marmi (5,000 people visited in two months in 2007) has secured its opening at least for the summer of 2008, and an expansion plan includes extra loungers and umbrellas, and a beach football area.

The beach opens from 10am till 10pm, provisionally from the end of June till the beginning of September, and is accessed from lungarno Serristori. Entrance and use of the facilities is free but ID must be shown to borrow a lounger.

Giovanni Dupré's bronze sculptures of Cain and Abel (Room 5) and Ottone Rosai's simple *Piazza del Carmine* in Room 30. Rooms 11, 12, 18 and 19 showcase the work of the Macchiaioli school.

Galleria Palatina & Appartamenti Reali
055 2388614. **Open** 8.15am-6.50pm Tue-Sun. **Admission** €7 (incl all Palazzo Pitti museums). No credit cards.

This gallery has 28 rooms of paintings, hung four- or five-high on the damask walls. You'll want to linger longest in the five planet rooms. The Sala di Venere (Venus) is dominated by a statue of Venus by Canova, but also contains Titian's regal *La Bella*. The Sala di Apollo houses the nine *Muses* and is crowded with works by Rosso Fiorentino and Andrea del Sarto. The Sala di Marte (Mars) is closed for restoration (Rubens' *Four Philosophers* and other works from this room are on show in the Sala delle Nicchie). The best place to look in the Sala di Giove (Jupiter) is up, in order to admire the lofty depiction of Jupiter. Look too for Raphael's lover, the so-called 'baker girl' Margherita Luti, in his *La Velata*. Finally, the Sala di Saturno (Saturn) contains some of Raphael's best-known works: among them the *Madonna of the Grand Duke*, which shows a distinct Leonardo influence, and his last painting, *Holy Family*, seemingly inspired by Michelangelo.

Museo degli Argenti
055 2388709. **Open** Oct-May, Sept 8.15am-6.30pm daily. June-Aug 8.15am-7.30pm daily. Year-round closed 1st & last Mon of mth. **Admission** €7 (incl Museo delle Porcellane, Museo del Costume, Giardino di Boboli & Giardino Bardini). No credit cards.

The extravagant two-tier museum section of the Pitti Palace houses not just silver, but an astonishing hoard of treasures amassed by the Medici, from tapestries and rock crystal vases to a banal collection of miniature animals.

Museo delle Carrozze
055 2388614. **Open** by appointment only; call ahead.

Grotta di Buontalenti, Giardini di Boboli p128

Hemingway p137

While plans are being made to move this fairytale collection of carriages that once belonged to the Medici, Lorraine and Savoy houses into the former Medici stables, anyone with a Cinderella complex can arrange a visit by appointment.

Museo del Costume
055 2388713. **Open** 8.15am-6.30pm (last entry 6.15pm) Tue-Sat, 2nd, 4th Mon of mth & 1st, 3rd, 5th Sun of mth. **Admission** €7 (incl Museo degli Argenti, Museo delle Porcellane, Giardino di Boboli and Giardino Bardini). No credit cards.

The sumptuous Costume Museum is in the Palazzina della Meridiana. Collections of formal, theatre and everyday costumes from the museum's 6,000 pieces and from a period spanning five centuries are shown in rotation, changing every two years. Some of the more important get-ups are permanently on display, among them Cosimo I's and Eleonora di Toledo's clothes, including her grand velvet creation from Bronzino's portrait.

Museo delle Porcellane
055 2388709. **Open** as per Boboli Gardens; p128. **Admission** €7 (incl Museo degli Argenti, Museo del Costume, Giardino di Boboli & Giardino Bardini). No credit cards.

This outhouse at the top of the Boboli Gardens was once a reception room for artists, built by Leopoldo de' Medici. The museum has ceramics used by the various occupants of Palazzo Pitti and includes the largest selection of Viennese china outside Vienna, but most visitors are more interested in the views.

Santa Felicita
Piazza Santa Felicita (055 213018). **Open** 9am-12.30pm, 3.30-6.30pm Mon-Sat; 9am-1pm Sun (except 9am & noon services). **Admission** free. **Map** p128 C2 ❼

This church occupies the site of the first church in Florence, founded in the second century AD by Syrian Greek tradesmen. The oldest surviving part is the portico, built in 1564; the interior mainly dates back to the 18th century. Most who come here do so to see Pontormo's *Deposition* altarpiece in the Cappella Barbadori-Capponi.

Santa Maria del Carmine & Cappella Brancacci
Piazza del Carmine (055 2768558/ bookings 055 2768224). **Open** *Chapel* 10am-5pm Mon, Wed-Sat; 1-5pm Sun. Phone to book. **Admission** €4. No credit cards. **Map** p128 A2 ❽

This blowsy Baroque church is dominated by a huge single nave adorned with pilasters and pious sculptures overlooked by a ceiling fresco of the Ascension – but this is not what visitors queue in droves for. The Brancacci Chapel, frescoed in the 15th century by Masaccio and Masolino, is one of the city's greatest art treasures. Masaccio died aged just 27, but reached his peak with this cycle of frescoes, especially the tangibly grief-stricken Adam and Eve in the *Expulsion from Paradise*, a fresco that entranced Michelangelo.

Santo Spirito

Piazza Santo Spirito (055 210030). **Open** *Winter* 8am-noon, 4-5pm Mon, Tue, Thur, Fri; 8am-noon Wed. *Summer* 8am-noon, 4-6pm Mon, Tue, Thur, Fri; 8am-noon Wed. **Admission** free. **Map** p128 B2 ⑨

Behind the exquisitely simple 18th-century cream façade is one of Brunelleschi's most extraordinary works. There was an Augustinian church on this site from 1250, but in 1397 the monks decided to replace it, commissioning Brunelleschi. Work started in 1444, two years before the great master died, and the façade and exterior walls were never finished. Santo Spirito's structure is a beautifully proportioned, Latin-cross church lined with a colonnade of dove grey-coloured pietra serena pilasters sheltering 38 chapels. Left of the church is the refectory housing the Cenacolo di Santo Spirito (p127).

La Specola

Via Romana 17 (055 2288251/guided visits 055 2346760/www.msn.unifi.it). **Open** 9am-1pm Mon, Tue, Thur, Fri, Sun; 9am-5pm Sat. **Admission** €4. No credit cards. **Map** p128 A3/B3 ⑩

A dream day out for older kids with horror fixations, La Specola is the zoology department of the Natural History Museum. The first 23 rooms are crammed with stuffed and pickled animals including famously extinct species, and up to here the museum can also be fun for younger children. From Room 24 onwards, however, the exhibits are more gruesome. A Frankenstein-esque laboratory is filled with wax corpses on satin beds, each a little more dissected than the last.

Villa Bardini

Via de' Bardi 1r (055 2638599/www. bardinipeyron.it). **Open** 10am-4pm daily. Closed 1st & last Mon of the month. **Admission** €5. No credit cards. **Map** p129 D3 ⑪

The newly restored Villa Bardini is home to a permanent exhibition of the fabulously extravagant creations of couturier Roberto Capucci. A new museum in the villa of the works of Italian artist Pietro Annigoni is due to open in spring 2008, preceded by a new bar/restaurant.

Eating & drinking

LibreriaCafé La Cité (p139) is as popular for its café and wine-, cheese- and olive oil-tasting nights as it is for its fantastic selection of books and cultural events.

Beccofino
Piazza degli Scarlatti 1r (055 290076/ www.beccofino.com). **Open** 7-11.30pm Tue-Sun. **€€€**. **Modern Tuscan**. **Map** p128 B1/B2 ⑫
When Beccofino opened in 1999, its combination of contemporary decor, innovative food and serious wines was unique in town, and it was an instant hit. After something of a decline, a re-launch in 2006 seems to have put things back on track; Anglo-Italian chef Roby Papin aims to exalt local recipes and seasonal ingredients. An autumn meal included potato-stuffed tortelli with a mixed mushroom sauce; plump for a *bistecca alla Fiorentina* with prized, properly sourced Chianina meat.

Borgo San Jacopo
Borgo San Jacopo 62r (055 281661/ www.lungarnohotels.com). **Open** 7.30-10.30pm Mon, Wed-Sun. **€€€**. **Italian/fish**. **Map** p128 B2 ⑬
The Hotel Lungarno's restaurant is well respected in Florence for its classy yet informal ambience and its delicious, unfussy food. Chef Beatrice Segoni hails from the Adriatic coast and several fish dishes from her home territory feature on the menu. Punchy meat options include a *millefoglie* of duck breast and pigeon with artichokes. A huge arched window allows for plenty of river-based sights, but you'll have to fight for a table on the terrace, with its incomparable views of ponte Vecchio.

Caffè degli Artigiani
Via dello Sprone 16r (055 291882/ www.oltrarno-firenze.net). **Open** *May-Sept* 8am-4pm Mon; 8am-midnight Tue-Sat. *Oct-Apr* 8.30am-10.30pm Mon-Sat. **Café/bar**. **Map** p128 B2 ⑭
This charming, laid-back gem of a café is worth seeking out for its country cottage atmosphere (think low ceilings and beautifully carved antique chairs). Staff are friendly and multilingual and a couple of outside tables appear in warm weather.

Caffè Ricchi
Piazza Santo Spirito 9r (055 215864/ www.caffericchi.com). **Open** *Summer* 7am-1.30am Mon-Sat. *Winter* 7am-10pm Mon-Sat. Closed last 2wks Aug, last 2wks Feb. **Café/bar**. **Map** p128 B2 ⑮
Ricchi is on the traffic-free piazza Santo Spirito, a charming setting for alfresco drinking. The place does a good lunch menu that changes daily. If it rains, the side room is a great place to relax with a coffee and a cake. The nearby eponymous restaurant has sadly gone downhill after a change in ownership.

Trattoria del Carmine p138

Da Camillo

Borgo San Jacopo 57r (055 212427).
Open 7.30-10.20pm Tue-Sun. €€€.
Tuscan. Map p128 B2 ⓰
You may pay over the odds to eat at this *trattoria* (favoured haunt of the Florentine aristocracy since the 1940s), but the food is top notch and prepared with the best ingredients. Chiara Masiero's varied menus feature Florentine classics, influences from Romagna, plus the results of her own experimenting, such as *ceciata di maiale* (a hearty stew of pork, chickpeas and spinach). Friday's menus always include fish. There's a fairly hefty mark-up on the wines, but the *vino della casa* is good and affordable.

Cavolo Nero

Via dell'Ardiglione 22 (055 294744/ www.cavolonero.it). **Open** 7.30-10.30pm Mon-Sat. €€€. **Italian**.
Map p128 A2 ⓱
This inviting restaurant is nestled on the street where Filippo Lippi was born. Chef/owner Arturo Dori's menus (divided equally between fish and meat)

have evolved to offer unfussy 'contemporary Italian' cooking that's often very good indeed. He and his wife Michela run their outfit with charm and enthusiasm and have a firm local fan base. Dishes come from all over Italy, but Mediterranean flavours dominate.

Filipepe

Via di San Niccolò 39r (055 2001397/ www.filipepe.com). **Open** 7.30pm-1am daily. Closed 2wks Aug. €€€.
Modern Italian. Map p129 E3 ⓲
Funky decor provides a sensual setting for the unusual food at Filipepe, one of the best deals in town. The two chefs hail from Calabria in Southern Italy and their regularly changing menus feature punchy, sunny flavours. Dishes are divided into *freddo e crudo* (cold and raw) and *caldo* (hot) sections, but you can mix and match as you wish. Choose from the likes of pasta with sardines, sultanas and pine nuts; and seared tuna with a balsamic mousse. The wine list is well priced. Look out for Filipepe's new sister restaurant Garbo (borgo San Frediano 233-25r, 055 213415), which

Le volpi e l'uva p138

was about to open as this guide went to press, and which promises to be as interesting as the original.

Il Guscio

Via dell'Orto 49 (055 224421). **Open** noon-2pm, 8-11pm Mon-Sat. Closed Aug. **€€. Tuscan.** Map p128 A2 ⑲
The vibe at this popular eaterie screams 'new-generation *trattoria*', while the menu offers carefully prepared, largely traditional Tuscan dishes. Francesco Gozzini runs front-of-house while his wife and mother prepare the food. In summer, the menu leans towards fish and seafood, while in winter, hearty meat choices prevail. The wine list features over 500 labels, starting at just €10. Pop in for a *divino panino* or bowl of soup at lunchtime – the price (€5) includes a glass of wine and a *caffè*.

Hemingway

Piazza Piattellina 9r (055 284781/ www.hemingway.fi.it). **Open** 4.30pm-1am Mon-Thur; 4.30pm-2am Fri, Sat; 3.30pm-1am Sun (brunch noon-2.15pm). Closed mid June-mid Sept. **Café/bar.** Map p128 A2 ⑳
This charming café has a huge selection of quality teas, unusual tea cocktails and at least 20 types of coffee, but it's best known for its chocolate delectables: the owner belongs to the Chocolate Appreciation Society, and the café's *sette veli* chocolate cake once won the World Cake Championship. Hemingway's high tea (6-7.30pm) tempts with sweet delights; there's also a Sunday brunch (book in advance).

La Mangiatoia

Piazza San Felice 8-10r (055 224060). **Open** noon-3pm, 7-10pm Tue-Sun. **€. Pizzeria/rosticceria.** Map p128 B3 ㉑
La Mangiatoia, a combination of *rosticceria* and pizzeria, is popular with a mix of local residents, students and tourists, thanks to its rock-bottom prices and good, honest home cooking. Order takeaway food from the counter, or go through to one of a series of rooms behind the shop, where, aside from standard *rosticceria*

fare (lasagne, spit-roast chicken, roast meats), there's a daily menu of specials and good pizzas.

Olio e Convivium

Via Santo Spirito 4 (055 2658198/ www.conviviumfirenze.com). **Open** *Food served* noon-3pm Mon; noon-3pm, 5.30-10.30pm Tue-Sat. Closed 3wks Aug. **Italian.** Map p128 B2 ㉒
Well-heeled locals call into this upmarket grocer to buy delicious food to go (sweet and savoury preserves, olive oils, wines and superlative treats), but two cosy restaurant rooms – with chequerboard floors, sparkling crystal, shelves stacked with wine, olive oil and other edibles – make fine spots in which to enjoy a quiet meal. Specials are chalked up on a board, and feature the likes of *taglierini* with lobster, broad bean and pecorino risotto.

Pane e Vino

Piazza Cestello 3 (055 2476956/ www.ristorantepaneevino.it). **Open** 7.30pm-midnight Mon-Sat. Closed 2wks Aug. **€€. Italian.** Map p128 A1 ㉓
Pane e Vino has a faithful following among foodies who appreciate the consistently high standards of cooking and keen prices. Tuscan-based cuisine features alongside influences from other regions, and more adventurous dishes have been appearing of late, like the cocoa-stuffed ravioli, and skewered rabbit with Tuscan herbs and a hint of curry. The fresh dates stuffed with caramel marscapone make a superb dessert. Honest mark-ups on the unusual wine list and late hours are added perks. On the downside, service can sometimes be sloppy and rude.

Il Rifrullo

Via di San Niccolò 55r (055 2342621/ www.ilrifrullo.com). **Open** 8am-2am daily. Closed 2wks Aug. **Café/bar.** Map p129 E3 ㉔
This long-time fave has something of the hospitable friend's house vibe, with chatty bar staff, well-worn upholstered chairs and a fire in winter. The atmosphere is laid-back during the day, but the mood mutates for

the evening *aperitivo*, when the music comes on, the back rooms open to accommodate the crowds and plates of homely snacks are served. Sunday brunch is another crowd-puller; it's not unknown for people to wander in for brunch and not emerge again until nightfall. The charming summer roof garden is another plus.

Sant' Agostino 23

Via Sant'Agostino 23 (055 210208). **Open** noon-2.30pm, 7.30-10.30pm Mon-Sat. **€€. Tuscan.** Map p128 A2 ㉕
A welcome addition to the Oltrarno eating scene comes in the form of this tastefully modernised *trattoria*, which serves up Florentine and Italian specialities; *tagliolini* with grated tuna roe, grilled *baccalà* (salt cod) with a rosemary-spiked chickpea purée, tripe, *orecchia di elefante* (literally 'elephant ear', a kind of super-thin Wiener schnitzel) and a fine hamburger and chips. The two-course lunchtime menu offers great value at €10.

Il Santo Bevitore

Via di Santo Spirito 64-66r (055 211264/www.santobevitore.com). **Open** 12.30-3pm, 7.30-11.30pm daily. Closed 3wks Aug. **€€. Italian.** Map p128 A1 ㉖
This restaurant/wine bar occupying a large, vaulted room has become hugely popular with a young crowd in the evenings. Lunchtimes, when there's a more limited menu, are quieter. The food is reliable, even very good at times, and prices are fair; varied and nicely priced wine list is another attraction. As well as the ever-present wooden platters laden with cheeses and cold meats, there's fresh pappardelle with lamb and artichoke sauce, potato soufflé with aromatic butter, and tartare of Chianina beef.

Al Tranvai

Piazza Torquato Tasso 14r (055 22519/www.altranvai.it). **Open** noon-2.30pm, 7-11pm Mon-Sat. **€€. Tuscan.** Map p128 A3 ㉗
Local artisans continue piling in to this place from their nearby workshops, especially at lunchtimes, for the wholesome, down-to-earth cooking and great prices. Dishes hail from the *cucina popolare* tradition; *ribollita* and *pappa al pomodoro* (or *panzanella* in summer), tripe and *lampredotto* (cow's intestine), *lesso rifatto con le cipolle* (a tasty beef and onion stew) and squid *'in inzimino'* (with Swiss chard). Puds are own-made and the house plonk is just fine.

Trattoria del Carmine

Piazza del Carmine 18r (055 218601). **Open** noon-2.30pm, 7.30-10.30pm Mon-Sat. Closed 3wks Aug. **€€. Tuscan.** Map p128 A1 ㉘
This pleasantly rustic, good-value neighbourhood *trattoria* is a step up, in terms of both food and service, from some of the other budget options in the area. The clientele is a mix of regular locals and tourists and the menu is divided between a seasonally inspired *menù del giorno* and a long, fixed menu. Tuscan standards (*ribollita*, spinach and ricotta ravioli, excellent *bistecca*) are always on offer, supplemented by daily specials.

Le volpi e l'uva

Piazza de' Rossi 1r (055 2398132/www.levolpieluva.com). **Open** 11am-9pm Mon-Sat. **Wine bar.** Map p128 C2 ㉙
In winter, the only seats at this squeeze of an *enoteca* are at the bar. In summer, there's much more room thanks to the terrace. Much of what's on offer will be unfamiliar to all but the most clued-up oenophiles: owners Riccardo and Emilio search out small, little-known producers from all over Italy, with an eye for value for money. A limited but delicious selection of nibbles includes cheeses, cured meats and panini *tartufati* (stuffed with truffle cream).

Shopping

Aprosio e Co

Via Santo Spirito 11 (055 290534/www.aprosio.it). **Open** 9.30am-1.30pm, 3-7pm Mon-Sat. Map p128 B2 ㉚
An aloof dog guards the intricate necklaces, bracelets, earrings, evening

Dolcissimo

bags and belts, all made from tiny glass beads, at this sleek showroom.

Arredamenti Castorina
Via Santo Spirito 13-15r (055 212885/ www.castorina.net). **Open** 9am-1pm, 3.30-7.30pm Mon-Fri; 9am-1pm Sat. Closed Aug. **Map** p128 B2 ③①

An extraordinary old shop full of all things baroque, including gilded mouldings, frames, cherubs, trompe l'ceil tables and fake malachite and tortoiseshell obelisks.

Beaded Lily
Sdrucciolo dei Pitti 13r (334 9763949/ www.beadedlily.com). **Open** 2-7pm Tue-Fri; 11am-1.30pm, 3.30-7pm Sat; 2-6pm 2nd & 3rd Sun of month . **Map** p128 B2/B3 ③②

American jewellery designer Lily Mordà's bead and jewellery shop is just around the corner from her glass bead-maker husband's studio, so the Venetian-style beads don't have far to travel. A treasure trove of necklaces, earrings and bracelets awaits, and there's scope for creating your own pieces.

Ceri Vintage
Via de' Serragli 26r (055 217978). **Open** 10am-1.30pm, 3.30-7pm Mon-Sat. **Map** p128 A2 ③③

See box p140.

Dolcissimo
Via Maggio 61r (055 2396268/ www.caffeitaliano.it). **Open** 8am-1pm, 2-8pm Tue-Sat; 9am-2pm Sun. **Map** p128 B3 ③④

A delightful shop from another age. Exquisite chocolates are displayed in gilded cabinets, and glass cake stands hold tempting concoctions, including an unmissable chocolate and pear cake.

Flair
Piazza Scarlatti 2r (055 2670154/ www.flair.it). **Open** 3.30am-7.30pm Mon; 10am-7.30pm Tue-Sat. **Map** p128 B1 ③⑤

Acutely stylish homeware (lamps, mirrors, furniture) and gifts. Black woods, glass and chrome create a masculine vibe. Vintage items are also stocked, and a wall is given over to beautifully boxed teas from Paris.

LibreriaCafé La Cité
Borgo San Frediano 20r (055 210387/ www.lacitelibreria.info). **Open** 10.30am-1am daily. **Map** p128 A1 ③⑥

La Cité has given this part of the Oltrarno a true Left Bank feel. As much cultural centre as bookshop, it organises readings and debates (mostly in Italian). The mezzanine café serves own-baked cakes, freshly made fruit and veg juices and Fairtrade coffees. Afternoon and

FLORENCE BY AREA

Old meaning new

Elio Ferrano

A burgeoning trend has recently emerged among Florentine shoppers that's rivalling the big-name designers monopolising prime central shopping streets. Several shops selling vintage clothing, accessories and homeware have sprung up all around the city, so that almost every shopping district now has at least one vintage shop worth stopping off at. Until recently, fashion-conscious Italians wouldn't have been seen dead in second-hand gear, but Florentines have finally embraced cast-off culture, albeit in this suitably snobby form (charity shop chic is still considered beyond the pale).

In the central Duomo area, **Boutique Nadine** (p76) is a lovely treasure trove of vintage stock mainly from the 1930s to the '60s, including Gucci bags and Louis Vuitton trunks. There are also stacks of old but unused stock such as cashmere twinsets and costume jewellery, while a back room is piled high with home-furnishing oddities.

Santa Maria Novella's vintage showcase is **Elio Ferraro** (p91), the first vintage store in the city.

The shop is known for unique, one-off designer pieces and accordingly high prices. Window displays flaunt an eccentric collection of original '50s and '60s furniture and accessories, including chairs by Giò Ponti and plates by Fornasetti. Many of the clothes are couture pieces from Chanel, Dior or Schiaparelli.

Santa Croce is home to **Soqquadro** (p123), a specialist source for retro furniture, lighting and accessories, particularly from the '60s and '70s. In the same street is **Maison Dumitru** (p123), with a section of 'reconstruction' clothing – original pieces reworked into contemporary styles.

Over in the Oltrarno is **Pitti Vintage** (p141). The shop has a more classically junk-shop feel, but stock is dominated by classy vintage clothing. Many Florentine brands are stocked, with a special line in 'museum pieces' from as far back as the turn of the last century. Also this side of the river is **Ceri Vintage** (p139), a cavernous vaulted emporium with a bizarre mix of period military garb, '60s prints, posters and Victoriana, such as corsets and lace-up boots.

early evening tastings of wines, oils and cheeses from local producers are held often, with live jazz in the background.

Lisa Corti

Via de' Bardi 58 (055 2645600/ www.lisacorti.com). **Open** 3.30-7.30pm Mon; 10am-7.30pm Tue-Sat; 11am-1.30pm, 2.30-7pm Sun. **Map** p129 C2 ③

A gorgeous range of shirts and dresses in printed crinkle cottons, pleated two-tone scarves and silk bags. See also p22 Lisa Corti Home Textiles Emporium in Santa Croce.
Other locations Via San Niccolò 97r (055 2001200).

Madova

Via de' Guicciardini 1r (055 2396526/ www.madova.com). **Open** 9.30am-7pm Mon-Sat. **Map** p128 C2 ③
Madova makes gloves in every imaginable style and colour in its factory, just behind this tiny shop.

Millesimi

Borgo Tegolaio 35r (055 2654675/ www.millesimi.it). **Open** 2-8pm Mon; 11am-8pm Mon-Fri. Closed 2wks Aug. **Map** p128 B3 ③
Home to one of the biggest selections of wine in town, Millesimi offers a wide range from Piemonte as well as Tuscan labels, and also has the best choice of French plonk.

Obsequium

Borgo San Jacopo 17 (055 216849). **Open** 10.30am-7.30pm Mon-Sat. **Map** p128 B2/C2 ④
Obsequium is a treasure trove for wine-lovers, housed in a 12th-century tower. As well as an incredible cellar of fine and everyday wines, spirits and liqueurs, the place stocks all manner of drink-themed gadgets. A good bet for presents.

Pitti Vintage

Sdrucciolo de' Pitti 19r (055 2302676/ www.pittivintage.it). **Open** 3.30-7.30pm Mon; 10am-1.30pm, 3-7.30pm Tue-Sat & 2nd, 3rd Sun of each mth. **Map** p128 B3 ④
See box p140.

Stefano Bemer

Borgo San Frediano 143r (055 222558/www.stefanobemer.it). **Open** 9am-1pm, 3.30-7.30pm Mon-Sat. Closed Aug. **Map** p128 A1 ④
Well-heeled Florentine men come here for handmade luxury shoes. The branch does a ready-to-wear line.
Other location Via Camaldoli 10r (055 222462).

Sugar Blues

Via de' Serragli 57r (055 268378). **Open** 9am-1.30pm, 4.30-8pm Mon-Fri; 9am-1.30pm Sat. *Sept-June* also 4.30-8pm Sat. **Map** p129 A2 ④
A great source of organic health foods and produce, eco-friendly detergents and ethical beauty products.

Il Torchio

Via de' Bardi 17 (055 2342862). **Open** 2.30-7pm Mon; 10am-1.30pm, 2.30-7.30pm Tue-Sat. **Map** p129 D3 ④
Watch bookbinding in action, and stock up on handmade paper boxes, stationery and albums.

Twisted

Borgo San Frediano 21r (055 282011). **Open** 9am-1pm, 3-7.30pm Mon-Sat. **Map** p128 A1 ④
A specialist jazz shop with rare recordings and more mainstream sounds. The stocked artists span 1950s trad jazz right through to acid and nu jazz.

Nightlife

Although sleepy during the day, café/bar Il Rifrullo (p137) livens up in the evening, when cocktails and *aperitivo* pull in the crowds.

Caffè la Torre

Lungarno Benvenuto Cellini 65r (055 680643/www.caffelatorre.it). **Open** 10.30am-3am daily. **Map** p129 F3 ④
Caffè La Torre forms the central hub of eastern Oltrarno's bar-crawl itinerary, sandwiched as it is between Plasma (p154), Negroni (p142) and Zoe (p142). There are (almost) nightly live acts, and the place is also popular as a mercifully mellow post-clubbing stop-off; tapas and pasta are served till late.

Obsequium p141

La Dolce Vita

*Piazza del Carmine 6r (055 284595/
www.dolcevitaflorence.com).* **Open**
5pm-2am Tue-Sun. Closed 2wks Aug.
Map p128 A2 ⁴⁷

La Dolce Vita is a club that lives up to
its name, and it's still going strong
after years of hegemony in the summer
nights-out stakes. Beautiful people
dancing to live Brazilian, jazz or contemporary music fill the swanky metal
and glass bar area, which leads off to
a cosier salon with sofas and soft lighting from crystal lamps. Crowds spill
out on to the square during warm
evenings. Drinks prices are a little
steep, but the atmosphere makes up for
it. Showing up in jeans and a T-shirt
might incur unwelcome glances.

James Joyce

*Lungarno Benvenuto Cellini 1r (055
6580856).* **Open** 6pm-2am Mon-Thur;
6pm-3am Fri-Sun. No credit cards.
Map p129 F3 ⁴⁸

The large enclosed garden with long
wooden tables makes this one of the
best of Florence's pubs in spring and
summer. JJ has a high-spirited vibe,
especially around happy hour (7.30-
9.30pm). To go with the name, there's
a small bookshop selling paperbacks,
some of them in English.

Muna

*Via Maffia 31r (055 287198/www.
munaciello.it).* **Open** 8pm-2am daily.
Admission free. **Map** p128 A2 ⁴⁹

A small, new locale defined by minimalist design and cocktails, and popular with the local gay community. It's
also a good place for dinner, in the
adjoining restaurant, O'Munaciello.

Negroni

*Via de' Renai 17r (055 243647/
www.negronibar.com).* **Open** 8am-
2.30am Mon-Sat; 6pm-2am Sun. Closed
2wks Aug. **Map** p129 E3 ⁵⁰

Named after Signor Negroni – the man
who invented the eponymous cocktail
while sitting at a bar that used to be on
this site – this is one of the coolest destinations in town. The sleek red and black
interior is a backdrop for art exhibitions,
while the garden square gets packed on
summer nights. The music works
around CD promotions run in conjunc-
tion with Alberti record shop (p101).

Zoe

Via de' Renai 13r (055 243111).
Open 8am-1.30am Mon-Thur; 8am-
2am Fri, Sat; 6pm-1am Sun. **Map**
p129 D3 ⁵¹

Zoe's red neon sign lures punters in with
the promise of the sexiest atmosphere of
the Oltrarno's many drinking holes. A

long thin bar area functions as a proxy catwalk and bassy beats pump out from the DJ room at the back. Zoe also has the best red cocktails in town, including the Crimson Zoe and the Red Caipiroska.

Arts & leisure

LibreriaCafé La Cité (p139) holds frequent cultural events.

British Institute Cultural Programme

Lungarno Guicciardini 9 (055 267781/ www.britishinstitute.it). **Open** *Lectures* from 6pm. *Film screenings* from 8.30pm. **Tickets** €5 plus €5 membership. No credit cards. **Map** p128 B1/B2 ⑫
The BI runs a Talking Pictures programme on Wednesday evenings. A movie is sandwiched between an introduction and a discussion, all in English. It also runs courses in Italian cinema.

Cango Cantieri Goldonetta Firenze

Via Santa Maria 23-25 (055 2280525/ www.cango.fi.it). **Seasons** Sept-Dec, May-June. No credit cards. **Map** p128 A3 ⑬
The term *'cantiere'* (building site) refers to this venue's status as a project-in-progress. In addition to classical music performances by the resident ensemble Virgilio Sieni, events include dance workshops, competitions and the Oltrarno Atelier festival in June (p34).

Chiesa Luterana

Lungarno Torrigiani 11 (055 2542775). **Map** p129 D3 ⑭
Organ recitals and other chamber music, often involving early repertoire, are held at Florence's Lutheran church all year – and are usually free.

Florence Beach

Off Lungarno Serristori (www.comune. fi.it). **Open** *June-Sept* 10am-10pm daily. **Admission** free. **Map** p129 F3 ⑮
See box p130.

Florence Dance Cultural Centre

Borgo della Stella 23r (055 289276/www. florencedance.org). **Map** p128 A2 ⑯

Directed by former étoile Marga Nativo and American choreographer Keith Ferrone, this eclectic centre hosts a range of dance classes as well as a programme of visual art events called Etoile Toy. It also organises the Florence Dance Festival, which takes place in July and December (p35 and p37).

Forte di Belvedere

Porta San Giorgio (entrance at Via di Belvedere) (055 2625908/www. fi-esta.com/www.firenze-oltrarno.net). **Dates** late June-late Aug. **Admission** free. **Map** p128 C3 ⑰
This star-shaped fortress was built in 1590 by Bernardo Buontalenti to protect the city from insurgents and was then used as a strongroom for the Medici Grand Dukes' treasures. After a painfully drawn-out restoration, the fort is open once again for temporary art exhibitions, film screenings, shows and events. It's worth the trek up the steep hill for the fabulous views alone. Bars and restaurants surround the terrace.

Sala Vanni

Piazza del Carmine 19 (055 287347/ www.musicusconcentus.com). **Tickets** prices vary. No credit cards. **Map** p128 A2 ⑱
Sadly underused, this large warehouse-like auditorium is a great place to hear progressive jazz and contemporary classical groups. The venue hosts a sparse but excellent series of concerts organised by Musicus Concentus in autumn and winter.

Teatro Goldoni

Via Santa Maria 15 (055 229651/ Teatro Comunale 055 213535). **Season** varies. No credit cards. **Map** p128 A3 ⑲
This divine little theatre dates from the early 1800s and seats only 400. A drawn-out restoration was finally finished in the late 1990s and the theatre is now partially under the direction of the Teatro del Maggio (p93). It's used – though not regularly enough – for chamber music, small-scale opera and ballet, including the winter season of the Florence Dance Festival (p37).

FLORENCE BY AREA

San Miniato al Monte p152

Outer Districts

The historic centre of Florence is home to the densest concentration of art treasures and sights in the world, but it's surprisingly small. This makes exploring beyond the central area, delineated by the eight surviving city gates, easy even without your own means of transport, and the rewards are fabulous views, sublime countryside, fascinating cultural sights and, in summer, some of the city's most lively nightlife.

The ATAF bus network has efficient services to the outer areas, and most of the places listed in this chapter can be reached directly by bus or with a short walk.

North of the river

North of the river, the old stone gates are linked by the *viali*,
traffic-clogged multi-lane arteries circling the city. To the north, the roads leading to **Fiesole** and **Settignano** are dotted with charming country houses. Travelling east is a more mixed experience of genteel suburbia and semi-industrial plots. **Firenze Nova**, the satellite city and administrative centre, constructed on reclaimed land north-west of the centre, has breathed new, though generally uninspiring, life into the area. Further out in this direction, dull housing and industrial development have claimed swathes of land, creating urban eyesores such as Brozzi and Campi Bisenzio, though there are still ancient convents and elegant villas on the hills, and the old town area of **Sesto Fiorentino** has a charm of its own.

Sights & museums

Cimitero degli Inglesi

Piazzale Donatello 38 (055 582608 afternoons). Bus 31, 32. **Open** 9am-noon Mon; 2-5pm Tue-Fri. **Admission** by donation.

Designated in 1827 and later given its oval shape by Giuseppe Poggi, the 'English Cemetery' reflects the prevalence of English artists living in Florence in the 19th century: Frederic, Lord Leighton, Roddam Spencer Stanhope and William Holman Hunt are among those who designed and sculpted the lichen-covered tombs. The cemetery houses the remains of many famous Anglo-Florentines, as well as Swiss, Russians and Americans. Among them are poet Elizabeth Barrett Browning, sculptor Hiram Powers and novelist Fanny Trollope.

Fortezza da Basso

Viale Filippo Strozzi.

Alessandro de' Medici commissioned Antonio da Sangallo to design this fortress in 1534; he later met his death within its ugly walls. The building is a prototype of 16th-century military architecture; restored in the 1990s, it's now Florence's main exhibition centre, and known for hosting many of the city's biggest fashion shows.

Museo del Cenacolo di Andrea del Sarto

Via San Salvi 16 (055 238 8603). Bus 6. **Open** 8.15am-1.50pm Tue-Sun. **Admission** free.

This refectory-cum-museum was part of the Vallombrosan monastery of San Salvi, and is chiefly notable for housing Andrea del Sarto's celebrated lunette-shaped Mannerist *Last Supper*.

Museo Stibbert

Via Stibbert 26 (055 486049/www. museostibbert.it). Bus 4. **Open** 10am-2pm Mon-Wed, 10am-6pm Fri-Sun. **Admission** €6.

This museum's bizarre, eccentric collection formerly belonged to Frederick Stibbert (1838-1906), a brother-in-arms with Garibaldi. Among the 50,000 items crammed into the 64 rooms and shown in rotation are Napoleon's coronation robes (Stibbert was a fan), a hand-painted harpsichord, a collection of shoe buckles, chalices, crucifixes and even an attributed Botticelli. The rambling garden makes for an interesting stroll.

Villa di Castello

Via del Castello 40 (055 454791). Bus 28. **Open** Times vary; call for details. **Admission** free.

Castello is known for its Il Tribolo-designed gardens and Ammanati's sculpture *Allegory of Winter*. The extravagant Grotta degli Animali is also here, filled with animal and bird statues and stone water features, planned by Il Tribolo and finished by Vasari.

Villa della Petraia

Via della Petraia 40 (055 452691). Bus 28. **Open** 8.15am-3.30pm Mon-Sun. Closed 2nd & 3rd Mon of mth. **Admission** free.

Sitting on a little hill, the grounds of Villa della Petraia – acquired by the Medici in 1530 – stand apart from the surrounding industrial mess. Originally a tower belonging to Brunelleschi's family, the fabulous formal terraced gardens by Il Tribolo are among the select few immortalised in Giusto Utens's lunettes.

Eating & drinking

Portofino

Viale Mazzini 25-27r (055 244140/ www.ristoranteportofino.it). **Open** 12.30-3pm, 7.30-11pm Tue-Sat; 12.30-3pm Sun. **€€€.** **Seafood.**

Proof of the fact that some of Florence's better eateries are in the suburbs, this relatively new fish restaurant is located near Campo di Marte train station. Fish and seafood dominate and Tuscan-based flavours are given a creative twist; expect the likes of courgette flowers stuffed with sole and prawns and tender chunks of sweetest squid nestling on a bed of chickpea purée. Mains include tuna steak in a sesame crust and sea bass fillet with cherry tomatoes and capers.

FLORENCE BY AREA

Povero Pesce

Povero Pesce

*Via Pierfortunato Calvi 8r (055 671218/
www.poveropesce.it).* **Open** noon-3pm,
7-11pm daily. **€€€. Seafood.**
Unpretentious fish and seafood dishes
make up the backbone of the menu at
this *trattoria* near the football stadium. With its modern, vaguely nauti-
cal-themed interior and keen prices,
it's become very popular. The menu
changes daily, but a typical meal
might feature a starter of the house
antipasto misto (five or six little
tasters), spaghetti *alle vongole* (clams)
or *bavette all' astice* (lobster). A tart
sorbetto al limone is a good way to finish. The wine list is quite limited and
on the pricey side.

Salaam Bombay

*Viale Rosselli 45r (055 357900). Bus
22.* **Open** 7.30-10pm Mon-Fri; 7.30pm-
midnight Sat, Sun. **€€. Indian.**
When you need a spicy change from
pasta *e fagioli*, head to one of Florence's
few Indian restaurants. Tapestries
adorn the walls of the single, galleried
room; sit upstairs if you want to look
down on the buzzy action below. The
menu offers the safe but decently
cooked standards found on the menus
of most Indian restaurants in Italy:

tandooris and mughlai dishes, vegetarian options, great naans and own-made
mango chutney. Good value.

Santa Lucia

*Via Ponte alle Mosse 102r (055
353255). Bus 30, 35.* **Open** 7.30pm-
midnight Mon, Tue, Thur-Sun. Closed
Aug. **€.** No credit cards. **Pizzeria.**
It may be a bit of a trek (a ten-minute
walk north-west of Porta al Prato),
but many Florentines reckon the
pizza at Santa Lucia to be the best in
town (although it now has a serious
rival, with the opening of Vico del
Carmine; p154). The pizzas are
authentically Neapolitan, and so is
the atmosphere. If you don't want
pizza, terrific fish dishes include
spaghetti *allo scoglio* (with mixed
seafood) and octopus in spicy tomato
sauce. Book in advance.

Targa

*Lungarno Cristoforo Colombo 7 (055
677377/www.targabistrot.net). Bus 14.*
Open 12.30-2.30pm, 7.30-11pm Mon-
Sat. Closed 1st 3wks Aug. **€€€.**
Florentine.
Gabriele Tarchiani's riverside 'Bistrot
Fiorentino' has a particularly inviting
interior – with lots of wood and glass,

low lighting and plenty of greenery. Local flavours and traditions dominate the seasonal menu, but there are also dishes from further afield: marinated *baccalà* (salt cod) with chickpeas, rigatoni with broccoli, fresh tuna and cherry tomatoes and rack of lamb. One of Tarchiani's classics is the hot chocolate soufflé: leave room. The cheeseboard is impressive and the hefty tome of a wine list is superb.

Zibibbo

Via di Terzollina 3r (055 433383). Bus 14. **Open** 12.30-3pm, 7.30-10pm Mon-Sat. Closed Aug. €€€.
Florentine/Italian.
This sunny restaurant may be some way from the centre, but the food justifies the effort. This is the domain of Benedetta Vitali, co-founder of Cibrèo (p118). Her superb, unfussy cooking finds roots in both Florentine and southern Italian traditions, using only seasonal ingredients. A faithful, mostly local clientele comes for the likes of tender octopus and potato salad and stuffed duck cooked in honey with a plum sauce. The wine list is excellent. Lunchtimes are more casual and, for a quick snack, you can have a plate of pasta at the bar.

Nightlife

Ambaciata di Marte

Via Mannelli 2 (055 6550786/www. ambaciatadimarte.org). Bus 3, 6, 10, 20, 44. **Open** times vary, but usually 10pm-2am Mon-Sat. Closed July, Aug. **Tickets** €5 annual membership. No credit cards.
One of the newest additions to Florence's music scene, Ambaciata di Marte is a one-stop locale for upcoming, alternative bands.

Auditorium FLOG

Via M Mercati 24B (055 487145/ www.flog.it). Bus 4, 8, 14, 20, 28. **Open** 10pm-late Tue-Sat. Closed June-Aug. **Tickets** €10-€15.
No credit cards.
At FLOG, music runs from rock to Tex-Mex rockabilly, with Fridays for reggae and ska, and a DJ after the bands. Dance parties and theatrical shows take place early in the week, and the venue hosts the Rassegna Internazionale Musica dei Popoli and Azione Gay e Lesbica parties. While the auditorium is closed in the summer, its grounds hosts a popular small outdoor pool – a great place to hang out on a baking hot day.

Central Park

Central Park

*Via Fosso Macinante 2, nr ponte della
Vittoria (335 8183400). Bus 1, 9, 26.*
Open *Summer* 11.30pm-4.30am Tue-
Sat. *Winter* 11pm-4am Fri, Sat.
Admission €16-€25.
The greatest of summer disco venues,
Central Park comes into its own in hot
weather, when the huge garden areas
with bars and outdoor dancefloors provide the perfect environment for sun-
frazzled dancing legs. The music is
progressive by Florentine standards.
You might heed the siren call of trance,
techno, garage, drum 'n' bass and deep
house classics. Frankie Knuckles
turned up in 2007. Then again, you
might stumble upon mediocre live acts
and play-by-rote hits.

Girasol

*Via del Romito 1 (055 474948/
www.girasol.it). Bus 14.* **Open** 7pm-
2am Tue-Sun. Closed June-Aug.
No credit cards.
One of the most colourful bars in
Florence, Girasol tops the list when it
comes to Latin (particularly Brazilian)
sounds, playing live music pretty well
nightly. Instructors from local dance
schools occasionally give free lessons
in tango and samba to get you in the
mood. Drinks are on the pricey side,

but the exotic mixes blend in perfectly
with the colourful decor. A pizzeria is
being added for 2008.

Meccanò

*Viale degli Tigli 1, nr ponte della
Vittoria (055 331371). Bus 1, 9, 16,
26, 27.* **Open** *Summer* 11.30pm-4am
Tue-Sat. *Winter* 11.30pm-4am Mon-Sat.
Admission €15-€20.
Meccanò caters to the masses, who
come out in force to play in its theme-
park atmosphere. It's easy to play
hide-and-seek in the labyrinthine tan-
gle of bars and dancefloors, especially
when the garden opens in the summer
months. Music is mostly Latin, commercial party and trashy pop, with a
sprinkling of hip hop and funky
house. The best perch is to be found
in the quieter upstairs bar.

Saschall-Teatro di Firenze

*Via Fabrizio de André, nr lungarno A
Moro 3 (055 6504112/www.saschall.it).
Bus 14.* **Tickets** prices vary.
This tent-shaped, 4,000-capacity venue
hosts a variety of mainstream acts
from Italy and abroad. The upper balconies have seating, but choose the
main standing hall downstairs if you're
there for sound rather than comfort.
Saschall's annual events include a St
Patrick's Day knees-up.

Stazione Leopolda
*Via Fratelli Rosselli 5 (055 89875/
3245485/www.stazione-leopolda.com).
Bus 1, 9, 12, 16.* **Tickets** prices vary.
This disused station is beloved of street-
chic designers, who host catwalk shows
here, but it's also occasionally called into
service by artists such as jazz pianist
Stefano Bollani and Liars, a US noise-
rock band. The Fabbrica Europa performing arts festival is held here (p33).

Tenax
*Via Pratese 46 (055 308160/www.
tenax.org). Bus 29, 30.* **Open** 10.30pm-
4am Thur-Sat & for gigs. Closed mid
May-Sept. **Admission** €20-€25.
The most influential and international
of the Florentine clubs is the ware-
house-style Tenax in Peretola. Far
enough outside the centre to make a
night out an adventure, but not too far
to be impractical without a car, it's best
known as a live venue for hip international bands and for its DJ exchanges
(Pete Tong and Tricky have hit the
decks here). The club has a huge raised
dancefloor and antechambers stuffed
with computers, pool tables and bars.

Arts & leisure

The small outdoor pool in the
grounds of **Auditorium FLOG**
(p147) is a great place to hang out
during the baking-hot months of
June, July and August. Call 055
484465 for opening hours.

Arena Raggio Verde
*Palazzo del Congressi, viale Strozzi
(055 4973222/www.ateliergroup.it).*
Dates late June-late Aug. Tickets
vary. No credit cards.
This stunning amphitheatre-style
open-air cinema, overlooking a 16th-
century villa, runs nightly double bills
during the summer months.

Cinema Arena di Marte
*Palazzetto dello Sport di Firenze, viale
Paoli (055 289318/www.ateliergroup.
it). Bus 10, 20, 34.* **Dates** late June-late
Aug. **Open** 8pm (shows 9.30pm daily).
Tickets €5. No credit cards.

One of the two screens at this major outdoor venue shows cult and non-main-
stream films (some in their original
language); the larger screen runs the
previous year's blockbuster movies.
There's a good outdoor restaurant.

Costoli
*Viale Paoli (055 6236027). Bus 10, 17,
20.* **Open** *June-Aug* 2-6pm Mon; 10am-
6pm Tue-Sun. *Sept-May* call for details.
Admission €4.10/hr; free-€4.50/hr
reductions. No credit cards.
Near the football stadium, this is a
swimmer's dream, with Olympic-size,
diving and children's pools, surrounded
by a lovely green park. There's also
an indoor pool for the winter months.
Membership required.

Ippodromo Le Cascine
*Via delle Cascine 3, Parco delle
Cascine (055 422591/www.ippodromi
fiorentini.it). Bus 17C.* **Open** Apr-
May, Sept-Oct. **Admission** free.
No credit cards.
Florence's *galoppo* (flat-racing) course.
Keep an eye out for leading Tuscan
jockeys such as Alessandro Muzzi and
Claudio Colombi.

Ippodromo Le Mulina
*Viale del Pegaso, Parco delle Cascine
(055 4226076/www.ippodromi
fiorentini.it). Bus 17C.* **Open** Nov-
Mar, June-July. **Admission** free.
No credit cards.
Florence's racecourse for *il trotto* (trotting), where the driver sits in a carriage
behind the horse. Enrico Bellei is the
jockey to watch – he's notched up 47
wins and 37 placements in all of his 118
races, and took the top spot in 2007 with
a win rate of nearly 40%. The Premio
Duomo in June is among Tuscany's
biggest equine events.

Parco delle Cascine
*Entrance nr ponte della Vittoria.
Bus 17C.*
Stretching west of the city on the right
bank of the Arno, Florence's largest park
hosts fairs and markets and is a popular
destination for a day out, especially at
weekends, with cycling children, in-line

Stadio Artemio Franchi

skaters, joggers and picnickers. There's a riding school, a swimming pool, a race track where horse racing and polo matches are held and tennis courts, and in summer the park is used as a venue for club nights, theatre and gigs.

Stadio Artemio Franchi

Viale Manfredo Fanti 14, Campo di Marte (055 503011/667566/www. acffiorentina.it). Bus 10, 11, 17. **Open** Aug-May. **Tickets** approx €20-€150; reduced prices for women and children. No credit cards.
Built in 1932 and enlarged for the 1990 World Cup, ACF Fiorentina's stadium has a capacity of 66,000. Home matches are generally held every other Sunday, with kick-off at 3pm. You can buy tickets at the stadium, online or up to three hours prior to a match at Chiosco degli Sportivi (via Anselmi, near piazza della Repubblica, Duomo & Around, 055 292363). The stadium also moonlights as a music venue.

Fiesole & around

The foundation of **Fiesole**, home to some 14,000 people, precedes that of Florence by centuries, and could be credited with the city's very existence – this stubborn Etruscan hill town proved so difficult for the Romans to subdue that they were forced to set up camp in the river valley below. When they eventually took Fiesole, it became one of the most important towns in Etruria, remaining independent until the 12th century, when Florence finally vanquished it in battle. It soon took on a new role as a refined suburb where Florentine aristocrats could escape the heat and hoi polloi. The road leading up to the town winds by lovely villas and gardens.

Sights & museums

Duomo

Piazza Mino (055 59400). Bus 7. **Open** *Nov-Mar* 7.30am-noon, 2-5pm daily; *Apr-Oct* 7.30am-noon, 3-6pm daily. **Admission** free.
Fiesole's recently restored main square is dominated by the immense honey-stone campanile of the 11th-century cathedral; inside sit columns topped with capitals dating from Fiesole's period under Roman occupation.

Museo Bandini

Via Portigiani 1 (055 59477/
598720). Bus 7. **Open** Call for details.
Admission €13 incl Teatro Romano
& Museo Archeologico.
The Bandini collection consists of
Florentine paintings dating from the
13th to 15th centuries. The house now
has two new rooms displaying previously unshown works, including several Andrea della Robbia terracottas.

Teatro Romano

Via Portigiani 1 (055 59477). Bus 7.
Open 10am-6pm Mon, Thur-Sun.
Admission as Museo Bandini, above.
Built in 1 BC, the 3,000-seat amphithe-
atre still stages a mix of concerts and
plays in summer. The complex houses
the remains of two temples, partially
restored Roman baths and a stretch of
Etruscan walls, as well as the Museo
Archeologico, with finds from Bronze
Age, Etruscan and Roman Fiesole, and
the Costantini collection of Greek vases.

Eating & drinking

L'Arte Gaia

Via Faentina 1 (055 5978498).
Bus 1A. **Open** 8-10.30pm Tue, Sun;

noon-2.30pm, 8-10.30pm Wed-Sat.
Closed 2wks Aug. **€€€**. **Seafood**.
On a small bridge crossing a scruffy
tributary of the Arno just below Fiesole
lies this modern, welcoming restaurant. It's a little hard to get to, but the
effort will be rewarded by an excellent
fish meal and an honest bill. Wood
floors, white tablecloths and soft lighting provide the background to colourful cooking, with dishes such as
smoked tuna and melon, mint-spiked
red mullet and aubergine kebabs, and
fregole (a Sardinian pasta) with clams
and mussels. At €35 and €39, the four-
course set menus are great value.

Arts & leisure

Scuola Musica di Fiesole

Villa La Torraccia, via delle Fontinelle
24, San Domenico (055 597851/
www.scuolamusica.fiesole.fi.it). Bus
7, then 10min walk. **Open** 8.30am-
8.30pm Mon-Sat.
One of Italy's most famous music
schools occupies a 16th-century villa in
beautiful grounds. It's the home of the
Orchestra Giovanile Italiana, the country's number one youth orchestra. The
annual Festa della Musica is held on 24

June, while the Concerti per gli Amici series takes place in the 200-seat auditorium from September/October to June.

South of the river

The gently winding, tree-lined avenues forming an umbrella round the south of the city are much more picturesque than the northern *viali* and are worth a drive or a bus-ride in themselves. Head south of the historic centre for the best walks, views and sights; as the steep hills practically rise from the banks of the Arno, you can walk in minutes from the town into real countryside dotted with villas, cypress and olive trees.

The most famous viewpoint in Florence is probably from **piazzale Michelangelo**, on the hill directly above piazza Poggi. Considered the city's balcony, this is a large, open square with vistas over the entire city to the hills beyond. Its stone balustrade is perennially crowded with tourists. Laid out in 1869 by Giuseppe Poggi, the piazzale is dominated by a bronze replica of Michelangelo's *David*.

Sights & museums

Certosa del Galluzzo
Via Buca di Certosa 2, Galluzzo (www.cistercensi.info). Bus 36 or 37. **Open** times vary. **Admission** by donation.
This imposing complex was founded in 1342 as a Carthusian monastery by Renaissance big-wig Niccolò Acciaiuoli and is the third of six built in Tuscany in the 14th century. It's been inhabited since 1958 by a group of Cistercian monks. The main entrance leads into a courtyard and the church of San Lorenzo, said to be by Brunelleschi.

San Miniato al Monte
Via delle Porte Sante 34 (055 2342731). Bus 12, 13. **Open** times vary; call for details. **Admission** free.

The façade of this exquisite church is delicately inlaid with white Carrara and green Verde di Prato marble, and the glittering gold mosaic dates from the 13th century. There has been a chapel on this site since at least the fourth century, and this is also the spot where, according to legend, St Miniato picked up his decapitated head and walked from the banks of the Arno up the hill. The chapel was replaced with a Benedictine monastery in the early 11th century. The church's interior is one of Tuscany's loveliest, its walls a patchwork of faded frescoes. One of its most remarkable features is the marble pavement in the nave, inlaid with the signs of the zodiac. Gregorian chant is sung daily by the monks (4.30pm winter, 5.30pm summer).

Eating & drinking

Area 51
Il Magnifico, Warner Village, via del Cavallaccio (335 8014085 mobile/ www.area51.it). Bus 1. **Open** 8am-4am daily. No credit cards. **Café**.
More 'internet' than 'café', Area 51 is the biggest gaming centre in the country. More than 40 PCs are set up for all the latest games, with the option to bring your own disc to be set up if the place doesn't already have it.

Bibe
Via delle Bagnese 1r (055 2049085). Bus 36, 37, then taxi. **Open** 7.30-10pm Mon, Tue, Thur, Fri; 12.30-2pm, 7.30-10pm Sat, Sun. Closed last wk Jan, 1st wk Feb & 1st 2wks Nov. **€€**. **Tuscan**.
Occupying an old farmhouse about 3km (2miles) south of Porta Romana, and entered through a bar and grocer's, Bibe is a good place to soak up the atmosphere of a rustic country restaurant without having to travel too far from the city. Try deep-fried courgette flowers stuffed with ricotta for a first course, and one of the classic Tuscan dishes for a main – deep-fried chicken, rabbit and brains is a speciality. Puddings and the wine list are several notches above your average rustic eaterie.

Fuori Porta

Via Monte alle Croci 10r (055 2342483/www.fuoriporta.it). Bus D. **Open** 12.30-3.30pm, 7pm-12.30am Mon-Sat. Closed 2wks Aug. **Wine bar**. Florence's best-known wine bar is situated in a lovely neighbourhood at Porta San Miniato and has a terrace overlooking the old city gate. It's a relaxed spot for a glass and a snack at lunchtimes; evenings are buzzier. There are between 500 and 650 labels on the list, with about 50 available by the glass and 250cl carafe. The daily menu has excellent pastas, *carpacci* and salads; the classic snack here is one of the delicious *crostoni*.

Omero

Via Pian de'Giullari 11r (055 220053). Bus 13, 38. **Open** noon-2.30pm, 7.30-10.30pm Mon, Wed-Sun. Closed Aug. **€€€. Florentine**. The entrance to Omero, in the quiet, exclusive hamlet of Pian de' Giullari, is on a narrow cobbled street. Head to the sunny room at the back of the grocer's

that fronts the restaurant from great rural views (downstairs is not so nice). The menu features traditional Florentine food, reliable, if not particularly exciting, and served at high prices. Never mind: you're here for the old-fashioned atmosphere, the respectful service and the wonderful location.

Da Ruggero

Via Senese 89r (055 220542). Bus 11, 36, 37. **Open** noon-2.30pm, 7.30-10.30pm Mon, Thur-Sun. Closed mid July-mid Aug. **€€. Florentine**. This tiny *trattoria*, run by the Colsi family for over 30 years, is one of the best places in Florence to eat genuine home cooking. The thing is, the locals all know it, so don't risk the trek to Porta Romana without booking. The menu of traditional dishes changes with the seasons, but always includes a hearty soup or two and an excellent spicy spaghetti *alla carattiera*. Among the roast meats, try the tasty pigeon or go for the exemplary *bollito misto* (mixed boiled meats) served with tangy, parsley-fresh salsa verde.

Moleria Locchi p154

Vico del Carmine

Via Pisana 40-42r (055 2336862).
Open 7-11pm Mon-Sat. **€**. **Pizzeria**.
Done out as a typical street in old
Naples (complete with washing lines),
this place is always full, and, for many,
the cacophony adds to the atmosphere.
Punters pile in for what is possibly the
best pizza in town, baked in an authentic Neopolitan pizza oven with ingredients that are strictly sourced from the
Campania region (as are most of the
wines). Highly recommended is the
remarkable *a chiummenzanza*: the fold-
ed-over crust is stuffed with ricotta
while the base is topped with smoked
scamorza cheese and cherry tomatoes.

Shopping

I Gigli

*Via San Quirico 165 (055 8969250/
www.igigli.it).* **Open** 9am-10pm daily. .
An authentic covered mall about 30
minutes by bus from the centre of
town, with over 120 Italian and international chains and restaurants.

Moleria Locchi

*Via Burchiello 10 (055 2298371/
www.locchi.com).* **Open** 9am-1pm, 3-
6.30pm Mon-Fri.
It's worth making the effort to visit this
unique old-fashioned glass and lead
crystal workshop, which offers a restoration service and creates bespoke replace-
ments for glass objects like chandeliers.

Nightlife

Pinocchio Jazz

*Viale Giannotti 13 (055 680362/www.
pinocchiojazz.it).* Bus 8, 23, 31, 32, 80.
Open 9pm-2am Sat. Closed May-Oct.
Tickets €10 membership; entrance
with membership €10-€15.
Pinocchio Jazz hosts internationally
recognised jazz stars such as Chris
Speed, Anthony Coleman and Richard
Galliano, as well as Italian artists. Later
in the evening, the atmosphere becomes
more mellow, with soft jazz filling the
air. The Pinocchio Jazz Live Festival is
held from January to March.

Plasma

*Piazza Ferrucci 1r (055 0516926/
www.virtualplasma.it).* Bus 23, D.
Open 7pm-2am Wed-Sun.
This spectacular bar on two floors,
with LED-lit vaults, a backlit water-
fall and a gallery of plasma screen art,
is refreshingly ahead of its time in
design-staid Florence. Indeed, the aes-
thetics alone might be enough reason
to make the trek up the lungarno. But
there are other draws: a cool repertoire of tunes and a 5m-long (16ft)
glass bar where the polychromatic
cocktails sit looking pretty. It's a sensory experience worthy of Miami,
London or New York's best.

Porto di Mare Eskimo Club

*Via Pisana 128 (328 7593125/
www.palcodautore.com).* **Open** 8pm-
3am nightly. Closed Aug.
This club is perfect if you're planning
a simple night out. Starting at the top
floor of the three-tiered club is a rustic pizzeria that makes a great penne
alle Calabrese. On the second floor
you'll find a quaint pub with a large
TV screen and comfy chairs. Head
down to the basement to catch a live
show – local rock and folk musicians
play seven days a week.

Arts & leisure

Parco Carraia

*Entrance off via dell'Erta Canina,
San Niccolò.* Bus 23.
This little-known park is just a stroll
up from Porta San Miniato but feels
miles away from the city. You'll find
swings and picnic facilities.

Teatro Cantiere Florida

*Via Pisana 111 (055 7131783/
www.elsinor.net).* Bus 6, 26, 27, 80.
Season Late Oct-Apr. No credit cards.
This bare-walled 288-seat theatre
aims to promote young actors, directors and playwrights, and to appeal
to young audiences. Productions – in
Italian – range from reworks of
Shakespearean classics to experimen-
tal pieces. Family shows are on
Sunday afternoons.

Siena's Piazza del Campo p157

Day Trips

Pisa

Pisa's elegant **Campo dei Miracoli** – where you'll find the **Duomo**, the **Baptistery** and the **Leaning Tower** – is the ultimate Catholic theme park, and the focus of the touristic onslaught that this city receives each summer. Venture beyond it, however, and you'll find that there's much more to Pisa than the sum of its most famous parts. Highlights from the list of worthy sights include **Museo Nazionale di Palazzo Reale** (lungarno Pacinotti 46), housing many Medici-related works; **Museo Nazionale di San Matteo** (piazza San Matteo in Soarta), containing Pisan and Islamic medieval ceramics, works by Masaccio, Fra Angelico and Ghirlandaio and Donatello; **Orto Botanico** (via Luca Ghini 5), the oldest university garden in Europe; as well as the churches of **San Nicola** (via Santa Maria 2) and

Santa Maria della Spina (lungarno Gambacorti). The **Arsenale Mediceo** (lungarno Simonelli) – 18 2,000-year-old ships – was discovered preserved beneath layers of silt in 1998, and bares witness to Pisa's early power and wealth. The fleet is being restored but you can arrange tours of the site by visiting www.navipisa.it.

Although it eventually ceded its power to Florence, Pisa retained its taste for intellectual advancement, and today's academic population lends the place a purposeful vibe and a youthful pulse: there are a good number of bars and clubs here, as well as some good eateries (try Osteria dei Cavalieri, via San Frediano 16, 050 580858 or café-restaurant-shop Pasticceria Salza, borgo Stretto 46, 050 580144) and shops. The beautiful **piazza dei Cavalieri** is a social focal point of the city; most of its 16th-century buildings were designed by Vasari.

Sights & museums

Listed below are the sights of the **Campo dei Miracoli**. Tickets are available from the **Museo delle Sinopie**. There are several types, including one that offers admission to all the sights (except the Leaning Tower) for €10.50. Call 050 3872210 for info, or visit www.opapisa.it.

Baptistery

050 3872210/www.opapisa.it).
Open *Apr-Sept* 8.30am-8pm daily. *Mar, Oct* 9am-6pm daily. *Nov-Feb* 10am-5pm daily. **Admission** €5.
The marble Baptistery was designed by Diotisalvi in 1152, with later decorative input by father and son Nicola and Giovanni Pisano. The magnificent pulpit (1260) is still there to be admired in situ, though most of the precious artwork is now in the Duomo's Museo dell'Opera del Duomo. The harmonious, onion-shaped dome was a later addition, from the mid 14th century.

Camposanto

Open *Apr-Sept* 8am-8pm daily. *Mar, Oct* 9am-6pm daily. *Nov-Feb* 10am-5pm daily. **Admission** €5.
The Camposanto (Holy Field), begun in 1277 by Giovanni de Simone, is a mix of various styles, including Gothic and Romanesque, and with more than 100 Roman sarcophagi. Allied bombardment in 1944 destroyed frescoes and sculptures, including a fabulous cycle by Benozzo Gozzolli. However, a few survived (including *Triumph of Death*, *Last Judgement* and *Hell*), and these are being restored as part of an ongoing project.

Duomo

050 3872210/www.opapisa.it.
Open *Mid Mar-Sept* 10am-8pm Mon-Sat; 1-8pm Sun. *Oct* 10am-7pm Mon-Sat; 1-7pm Sun. *Nov-mid Mar* 10am-1pm, 2-5pm Mon-Sat; 1-5pm Sun. **Admission** €2.
Begun in 1063 by Buschetto, Pisa's cathedral is one of the finest examples of Pisan Romanesque architecture. The white marble four-tiered façade incorporates Moorish mosaics and glass within the arcades. The main entrance features bronze doors by Bonanno da Pisa (1180). The brass doors by the Giambologna school were added in 1602 to replace the originals, destroyed in a fire in 1595.

After the fire, the Medici family came to the rescue, but nothing could be done at the time to save Pisano's superb Gothic pulpit (1302-11), which lay dismembered in crates until the 1920s. Crane your neck to admire the Moorish dome with its *Assumption* fresco. Behind the altar is a mosaic by Cimabue (1302); Giuliana Vangi's 2001 pulpit and altar are noticeably more modern.

Leaning Tower

050 3872210/www.opapisa.it.
Admission *Guided tour* €15; restrictions apply – see below.
Begun in 1173 by an unknown architect, Pisa's famous tower – the Duomo's campanile – started to lean almost as soon as it was erected, and many years before the top level, housing the seven bells, was added in 1350. Architect Giovanni di Simone attempted to correct the tilt in the 13th century by building floors that had one side higher than the other, but this only served to make the tower lean in the opposite direction (which is why it's now, in fact, curved). It was closed to the public in 1990, and reopened, after a long restoration, in 2001 – but with heavy restrictions: the tower is open only for guided tours, and then only to groups of 30 willing to pay €15 a head to climb its 294 steps. Under-eights aren't allowed; children aged eight to 18s must be accompanied by a grown-up.

Museo dell'Opera del Duomo

050 3872210/www.opapisa.it.
Open *Apr-Sept* 8am-8pm daily. *Mar, Oct* 9am-6pm daily. *Nov-Feb* 10am-6pm daily. **Admission** €5.
This museum contains works from the monuments of the Campo dei Miracoli. Notable among the exhibits are a series of sculptures from the 12th to 14th centuries, including several works by Pisano. Bonanno's restored medieval doors from the Duomo (above) are now on show.

Leaning Tower

Museo delle Sinopie

050 560547/www.opapisa.it. **Open** *Apr-Sept* 9am-8pm daily. *Mar, Oct* 9am-6pm daily. Nov-Feb 9am-5pm daily. **Admission** €5. No credit cards.
The 1944 bombings and subsequent restoration work uncovered the sinopie (reddish-brown preliminary sketches) from beneath the Camposanto's frescoes (p156). They were meant to be hidden forever, after the artist covered the *arriccio* (dry plaster) with a lime-rich plaster called *grassello*. The sinopie show what brilliant draftsmen the painters were.

Torre di Santa Maria

Open 10am-6pm daily. **Admission** €2. No credit cards.
Head here for a good overview of the Campo dei Miracoli.

Getting there

By train

The best way of getting to Pisa is by train; frequent services run between Stazione Santa Maria Novella and Pisa Centrale (journey time: 1hr).

By car

To get to Pisa by car, take the Firenze–Pisa–Livorno road.

Tourist information

Turistica APT *Campo dei Miracoli (no phone/www.pisa.turismo.toscana.it).* **Open** 9am-6pm Mon-Sat; 10.30am-6.30pm Sun.
Other locations piazza della Stazione 11; piazza Vittorio Emanuele II 16.

Siena

The Sienese are fond of saying that theirs is the most perfect medieval city in the world, and it's easy to agree. Not only has Siena preserved its exquisite monuments, it has also maintained its traditions and its passion for local cuisine. Head for the 13th-century **piazza del Campo** – often described as one of Italy's most beautiful squares. The piazza is uniquely shell-shaped, fanning out in nine segments of herringbone paving. It houses the **Torre del Mangia** – medieval Italy's tallest tower (€6 to climb its 503 steps) – and the **Palazzo Pubblico**, itself home to the superb **Museo Civico**. On a summer's night, the square turns into a great eating bowl; best bets are **Al Mangia** (no.43) and **L'Osteria Bigelli** (no.60).

The historic centre is divided into three sections. **Terzo di Città** was the original residential nucleus and includes the **Duomo**; **Terzo di San Martino** grew around the via Francigena, the pilgrim route heading south to Rome; and the **Terzo di Camollia** contains churches and basilicas to the north. These three sections house the 17 *contrade* (city districts). In summer, citizens commit their spirit to their *contrada* with an unequalled fervour, for the **Palio**, the world-famous horse race held in the piazza del Campo in both July and August.

FLORENCE BY AREA

While the tourist corridor between the piazza and the **Duomo** has lots to offer, ambling through the quiet alleys is the best recommendation for the idle traveller. Head north-west of the campo for beautiful **piazza Salimbeni**, flanked by three glorious palazzi: **Tantucci**, **Spannocchi** and **Salimbeni**. North-east of here is **piazza San Francesco**, with its eponymous Gothic church, built in 1326 by the Franciscans, as well as the 15th-century **Oratorio di San Bernardino**, with its magnificent fresco cycle (1496-1518) by Sodama, Beccafumi and Girolamo del Pacchia.

Sights & museums

Battistero

Piazza San Giovanni (0577 283048).
Open *May-Aug* 9.30am-8pm daily.
Sept-Nov, Mar-May 9.30am-7pm daily.
Nov-Feb 10am-5pm daily. **Admission** €3. No credit cards.
Under the apse of the Duomo, the Baptistery is rectangular rather than octagonal. The unfinished Gothic façade includes three arches adorned with busts, while inside, colourful frescoes (mainly Vecchietta) fill the room. The focal point is the central font (1417-34): designed by Jacopo della Quercia and considered one of the masterpieces of early Renaissance Tuscany; it features bronze bas-reliefs by Jacopo, Donatello and Lorenzo Ghiberti. In the same complex is the newly restored Crypt.

Complesso Museale di Santa Maria della Scala

Piazza del Duomo 2 (0577 224811/ www.santamariadellascala.com).
Open 10.30am-6.30pm daily.
Admission €6. No credit cards.
This is the site of Siena's newest museum, the brilliant Museo Archeologico, and various spectacular temporary exhibitions. Founded in the ninth century, it was previously a hospital – one of Europe's oldest. Entry to the museum is at the Pellegrinaio (Pilgrim's Hall), decorated by, among others, Domenico di Bartolo (1440-43), with elaborate frescoes depicting the history of the hospital. The archaeological museum lies underground, in a labyrinth of chambers.

Duomo

Piazza del Duomo (0577 283048).
Open *Summer* 10.30am-8pm Mon-Sat; 1.30-8pm Sun. *Sept, Oct, Mar-May* 10.30am-7.30pm Mon-Sat; 1.30-8pm Sun. Nov-Feb 10.30am-6.30pm Mon-Sat; 1.30-8pm Sun. **Admission** €3; €6 19 Aug-31 Oct. An all-inclusive (Duomo, Baptistery and Crypt) ticket is also available. No credit cards.
Construction on Siena's Duomo started in 1150 on the site of an earlier church, but plans had to be abandoned because of the Black Death. The resulting structure is Gothic in style but Romanesque in spirit. The black and white marble façade was started in 1226; 30 years later work began on the dome, one of the oldest in Italy. The lower portion of the façade and the statues in the centre of the three arches were designed by Pisano.

Inside, the cathedral's polychrome floors are its most immediate attraction; the inlaid boxes are usually covered by planks, but are visible between mid August and late September. In the apse is a carved wooden choir, built between the 14th and 16th centuries. Above it is a recently restored rose stained-glass window made by Duccio di Buoninsegna in 1288 – probably the earliest Italian example of a stained-glass window. The tabernacle has Bernini's *Maddalena* and *San Girolamo* statues.

Another highlight is the pulpit. The Piccolomini altar includes four statues by a young Michelangelo (carved 1501-04). At the far end of the left aisle, a door leads to the Libreria Piccolomini (admission €3), built in 1495 to house the library of Aeneas Silvius Piccolomini, who became Pope Pius II. It was frescoed by Pinturicchio (1502-09, his last work), reportedly assisted by a young Raphael

The Duomo's never-completed nave houses the Museo dell'Opera del Duomo.

Museo Civico

Palazzo Pubblico, piazza del Campo (ticket office 0577 292263/www.

comune.siena.it). **Open** *Mid Feb-mid Mar, Oct-late Nov* 10am-6.30pm daily. *Mid Mar-Oct* 10am-7pm daily. *Late Nov-mid Feb* 10am-5.30pm daily. **Admission** €7. No credit cards.

In the Anticappella of the Museo Civico you can admire frescoes by Taddeo di Bartolo (1362-1422) plus a *Madonna and Child with Saints* by Sodoma. The Sala del Mappamondo was decorated by Lorenzetti around 1320-30, its cosmological frescoes depicting the universe. This room also houses one of Siena's jewels: the *Maestà* fresco, painted by Simone Martini in 1315 and considered one of the first examples of political art. In the Sala della Pace is an extraordinary fresco cycle by Lorenzetti (1338-40; severely damaged), the largest secular fresco since Roman times.

Pinacoteca Nazionale

Palazzo Buonsignori, via San Pietro 29 (0577 286143). **Open** 8.30am-1.30pm Mon, Sun; 8.15am-7.15pm Tue-Sat. **Admission** €4. No credit cards.

This lovely 15th-century palazzo holds one of Italy's foremost art collections, and is renowned for its *fondi d'oro* (paintings with gilded backgrounds). The second floor is devoted to Sienese masters from the 12th to the 15th centuries; the first houses works by the Sienese Mannerist school; the third floor holds the Spannocchi Collection, with works by northern Italian and European artists of the 16th and 17th centuries.

Getting there

By bus

Tra-in runs most of the services between Florence and Siena (0577 204225). The direct service takes 75mins, and buses leave every 30 mins. Visit www.trainspa.it info.

By car

The raccordo dual carriageway links Florence and Siena (45mins), or there's the more rural SS2.

By train

There are some direct trains between Florence's SMN station and Siena,

but you'll normally have to change at Empoli (journey time up to 2hrs).

Tourist information

Centro Servizi Informazioni Turistiche Siena (APT) *Piazza del Campo 56 (0577 280551/www. terresiena.it).* **Open** 9am-7pm daily.

Lucca

Wealthy and conservative Lucca stands protected behind its perfectly preserved 16th-century walls. The city has few must-see sights, with its appeal lying in its handsome *piazze*, tree-shaded fortifications and cultured but reserved ambience. Much of the city is pedestrianised, and the best way to discover it is on foot – the ornate white façades of the old town's Romanesque churches all appear unexpectedly when strolling around the historic centre.

The distinctively oval-shaped **piazza dell'Anfiteatro** is a focal point of the *centro storico*, while the tree-lined 16th- to 17th-century **ramparts** (Italy's best-preserved city fortifications, used by locals for jogging, strolling and picnicking) and the oak-topped **Torre Guinigi** afford splendid views of the tight cityscape. Other good spots for a stroll or quiet sit-down include the **Giardino Botanico** (via del Giardino Botanico 14) and the peaceful gardens of **Palazzo Pfanner** (via degli Asili 33).

Other focal points are the huge **piazza Napoleone** and, directly to its north, **piazza San Michele** – the old town's social hub. Lucca is the birthplace of operatic composer Giacomo Puccini, and the charming **Casa Natale di Giacomo Puccini** (Corte San Lorenzo 9, off via di Poggio) lies to the west of piazza San Michele, but it's closed for restoration until 2009 (contact the tourist office (p161) for further info).

Piazza dell'Anfiteatro p159

Sights & museums

Duomo (Cattedrale di San Martino)

Piazza San Martino (0583 957068).
Open *Duomo* Summer 9.30am-5.45pm daily. Winter 9.30am-4.45pm daily. *Sacristy* Summer 9.30am-5.45pm Mon-Fri; 9.30am-6.45pm Sat; 9-9.50am, 11.20-1.50pm Sun. Winter 9.30am-4.45pm Mon-Fri; 9.30am-6.45pm Sat; 11.20-11.50am, 1-4.45pm Sun. No entry during services. **Admission** *Duomo* free. *Sacristy* €2.50; €6 incl Museo della Cattedrale & San Giovanni e Reparata.
The eccentric asymmetry of Lucca's 12-century Romanesque cathedral is due to the fact that its Lombard bell tower actually slightly predates it. Its interior, meanwhile, is so dimly lit that coin operated lights are on hand to illuminate paintings such as Tintoretto's *Last Supper*. Midway up the left nave is Matteo Civitali's octagonal marble Tempietto (1484), home to a 13th-century copy of the Volto Santo (Holy Face) wooden crucifix, which was an object of pilgrimage throughout Europe.

Museo della Cattedrale

Via Arcivescovado (0583 490530).
Open *May-Oct* 10am-6pm daily.

Nov-Apr 10am-6pm Mon-Fri; 10am-5pm Sat, Sun. **Admission** €4; €6 incl San Giovanni e Reparata. No credit cards.
This modern museum houses many treasures transferred from the Duomo and nearby San Giovanni (below).

Museo Nazionale di Palazzo Mansi

Via Galli Tassi 43 (0583 55570). **Open** 9am-7.30pm Tue-Sat; 8.30am-2pm Sun. **Admission** €4; free reductions; €6.50 incl Villa Guinigi. No credit cards.
Lucca's most remarkable example of Baroque exaggeration is this 16th- to 17th-century palazzo, home to a (largely uninspiring) collection of Tuscan art.

Museo Nazionale di Villa Guinigi

Via della Quarquonia (0583 496033). **Open** 8.30am-7pm Tue-Sat; 8.30am-1.30pm Sun. **Admission** €4; free reductions. No credit cards.
This pink-brick villa (1403-20) houses art from Lucca and around. Highlights include Roman and Etruscan finds, Matteo Civitali's *Annunciation*, some ornate altarpieces by Amico Aspertini and Fra Bartolomeo and intarsia panels by Ambrogio and Nicolao Pucci.

San Frediano

Piazza San Frediano (0583 493627).
Open 8.30am-noon, 2.30-5.30pm Mon-Sat; 9-11.30am, 3-6pm Sun; 10.30am-5pm public hols. **Admission** free.
San Frediano's strikingly resplendent Byzantine-like mosaic façade is unique in Tuscany, rivalled only by that above the choir of San Miniato al Monte (p152). Inside the 12th-century church is a small gem: the *fonte lustrale* (or baptismal font). Behind it is a glazed terracotta *Ascension* by Andrea della Robbia.

San Giovanni e Reparata

Via del Duomo (0583 490530).
Open *Mid Mar-Oct* 10am-6pm daily. *Nov-mid Mar* 10am-5pm Sat, Sun. **Admission** San Giovanni €2; Museo della Cattedrale €4; sacristy €2.50. No credit cards.
Originally Lucca's cathedral, the 12th-century basilica of San Giovanni is on the site of a pagan temple. Apart from

its magnificently ornate ceiling, the church's main draw is the architectural remains uncovered by excavations in the 1970s, ranging from a second-century Roman bath to a Paleo-Christian church.

San Michele in Foro

Piazza San Michele (0583 48459).
Open 8am-noon, 3.30-6pm daily.
Admission free.
San Michele's Pisan-Romanesque façade is among the finest in Tuscany, and remains Lucca's most alluring sight. Every element in the church's elaborate exterior lightly plays off against the other. The façade contrasts sharply with its sombre interior. On the right as you enter is a *Madonna and Child* by della Robia. Further on, you'll find Filippino Lippi's simple and serene Saints Jerome, Sebastian, Rocco and Helena, arguably Lucca's greatest artistic asset.

Torre Guinigi

Via Sant'Andrea 14 (0583 316846).
Open *Nov-Feb* 9.30am-6pm daily. *Mar* 9am-5pm daily. *Apr* 9.30am-9pm daily. *May, Oct* 10am-6pm daily. *June-Sept* 9am-midnight daily. **Admission** €3.50; €2.50 reductions. No credit cards.
It may be something of a slog, but it's worth the climb to reach the tranquil, leafy summit of this 14th-century, 44m (144ft) tower, for spectacular views.

Getting there

By bus

LAZZI (www.lazzi.it) runs frequent services (at least one bus an hour) between Florence and Lucca. Buses arrive at Lucca's piazzale Verdi.

By car

The A11 *autostrada* connects Florence and Lucca. Journey time is about an hour.

By train

Trains from Florence to Viareggio stop at Lucca; the trip takes about 1hr 20mins, with trains leaving Florence's Santa Maria Novella station almost every hour until 10pm. Visit www.trenitalia.com.

Tourist information

Comune di Lucca Tourist Office
Piazzale Giuseppe Verdi (0583 442944/www.luccaturismo.it). **Open** 9.30am-5.30pm daily.
Other locations piazza Santa Maria, viale Luporini, porta Elisa.

Arezzo

Arezzo has recreated itself from a gold-orientated semi-backwater to a modern tourist destination offering art, antiques and… okay, the gold is still a big draw. The town is an essential stop on any **Piero della Francesca** trail, housing his *Legend of the True Cross* in the church of **San Francesco** and a *Mary Magdalene* in the **Duomo**.

Most of Arezzo's sights lie in the quiet, hilly streets of the old town, the political heart of which is the **piazza Grande**, a bonanza of architectural irregularity. The jumble of styles includes Baroque **Palazzo del Tribunale**, the Romanesque **Pieve di Santa Maria** and the **Palazzo della Fraternità dei Laici**, designed mostly by Bernardo Rossellino. Vasari designed the arcaded **Palazzo delle Logge**, presiding over the medieval homes around the rest of the square.

Anyone interested in Giorgio Vasari can visit the **Casa Vasari** (via XX Settembre 55) to get an insight into this prodigious artist. Nearby is **Santa Maria delle Grazie** (via Santa Maria), housing the Renaissance's first porticoed courtyard, by Antonio da Maiano.

Arezzo's only park – **Il Prato** – is located between the Duomo and the **Fortezza Medicea** in the east. In the lower part of town are the **Anfiteatro Romano** and the nearby **Museo Archeologico Mecenate** (via Margaritone 10), with its estimable collection of Etruscan and Roman artefacts.

FLORENCE BY AREA

Badia di Santi Fiora e Lucilla

Piazza di Badia (0575 356612).
Open 8am-12pm, 4-7pm Mon-Sat;
7am-12.30pm Sun. **Admission** free.
As well as a *Crucifixion* by de Segna
and a marble-effect altar by Vasari,
Arezzo's Badia boasts an ingenious illusory drawn dome by Andrea Pozzo.

Duomo (Cattedrale di San Donato)

Piazza del Duomo (0575 23991).
Open 7am-12.30pm, 3-7pm daily.
Admission free.
Construction on Arezzo's Gothic Duomo
began in 1277, but the finishing touches
weren't made until the early 1500s; it
was a further 300 years before its campanile was erected. The main attractions are along the left aisle: Piero della
Francesca's *Mary Magdalene* (c1465),
and the screened-off Cappella della
Madonna del Conforto.

Museo d'Arte Medioevale e Moderna

Via San Lorentino 8 (0575 409050).
Open 8.30am-7.30pm Tue-Sun.
Admission €4. No credit cards.
An interesting collection of medieval to
19th-century art, including Vasari's
*Wedding Feast of Ahasuerus and
Esther* (1548), and one of Italy's finest
collections of 13th- to 17th-century
ceramics from the della Robbia school.

San Domenico

Piazza San Domenico 7 (0575 23255).
Open 8.30am-1pm, 3.30-7pm daily.
Admission free.
San Domenico was started by the
Dominicans in 1275, around the same
time as their Franciscan brothers were
getting under way with San Francesco
(below). It has an attractive quaintness,
accentuated by its uneven Gothic campanile. Inside is a crucifix by Cimabue.

San Francesco

*Piazza San Francesco (0575 20630/
3527270 to reserve tickets).* **Open**
8.30am-7pm daily. **Admission** free.

San Francesco's interior, begun by
Franciscan friars in the 13th century,
was adorned with frescoes, chapels
and shrines during the 1500s, thanks
to Arezzo's merchant class. By the 19th
century, it was being used as a military
barracks. Happily, however, *The
Legend of the True Cross*, Piero della
Francesca's magnum opus, survived,
and was unveiled in a ceremony in
2000 after a decade-long restoration.
One of the most important fresco cycles
ever produced, it was begun in 1453,
the year Constantinople fell to the
Ottoman Turks, and portrays the fear
this induced in the Christian world. A
separate ticket (€6) gains you an audio
guide and access to the chapels (it's
best to book in advance in high season),
but note that some of the frescoes are
too high to be appreciated by the naked
eye: take a pair of binoculars if you can.

Getting there

By bus

Bus services from Florence are best
avoided, being slow and irregular.
Arezzo's bus terminal is opposite
the train station.

By car

Arezzo is off the A1 (Florence–Rome)
autostrada. Journey time from
Florence is an hour. Parking can be
difficult in Arezzo. The new car
park on the north side is the best.

By train

Intercity and **InterRegionale**
(892021, www.trenitalia.it) trains
link Arezzo with Florence (50-
60mins). Arezzo's train station is
located at piazza della Repubblica.

Tourist information

**Azienda di Promozione Turistica
(APT)** *Piazza della Repubblica 28
(0575 377678/www.apt.arezzo.it).*
Open *Oct-Mar* 9am-1pm, 3-7pm
Mon-Sat; 9am-1pm 1st Sun of mth.
Apr-Sept 9am-1pm, 3-7pm Mon-Sat;
9am-1pm Sun.

Essentials

Casa Howard p171

Hotels

While room rates remain among the highest in Italy, the positive side to accommodation in Florence is the sheer variety of options. Whether your bed of choice lies in a boutique hotel with a sharp design edge or a homely B&B on the top floor of an ancient palazzo, chances are that you'll find something to appeal; in fact, just about the only thing missing in this city (and this is a firm positive) is big chain hotels.

There has been a steady stream of new openings over the past few years. Most significant has been the huge increase in the number of B&Bs, *afittacamere* (rooms to rent) and *residenze d'epoca* (listed buildings with no more than 12 rooms). These range from spartan rooms with threadbare towels and no breakfast to homely pads furnished with antiques where

you start off the day with warm brioches. The ones listed here are among our favourites.

There are also several new hotels in the upper price brackets, and the most keenly anticipated new opening for years – the long-awaited **Four Seasons Firenze** – is due to receive its first guests in July 2008 (see box p175).

If you're staying in the city centre during the long hot summer, a terrace or balcony can make a big difference. Alternatively, head for the hills, where, within a short distance of the city centre, you'll find lodgings set in wonderful rural locations.

Booking and prices

High season for Florence's hotels runs roughly from Easter until late July, and September up to early November. It also covers Christmas, New Year, Italian public holidays and the Pitti fashion fairs in early January. Hotel rooms at these times are at their most expensive and much in demand. On the other hand, low season offers great potential for bargains, especially among the upper-end establishments (where it's often worth haggling).

Duomo & Around

B&B Novecento

Via Ricasoli 10 (055 214138/ www.bbnovecentofirenze.it). €€.
Franco and Sawako run their cosy six-room B&B with great enthusiasm and have an excellent record of return guests. The space occupies the third floor of a building between the Duomo and piazza della SS Annunziata and has a small roof terrace where you can enjoy a glass of wine to the spectacular backdrop of Florence's skyline. The pretty rooms are mostly on the small side, but have been furnished with nice touches like orthopaedic mattresses. Breakfasts are above average.

Cestelli

Borgo SS Apostoli 25 (055 214213/ www.hotelcestelli.com). €.
The Cestelli is a thoughtful conversion of an old one-star hotel: super-friendly owners Alessandro and Asumi have done a wonderful job in maintaining an old-fashioned feel while updating what was once a shabby property. It's one of the best deals in Florence for simple, pristine, generously sized rooms. The building's antique parquet floors have been scrubbed up, and a complementary mix of antique and new furniture presides within. Five of the eight rooms come with a private bathroom.

Gallery Hotel Art

Vicolo dell'Oro 5 (055 27263/ www.lungarnohotels.com). €€€€.
Florence's original hip hotel opened in 1999, back when its East-meets-West design aesthetic was refreshingly

ESSENTIALS

Helvetia & Bristol

different from the norm. Located in a tiny piazza next to the Arno, the place has a cosy library with squashy sofas and mountains of arty books. Also here is the stylish Fusion Bar (p75), serving *aperitivi*, brunches, light lunches and dinners, while the public rooms on the ground floor double as show-space for contemporary artists. The bedrooms are super comfortable, and the bathrooms are a dream.

Helvetia & Bristol
Via de' Pescioni 2 (055 26651/ www.royaldemeure.com). €€€€.
Since 2005, a new, energetic management has been breathing fresh life into the venerable H&B, open since the late 1800s. The place is filled with antiques, oil paintings and pietra serena fireplaces, but the historic space now has a decidedly hip edge, especially evident in its restaurant. The bedrooms have been updated, leaving an air of discreet luxury, where fine fabrics and period furniture rub alongside flatscreen TVs. One of Florence's best smallish hotels.

Hotel Continentale
Vicolo dell'Oro 6r (055 27262/ www.lungarnohotels.com). €€€€.

Another distinguished member of the Ferragamo family's Lungarno group, the Continentale is situated across from the Gallery Hotel Art (p165). Both boast a contemporary style, but the Continentale is the feminine flipside to the Gallery's more masculine image. Splashes of zingy colour are supplied by 1960s pieces, but otherwise the design is free of fuss: blonde woods, creamy fabrics, filmy white curtains and huge glass vases. Bedrooms have modern four-posters and fabulous bathrooms; 'superiors' have full-on views of the river and ponte Vecchio. There's a spectacular roof terrace and bar and a wonderfully calm first floor Relax Room with daybeds.

Lungarno Suites
Lungarno Acciaiuoli 4 (055 27268000/ www.lungarnohotels.com). €€€€.
Ideal for travellers seeking the comforts typical of a four-star hotel, while maintaining a little more independence, the stylish Lungarno Suites – part of the Ferragamo hotel group, and sharing its design aesthetic – offers fully serviced self-catering apartments. Around half the apartments have river views; those on the

ESSENTIALS

Cheap and chic

N4U

Stylish, affordable accommodation in Florence is no longer an oxymoron thanks to a glut of excellent B&Bs and guesthouses (known officially as *affittacamere* or *residenze d'epoca*) where, instead of endless facilities and 24-hour room service, you'll find a warm welcome and plenty of personal input from the owners. Such places are at last offering a real challenge to more upmarket (and often overpriced) hotels.

The pioneers of the chic yet value-for-money formula were Lea Gulmanelli and Johanan Vitta of the mini Johanna/Johlea chain of *residenze*, of which there are now five in Florence. They opened their first *residenza* in 1994 and the original concept has been maintained; none of the *residenze* exceed six rooms, all are centrally located yet away from the tourist hordes and all are decorated to a high standard. Most significantly, they are reasonably priced. The latest project is the recently revamped **Antica Dimora Johlea** (p174), the most upmarket of the group. The X-factor here is the stunning little roof terrace with its 360° views of the city. The retro-chic decor at **Casa Rovai** (p176) is a bit more spartan, but the rooms are very comfortable nevertheless and the position, away from the crowds but near to Santa Croce and the buzzy Sant' Ambrogio market, is great. **Palazzo Galletti** (p176) is housed in a full-blown 18th-century mansion, its grand space totally belying the value offered by the nine lovely rooms. The pretty first floor rooms at the super-friendly **Relais Grand Tour** (p174) are cheaper (and simpler) than those on the ground floor, but for a few euros more, you can sleep in a palatial suite. One of the most recent openings of this genre is **N4U** (p169), providing hip, colour-themed rooms just a few minutes walk south of the Duomo. An excellent addition to the pack.

top floors have terraces. Each unit has a cleverly hidden and fully equipped kitchen, but you can have your shopping done for you or order meals from the Gallery Hotel Art (p165).

Dei Mori
Via Dante Alighieri 12 (055 211438/ www.deimori.it). €€.
This guesthouse in the heart of the medieval city was one of Florence's first B&Bs, and it's still one of the best. Rooms are keenly priced and comfortable: the ones on the first floor are more traditional (and some don't have bathrooms), while those upstairs are smarter and all en suite. The welcome is exceptionally warm: fresh flowers, bright rugs, cheerful paintings and a sitting room with books and magazines. There's also a terrace.

N4U
Via Proconsolo 5 (055 0515147/ www.n4uguesthouse.it). €€.
The owners of this chic new guesthouse, a stone's throw from the Duomo, set out to offer central, stylishly designed, personalised accommodation at more-than-honest prices. If you want room service, TV and a breakfast buffet, this place is Not 4 You, but the six rooms are comfortable, spacious and deliciously quirky. Rooms have electric kettles and morning coffee and brioche will arrive on a tray. All should be en suite by the time this guide is published. See also box p168.

Perseo
Via de' Cerretani 1 (055 212504/ www.hotelperseo.it). €€.
Occupying the shell of its rather down-at-heel predecessor, the new-look Perseo opened in April 2006, offering 20 stylish rooms, good prices and a super-central location. The owners have gone for a clean, contemporary look so expect modern wood furniture, a palette of earthy colours, flatscreen TVs, sharp light fittings and sparkling new bathrooms. The sitting room is well supplied with books and magazines while a complimentary *aperitivo* is offered to guests each evening.

Relais degli Uffizi
Chiasso del Buco 16, off chiasso de' Baroncelli (055 2676239/ www.relaisuffizi.it). €€.
Perhaps the best-positioned place for the Uffizi and Palazzo Vecchio, this smart hotel is nevertheless a little tricky to locate, down a tiny alley off the south side of piazza della Signoria. Once you're upstairs, settle down in the sitting room and enjoy its fab views, or relax in the comfort of your own room. The ten rooms vary in shape but are all spacious; iron beds and parquet floors set the aesthetic tone, which is consolidated by well-chosen antiques and paintings.

Residenza d'Epoca in Piazza della Signoria
Via de' Magazzini 2 (055 2399546/ www.inpiazzadellasignoria.com). €€€.
A hotel for visitors who want to be in the heart of the cultural action. Most rooms have views of piazza della Signoria ('Leonardo' and 'Michelangelo' have the best views), and are furnished in a fairly traditional, unfussy style, with antiques, canopied beds, oriental rugs, pastel walls and wooden floors. Imaginatively fitted bathrooms give a sense of the opulence of a bigger hotel. A hearty breakfast is served at the huge table on the third floor.

Savoy
Piazza della Repubblica 7 (055 283313/ www.hotelsavoy.com). €€€€.
Today's Savoy doesn't bear much of a resemblance to its 19th-century predecessor. Now one of the city's most popular all-rounders, big with the business and celebrity brackets, the hotel was added to the Rocco Forte portfolio in the late 1990s. Designer Olga Polizzi has created a stylish and calm ambience in the period space. The top-of-the-range Brunelleschi and Signoria suites have their own steam rooms, and there's a rooftop gym. The L'Incontro bar and brasserie is great for people-watching.

Torre Guelfa
Borgo SS Apostoli 8 (055 2396338/ www.hoteltorreguelfa.com). €€.

ESSENTIALS

Time Out
Travel Guides

Worldwide

All our guides are
written by a team of
local experts with a
unique and stylish
insider perspective.
We offer essential tips,
trusted advice and
honest reviews for
everything you need
to know in the city.

Over 50 destinations
available at all good
bookshops and at
timeout.com/shop

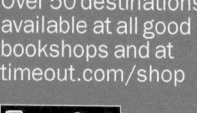

This popular hotel now occupies the whole of the 14th-century palazzo, which incorporates the tallest privately owned tower in Florence; evening drinks come with stunning views at the tower-top bar. Breakfast is served in a glassed-in loggia, where there's also an elegant sitting room (with Wi-Fi). Bedrooms are decorated in pastel colours with wrought-iron beds; some are huge. Number 15 is a romantic little den with its own roof garden – book at least six months in advance for this.

Santa Maria Novella

Abaco
Via de' Banchi 1 (055 2381919/ www.hotelabaco.it). €.
It's a bit of a climb up to the second floor of this 550-year-old building; once you've made it, you'll find a modest shell housing a handsome hotel. The friendly owner has decorated the less-than-grand place in grand style: the seven bedrooms are full of sumptuous fabrics and framed reproductions of works. Three are fully en suite, others have only a shower. Breakfast is free if you pay in cash (and there's a 10% discount in November and December).

Beacci Tornabuoni
Via de' Tornabuoni 3 (055 212645/ www.tornabuonihotels.com). €€€.
Comfortable and characterful Beacci Tornabuoni is situated on the top floors of the 15th-century Palazzo Minerbetti Strozzi and, though featuring all mod cons, it has a delightful Edwardian feel. The wonderful flower-filled roof garden is used for breakfast and dinners in summer; inside, old parquet floors creak and groan under the weight of the antique furniture. The lovely old reading room smells of floor wax and wood smoke, the latter from a pietra serena fireplace.

Casa Howard
Via della Scala 18 (06 69924555/ www.casahoward.com). €€€.
The owner of this stylish pied-à-terre has set out to offer comfortable, upmarket accommodation at reasonable

rates in the discreet atmosphere of a private home. The 12 rooms are classy and vaguely eccentric, decorated with strong colours and a mix of antique and custom-made furniture. Visit the website to choose the one you like best: the large, dramatic Drawing Room, perhaps, or maybe the sexy Hidden Room with its sunken bath and deep-red walls hung with Japanese erotic prints. There's a Turkish bath to ease museum-weary muscles and each floor has an 'honesty fridge'.

Ferretti
Via delle Belle Donne 17 (055 2381328/www.hotelferretti.com). €.
This friendly, spotlessly clean little one-star hotel enjoys a great location in a network of quiet, medieval streets. All 16 rooms are pleasant (and all have ceiling fans), but the best are at the top of the old building; bright and sunny, they have recently been redecorated and have crisp cotton covers on iron bedsteads and lovely marble floors. There's a cosy breakfast room with a free internet point. Only about half the rooms have a private bathroom.

Grand Hotel
Piazza Ognissanti 1 (055 27161/www. luxurycollection.com/grandflorence). €€€€.
While its rooms are no less luxurious than those at its sister hotel across the piazza, the Grand is decidedly different in character to the Westin Excelsior (p174). The reception area is light and airy, while the Conservatory, with its stained-glass ceiling and pietra serena columns, offers old-fashioned opulence. Less oppressive is new eaterie InCanto, offering modern Tuscan food. Roughly half of the 107 bedrooms and suites are done up in faux-Renaissance style, complete with frescoes, painted ceilings and heavy traditional fabrics. If your roommate is canine, you'll be given a dogs' welcome kit.

Grand Hotel Minerva
Piazza Santa Maria Novella 16 (055 27230/www.grandhotelminerva. com). €€€.

Once an annexe hosting guests to the adjacent convent, the Minerva has been a hotel since the mid 1800s. It was given a colourful revamp in the 1990s and is today staffed by a young, dynamic team. Many rooms have views over the piazza (it can get noisy in summer), while extras include in-room kettles, a kids' package of videos and games and a shiatsu masseuse on request. Pet owners get a special deal, as do lone women travellers. There's a small pool and bar on the roof garden.

Hostel Archi Rossi

Via Faenza 94r (055 290804/ www.hostelarchirossi.com). **€**.
This hostel's reception is covered with renditions of famous frescoes, done by guests. The maximum number of beds in the light rooms is nine, but many are smaller. Just ten minutes' walk from the station, it's a good choice for early departures or late arrivals. There are 147 beds in total, including four doubles in an annexe, with private bathrooms. The management allows mixed-sex rooms as long as everyone knows each other. There's a lovely garden and free guided tours of the city.

Hotel Santa Maria Novella

Piazza Santa Maria Novella 1 (055 271840/www.hotelsantamaria novella.it). **€€€€**.
Owned by clothing manufacturer Rifle, this 45-room hotel is due to open another 25 rooms in an adjacent building by mid 2008. The property is done out in rich colours, painted wood panelling and fancy marquetry, but contemporary decorative touches mean it never feels oppressive. Bedrooms come with canopied beds, silk curtains and plasma TVs; marble bathrooms contain goodies from Profumo-Farmaceutica di Santa Maria Novella (see box p89). There's a panoramic bar on the roof.

JK Place

Piazza Santa Maria Novella 7 (055 2645181/www.jkplace.com). **€€€€**.
The ultra-sophisticated, 20-room JK Place occupies an attractive old townhouse. The style is a contemporary take on a neoclassical look, where muted colours beautifully offset fine antiques, old prints, black and white photos and artful flower arrangements. No two bedrooms are alike, though all are luxurious and lack nothing in the way of facilities: several of the larger ones overlook the piazza. The top-floor penthouse suite has a 360° sweep of the city, as does the roof terrace.

Ostello Monaco 34

Via Guido Monaco 34, Santa Maria Novella (055 321018/www.ostello monaco34.com). **€**.
Offering stylish budget accommodation and excellent facilities, this 50-bed hostel opened in July 2007 near the station. The 1960s building previously housed five residential floors, and rooms (doubles, triples and quads) are still arranged so that each floor is self-contained, with bedrooms sharing a well-equipped kitchen and two bathrooms. All rooms all have flatscreen satellite TVs, air-conditioning and Wi-Fi. Good double glazing takes care of the traffic noise, but a couple of rooms on the top floor are windowless.

Residenza del Moro

Via del Moro 15 (055 2648494/ www.residenzadelmoro.com). **€€€€**.
The splendid piano nobile of 16th-century Palazzo Niccolini-Bourbon has been exquisitely restored and now houses this luxurious *residenza*. You'll find eleborate stucco work, impressive frescoes and painted ceilings – along with well-chosen contemporary art. The 11 bedrooms vary enormously in shape and size (and price), from the cosy, almost-affordable Biblioteca to the palatial, super-priced Marchese Suite, but all feature precious antiques, rich fabrics, canopied beds and marble bathrooms. Breakfast is served in the beautiful hanging garden.

Scoti

Via de' Tornabuoni 7 (055 292128/ www.hotelscoti.com). **€**.
If you want to secure a room in the wonderful Scoti, housed on the second floor of a 15th-century palazzo, book

well ahead: it's popular with visitors worldwide. After extensive renovation a couple of years back, the lofty bedrooms are simple but bright and sunny and all en suite; the frescoed salon has retained its air of faded glory. Breakfast is served around a big communal table or in the rooms.

Westin Excelsior
Piazza Ognissanti 3 (055 27151/www. westin.com/excelsiorflorence). €€€€.
While it still offers old-world luxury, the Westin has recently introduced some contemporary touches; there's now a health and fitness area, and the restaurant offers a special menu of low-cal dishes. The traditional framework remains, however: doormen are dressed in maroon and grey livery, and the grand public rooms have marble floors, neoclassical columns, painted wooden ceilings and stained glass. The 171 rooms and suites are sumptuously appointed; some boast terraces with views over the river.

San Lorenzo

Antica Dimora Johlea
Via San Gallo 72 (055 4627296/ www.johanna.it). €€.
Lea Gulmanelli and Johanan Vitta's latest project is the most expensive in their mini-chain. Classical music and a warm glow set the scene upon entering. The cosy bedrooms, all with four posters, are a riot of tasteful colours with kilims on marble or parquet floors and Indian print covers on the beds. Defying the low rates, all have flatscreen TVs, DVD players, digital radios and electric kettles. Breakfast is served at the top of the house, and there's a lovely roof terrace. If there's no room here, check the other – cheaper – hotels in the group's portfolio (same website). See also box p168.

Casci
Via Cavour 13 (055 211686/ www.hotelcasci.com). €€.
The super-helpful Lombardi family runs this friendly *pensione*, which occupies a 15th-century palazzo just north of the

Duomo, where opera composer Giacomo Rossini lived from 1851 to 1855. The open-plan bar and breakfast area has frescoed ceilings, while the 24 bedrooms are comfortable and come with up-to-date bathrooms. Bedrooms at the back look on to a beautiful garden; two sizeable family rooms sleep up to five. There's now Wi-Fi throughout.

Locanda degli Artisti
Via Faenza 56 (055 213806/ www.hotelazzi.it). €€.
Housed on the first two floors of a rambling old palazzo near the station, the Locanda degli Artisti is an interesting and comfortable little hotel with good prices and a lovely terrace. The big reception area has a retro vibe and you'll be greeted by classical music or jazz on the sound system. Eco-friendly materials and natural colours have been used in the 29 sunny bedrooms, and organic produce is served at breakfast. The Suite Blu has a big jacuzzi bath.

Relais Grand Tour
Via Santa Reparata 21 (055 283955/ www.florencegrandtour.com). €€.
Those 17th-century folk well-heeled enough to undertake the Grand Tour would have been delighted to rest their overexcited heads in one of the suites in this 16th-century building. The imaginatively restored B&B is run by welcoming couple Cristina and Giuseppe. The Mirrors Suite is much loved by, ahem, honeymooners, while the Theatre Suite occupies a private playhouse – the bed is on the stage, faced by several rows of seats. An basket of croissants can be left outside the room each morning. See also box p168.

San Marco

Loggiato dei Serviti
Piazza della SS Annunziata 3 (055 289592/www.loggiatodeiservitihotel.it). €€€.
One of the most beautiful three-star hotels in Florence, housed in a 16th-century former convent. The interior is a stylish mix of original architectural

Seclusion of grandeur

The Four Seasons Firenze opens its doors.

After a seven-year, multi-million-euro restoration project involving armies of workmen, restorers and gardeners and several delays, the **Four Seasons Firenze** (p177) is finally due to receive its first guests in July 2008.

Few casual visitors to Florence are aware of the five-hectare, walled Giardino della Gherardesca that lies inside the north-eastern part of the traffic-choked ring road, which incorporates 15th-century Palazzo della Gherardesca and a 16th-century ex-convent. More a resort than a mere hotel, yet only ten-minutes walk from the Duomo, guests to the property will be able to enjoy the unique garden (with rare trees and shrubs and a neo-classical *tempietto*), an outdoor heated pool, an impressive spa, a hair and beauty salon and a big fitness centre alongside all the bells and whistles associated with a five-star hotel. The property is so extensive that there will be golf carts to ferry guests to and fro.

Once inside, the grandeur of the original Renaissance building is immediately apparent. Public spaces on the ground floor are built around a graceful courtyard and decorated with elaborate stucco work, bas-reliefs and magnificent frescoes. The main bar occupies a glassed-in courtyard, while the Il Palagio restaurant is housed in a cool vaulted room with a big terrace.

Eighty-odd bedrooms are suites, housed in the main palazzo, while a further 37 are located in the *conventino* (to open in late 2008). In terms of decor, the yellow- or green-themed rooms push no buttons, but there's no denying their luxury. Veteran Four Seasons interior designer Pier-Yves Rochon has gone for a fairly restrained 'classic' look, with Empire-style furniture, opulent fabrics and luxurious marble bathrooms.

At €500 per night (excluding breakfast), the standard rooms will be among the most expensive in Florence; but with its plush facilities, the hotel will still provide stiff enough competition for the city's other luxury pads.

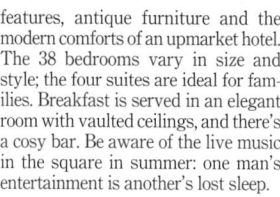
Palazzo Galletti

features, antique furniture and the modern comforts of an upmarket hotel. The 38 bedrooms vary in size and style; the four suites are ideal for families. Breakfast is served in an elegant room with vaulted ceilings, and there's a cosy bar. Be aware of the live music in the square in summer: one man's entertainment is another's lost sleep.

Palazzo Galletti
Via Sant'Egidio 12 (055 3905750/ www.palazzogalletti.it). €€.
Offering great value and situated just a few minutes' walk east of the Duomo, Galletti occupies the first floor of an 18th-century mansion. All the elements of a grand palazzo are here (weathered cotto floors, lofty ceilings, frescoes, the odd chandelier), but the overall effect is not at all pompous thanks to some carefully chosen contemporary design details. All but two of the nine lovely bedrooms face the quiet internal courtyard and have a tiny terrace. Even the smallest are a good size, while the two entirely frescoed suites are vast. See also box p168.

Residence Hilda
Via de' Servi 40 (055 288021/ www.residencehilda.com). €€€.
Boasting a prime location five minutes' walk north of the Duomo, RH provides stylish self-catering accommodation ranging from small units for two people to larger apartments for five. All of the super-modern apartments come with well-equipped kitchen units that can be hidden away behind sliding doors when required. The furnishings throughout are stylishly spare, with Philippe Starck chairs and other modern classics sitting on blonde wood floors. Staff will even deliver your shopping.

Santa Croce

Casa Rovai
Via Fiesolana 1 (055 2469856/ www.casarovai.com). €€.
This reasonably priced, retro-stylish guesthouse occupies the first floor of a 16th-century building not far from Sant'Ambrogio market. Expect

19th-century terrazzo floors, cream and dove-grey paintwork, the odd fresco, and a mix of late 19th- and early 20th-century furniture picked up at flea markets. The six bedrooms vary in shape and size, but all are comfortable and have modern bathrooms. Continental breakfast is included in the rate, but for an extra €5 you can order eggs, prosciutto and cheeses. See also box p168.

Dalí
Via dell'Oriuolo 17 (055 2340706/ www.hoteldali.com). €.
Run with genuine care by a young couple, Samanta and Marco, this little gem just east of the Duomo offers spotless, homely rooms at budget prices and – a miracle in central Florence – free car parking. Only four of the ten rooms are en suite, but all are thoughtfully decorated with hand stencilling, pretty bedcovers and old bedheads; all have ceiling fans. Rooms at the back overlooking the courtyard are sunny and quiet. Breakfast is not provided, but there are electric kettles and fridges in the rooms.

Four Seasons Firenze
Borgo Pinti 99 (055 26261/www. fourseasons.com/florence). €€€€.
See box p175.

Relais Santa Croce
Via Ghibellina 87 (055 2342230/ www.relaissantacroce.com). €€€€.
This hotel offers contemporary style and personalised service in the shell of 18th-century Palazzo Ciofi-Jacometti. The public rooms are suitably grandiose; bedrooms, meanwhile, have clean, modern lines with quirky design details. Two Royal Suites offer the full VIP treatment. Rear-facing rooms on the upper floors have views over a jumble of rooftops to Santa Croce church. The Relais shares its entrance with one of Italy's best restaurants, Enoteca Pinchiorri (p119).

Oltrarno

Annalena
Via Romana 34 (055 222402/ www.annalenahotel.com). €€.

The Annalena is housed in a 15th-century building opposite the back entrance to the Boboli Gardens. At various times it's been used as a refuge for young widows, and lodgings for refugees from Mussolini's Fascist police. After a period of decline, it has recently been taken over by an enthusiastic new management. The huge salon that serves as lounge, bar and breakfast room has been brightened up, while the pleasant, spacious bedrooms have been given a lick of paint. Rooms at the back overlook the gorgeous Annalena gardens.

Casa Pucci
Via Santa Monaca 8 (055 216560/ www.casapucci.artwork-inform.com). €.
Signora Pucci's cosy ground-floor apartment occupies part of a former 15th-century convent. Three of the five rooms lead off a plant-filled courtyard where a huge rustic table is laid for summer breakfasts. The whole place has a nice, lived-in feel, from the big kitchen (which guests can use) to the spacious, homely rooms furnished with family antiques. Romantics should go for room five with its four-poster bed and stone fireplace. Book well ahead.

Istituto Gould
Via de' Serragli 49 (055 212576). €.
Run by the Valdese Church, Istituto Gould offers excellent budget accommodation in a well-kept 17th-century palazzo with a serene courtyard, stone staircases, terracotta floors and lots of atmosphere. There are now some 41 rooms on site: two-thirds are doubles, while the others accommodate a maximum of four. All rooms but two have private bathrooms. The quieter rooms are at the back. You need to check in during office hours, but once that's done, you get your own key.

Lungarno
Borgo San Jacopo 14 (055 27261/ www.lungarnohotels.com). €€€€.
The most coveted rooms in this stylish hotel have terraces overlooking the Arno. However, the waterside setting

can also been enjoyed from the breakfast room and lounge/bar, or the outside seating area. More classic in feel than other Ferragamo-owned hotels, the Lungarno is decorated in cream and navy-blue with lovely mahogany and cherrywood antique furniture, plus a collection of fine artworks (including an original Picasso). Bedrooms are stylish and comfy but, with the exception of the spacious suites, fairly small.

Palazzo Magnani Feroni

Borgo San Frediano 5 (055 2399544/ www.florencepalace.it). €€€€.
Expect top-class service and facilities at this grand palazzo. All but one of the 12 suites have separate sitting rooms elegantly furnished with squashy sofas, armchairs and antiques. The most charming room of all is actually the smallest: a romantic junior suite with floor-to-ceiling frescoes and a little private garden. Bathrooms are super-smart. The roof terrace – complete with a bar serving light meals – offers views of the whole city.

La Scaletta

Via de' Guicciardini 13 (055 283028/ 214255/www.hotellascaletta.it). €€.
A change of management in 2005 swept away the figurative cobwebs of the old-style Scaletta, housed in a grand 15th-century palazzo, in favour of cleaner lines. The 16 buttermilk bedrooms have elegant curtains and bedspreads and wrought-iron bedheads. Most are quiet; numbers 21, 22 and 23 overlook the Boboli Gardens, while those on noisy via Guicciardini boast effective double glazing. All have bathrooms. There are three roof terraces that offer breathtaking views of Boboli and the city skyline; one has a bar.

Outer Districts

Una Hotel Vittoria

Via Pisana 9 (055 22771/ www.unahotels.it). €€€€.
Architect/designer Fabio Novembre's exuberant hotel (just outside Porta San Frediano) is geared towards an upmarket business clientele, but will appeal to anyone looking for something different decor-wise. Novembre's idiosyncratic designs include a huge swooping mosaic in the entrance hall based on a 19th-century floral brocade, and a long, curved table in the restaurant influenced by refectory tables found in Tuscan monasteries. The spacious bedrooms are equipped with a plethora of gadgetry.

Ostello per la Gioventù

Viale Augusto Righi 2-4, Outside the City Gates (055 601451/www.iyhf.org). Bus 17A, 17B. €.
If you visit Florence during the torrid summer, head for the hills and this YHA youth hostel, just below Fiesole. It may be some way from the action, but its location, in the impressive Villa Camerata will keep you cool. Most of the 322 beds are in dorms with shared bathrooms, but there are some en suite doubles, triples and quads plus bungalows sleeping two people and camping facilities. If you aren't a member of the YHA, you can join on the spot for an extra €3 a day (for the first six days).

Pensione Bencistà

Via Benedetto da Maiano 4, Fiesole (055 59163/www.bencista.com). Bus 7. €€.
The characterful old Bencistà has taken a few steps towards the 21st century (a website, credit cards, a lift) in recent years, but not so many as to destroy its delightful old-world atmosphere. Run as a *pensione* by the Simoni family since 1925, it has a fabulous setting on the hillside just below Fiesole. No two bedrooms are alike – those at the front enjoy unrivalled city views as does the flower-filled terrace. The restaurant serves homely food.

Relais Marignolle

Via di San Quirichino a Marignolle 16 (055 2286910/www.marignolle.com). No bus. €€€.
Set in rambling grounds on a hillside at Marignolle, the Bulleri family's converted farmhouse makes the most of elegant country living while still keeping the sights of the city within easy

reach. Sun pours into the living room, where comfortable armchairs, an open fire and an honesty bar encourage lingering. Breakfast is served on a veranda. The nine bedrooms vary in shape and size, but all are tastefully decorated. Signora Bulleri serves light meals on request and holds cooking classes. The attractive pool is another perk.

Riva Lofts
Via Baccio Bandinelli 98 (055 7130272/www.rivahotel.it). €€€.
A welcome jolt was given to Florence's predominantly traditional hotel scene by the 2006 opening of Riva Lofts, occupying a complex of 19th-century artisan workshops on the Arno. Riva's heart is its open-plan living room with vaulted ceiling, exposed brick and a huge fire. Natural elements (wood, stone) warm the spare design, while furniture is an eclectic mix of modern classics and vintage. The nine suites (all but one with kitchen) range in size from 30 to 100sq m (320-1,080sq ft); top of the pile are the two spectacular lofts themselves. All rooms have electronic gadgets and super-hip bathrooms, and there's a garden, a pool and vintage bikes to get you into town.

Villa Poggio San Felice
Via San Matteo in Arcetri 24 (055 220016/www.villapoggiosan felice.com). €€.

The hills around Florence are dotted with elegant old houses, of which this 15th-century villa is a prime example. Set in a rose-filled garden with a small pool, it was rescued from decay by the present owners, who were careful not to spoil it with heavy-handed restoration. There are five bedrooms; one of them, La Camera dei Nonni, has a terrace overlooking the city. All in all, it offers the vibe of a cultured private home a ten-minute drive from central Florence. There's a complimentary shuttle service to and from the city.

Villa San Michele
Via Doccia 4 (055 5678200/ www.villasanmichele.com). Bus 7.
Closed late Nov-late Mar. *€€€€.*
The rooms in this fabulous yet understated hotel, much beloved on the celebrity circuit, are among the most expensive in Italy. Housed in a 15th-century monastery, Villa San Michele enjoys a superb location, nestled in a beautiful terraced garden on the hillside below Fiesole. Understated elegance, combined with subtle nods to the past, inform the style. The views down to the city are splendid: dinner under the loggia at sunset is an unforgettable experience, though the bill will be too. Service is immaculate.

Relais Santa Croce p177

ESSENTIALS

Getting Around

Arriving & leaving

By air

Florence Airport, Peretola (Amerigo Vespucci)
055 3061300/flight information 055 3061700/www.aeroporto.firenze.it.
Flying to Peretola, about 5km (3 miles) west of central Florence is the easiest way to reach the city; Meridiana flies here from London Gatwick. Bus shuttle **Volainbus** runs half-hourly (6am-11.30pm), to and from the SITA station at via Santa Caterina da Siena 15. Buy tickets (€4.50) on board, at the airport bar or at bus ticket outlets (p181). Bus season tickets are valid. A taxi to Florence costs from €20 and takes about 20 minutes.

Pisa International Airport (Galileo Galilei)
050 849111/flight information 050 849300/www.pisa-airport.com.
Trains to Florence's Santa Maria Novella (SMN) station from Pisa Aeroporto take around an hour. Buy tickets (single €5.50) to the right of arrivals in the main airport concourse. You may need to change at Pisa Centrale. Trains between Pisa Aeroporto and Centrale generally leave from and arrive at Platform 14 (reached via an underpass).

Terravision (050 26080, www.terravision.eu) runs a 70-minute coach service departing outside airport arrivals in Pisa airport to the steps of Florence SMN and back. Buy tickets (single €8) from the airport kiosk, hotel reservations booth at platform 16 of Florence SMN, online or by phone.

To get to Florence by car, take the Firenze–Pisa–Livorno road.

Bologna Airport (Guglielmo Marconi)
051 6479615/www.bologna-airport.it.
A bus stops outside terminal A (arrivals) and leaves for Bologna train station every 15 minutes between 6am and 11.40pm (30 minutes, tickets €5 on board). A taxi costs about €18. From Bologna Centrale, trains to Florence are frequent and take between 50 and 90 minutes; prices vary. The fastest trains are the Eurostars (single ticket €15); Intercities (single €11.50) are less regular. If you're flying into Bologna try to book a ticket in advance as trains into Florence are often fully booked.

Travelling by car, Florence is about 90 minutes south on the A1.

By rail

Buy train tickets from ticket desks, station vending machines, Ticket Point LAZZI (p181), www.trenitalia .com or some travel agents. Before boarding trains, stamp (*convalidare*) your ticket in the yellow machines by the platforms. Boarding without a ticket, or not stamping it, will land you a €50 fine. For details on train services in Italy call 892021 (7am-9pm daily) or visit www.trenitalia .com/en/index.html. For info on disabled access visit the assistance desk on platform five at SMN or call 055 2352275 or 199 303060.

Campo di Marte *via Mannelli (disabled assistance 055 2352275). Bus 12, 70 (night).* **Open** *Ticket office* 6.20am-9pm.
Florence's main station when SMN is closed at night. Many long-distance trains stop here.

Santa Maria Novella *piazza della Stazione.* **Open** 4.15am-1.30am daily. *Information office* 7am-9pm daily. *Ticket office* 5.50am-10pm daily.

By road

By coach, you'll arrive at either the SITA or the LAZZI coach stations, both near SMN train station.

Ticket Point LAZZI *piazza Adua, 055 215155/www.lazzi.it*
SITA *via Santa Caterina da Siena 15, 055 4782870/www.sitabus.it.*

Public transport

The ATAF bus network is comprehensive but strikes are still frequent and weekend and evening waiting times can be long. However, regular train services run between the city's three train stations, SMN, Campo di Marte in the east and Rifredi in the west. The new Tramvia tram system is under construction. For updates, visit www.tramvia.fi.it.

Bus services

Most daytime ATAF routes run every ten to 30 minutes. The orange and white *fermate* (bus stops) list the main stops along the route. After 9pm, night services 67, 68, 70, 71 and 304 run on main routes until 12.30am/1am (70 runs all night, leaving SMN every hour for Campo di Marte station and back). A useful network of electric buses, **A**, **B** and **C**, covers central routes; use normal bus tickets or season tickets. Most buses are wheelchair accessible.

ATAF *piazza della Stazione, opposite north-east exit of train station (800 424500/199 104245 from mobiles/www.ataf.net).*

Tickets

Buy tickets from the ATAF office (above; except for season tickets), machines, *tabacchi*, news-stands and many bars. When you board, stamp the ticket in a validation machine. If using a ticket for two consecutive journeys, stamp it on the first bus only, but keep it till you complete your journey; stamp another when the time limit is up. If you're caught without a valid ticket the fine is €50. Prices are as follows: 70-min ticket €1.20 – valid for 70 minutes of travel on all city area buses; on-board ticket €2; multiple ticket €4.50 for four tickets; three-hour ticket €1.80; 24-hour ticket €5; three-day ticket €12; seven-day ticket €16; AGILE swipe card €10/€20; monthly pass (*abbonamento*) €34 (€23 students). Buy passes from the ATAF office at SMN station or from any outlet with an 'Abbonamenti ATAF' sign. For student passes, go to the Ufficio Abbonamenti in piazza della Stazione with ID and two passport photos.

A 24-hour sightseeing bus ticket, **Firenze Passepartour**, costs €22.

Taxis

Licensed cabs are white with yellow graphics, with a code name of a place plus ID number on the door, e.g. 'Londra 6'. When phoning for a cab you'll be given the taxi code and a time, e.g. '*Londra 6 in tre minuti*'. You can only get a cab at a rank or by phone: they can't be flagged in the street. When the taxi arrives, the meter should read €3.20 during the day, €5.10 on Sundays and on public holidays, and €6.40 at night. Lone women pay ten per cent less after 9pm, but only if they request the discount. Phoning for a cab carries a surcharge of €1.90; each item of luggage in the boot is €1, and destinations beyond the official city limits cost more. For details, see the tariff card that cabs are required to display. Taxis between the airport and anywhere in the city centre have a fixed tariff of €20 in the day, €26.40 at night. Useful taxi numbers are 055 4390, 055 4798, 055 4242 and 055 4499.

ESSENTIALS

Driving

Access to the centre is limited according to Traffic-Free Zones (ZTL), as well as summer/weekend air-quality limitations. Access rules change regularly so check the local press or with the municipal police (800 055055). Speed limits are 50km/h (45km/h on motorbikes and mopeds) in the city, 90km/h on the *superstrada* and 130km/h on the motorway (*autostrada*). Legal drink drive limits are 0.5g/litre (reached by around a quarter litre of wine or a half litre of beer). Seatbelts are compulsory in front and back seats.

Major motoring organisations have reciprocal breakdown service arrangements with the Automobile Club d'Italia (055 24861/24hr info in English 166 664477/24hr emergencies 803116/www.aci.it). In a traffic emergency, call 055 3285 (055 328 3333 for less urgent situations). For general traffic or parking information, call 800 055055 (8am-8pm Mon-Sat).

All petrol stations sell unleaded fuel (*senza piombo*). Diesel fuel is *gasolio*. Normal hours are 7.30am-12.30pm and 3-7pm daily except Sundays. AGIP stations on via Bolognese, via Aretina, viale Europa, via Senese and via Baracca have 24-hour self-service machines.

Toll-charged motorway are indicated by green signs; take a ticket then hand it in and pay when you come off. Payment is by Viacard (from newsagents and the ACI), cash or credit cards.

Parking

Parking in central Florence is a headache as most main streets are no-parking zones for non-residents. Parking is forbidden where you see *passo carrabile* (access at all times) and *sosta vietata* (no parking) signs. In unrestricted areas, parking is free in most side streets. Blue lines denote pay-parking; there will be either meters or an attendant to issue timed tickets. Yellow stripes denote (free) disabled spaces. *Zona rimozione* (tow-away area) signs are valid for the whole street length, while temporary tow zones are marked at each end. If your car's not where you left it, check if it's been towed on 055 4224142. The central car pound, **Depositeria SaS** (24hrs), is in via Allende; car owners must take ID and proof of ownership to regain possession. The safest place to leave a car is a 24hr underground car park (*parcheggio*).

Parcheggio Parterre *via Madonna della Tosse 9, off piazza della Libertà, (055 5001994/www.firenzeparcheggi.it).* €1.50/hr; €18/24hrs; €65/wk.
Parcheggio Piazza Stazione *via Alamanni 14/piazza della Stazione 12-13 (055 2302655).* €2/hr for 1st 2hrs, then €3/hr; 5 days €140.

Vehicle hire

Alinari moped and bike hire *055 280500/www.alinarirental.com*
Avis *055 213629/www.avis.it.*
Europcar *055 290438/ www.europcar.it.*
Firenze by Car electric car hire *055 22825/333 1816919/www.firenzebycar.com.*
Hertz *055 2398205/www.hertz.com.*
Maxirent Car & moped hire *055 2654207/www.maxirent.com.*

Cycling

Cycle lanes skirt the main city avenues, but that's no guarantee they'll only be used by bikes. Bikes can be hired from the following places:

Florence by Bike *055 488992/ www.florencebybike.it*
Mille e Una Bici: council scheme with hire points around the city. €1.50/hour or €8/day, or 50¢/hour, €1/day or €15/month for residents and holders of train or bus passes.

Resources A-Z

Accident & emergency

For general **emergency services & state police** call 113; the **Carabinieri** police (English-speaking helpline) 112; **fire service** 115; **ambulance** (*ambulanza*) 118; **car breakdown** Automobile Club d'Italia (ACI) 803 116; **city traffic police** 055 3285.

For night and all-day Sunday emergency home doctor's visits, call the **Guardia Medica** (Central Florence: 055 2339456; Oltrarno: 055 215616). The hospitals below offer 24hr A&E services, unless otherwise stated:

Ospedale di Careggi *viale Morgagni 85 (055 7949644/www.ao-careggi. toscana.it). Bus 2,8,14C.* The main hospital for most emergencies.
Ospedale Meyer (Children) *via Luca Giordano 13 (055 56621/www.ao-meyer.toscana.it). Bus 11,17.*
Ospedale Torregalli *via Torregalli 3 (055 71921). Bus 83.*
Ospedale Palagi (eye hospital) *viale Michelangiolo 41 (055 65771).* **Open** 8am-8pm daily. Bus 12,13. For eye emergencies outside these opening hours, go to Careggi.
Santa Maria Nuova *piazza Santa Maria Nuova 1 (055 27581).* The most central hospital.

For translators to help out at the hospital, contact **AVO** (Association of Hospital Volunteers) via G Carducci 8 (24hrs 055 2344567).

Pharmacies

Pharmacies (*farmacie*), identified by a red or green cross, have a duty rota system. A list by the door of all pharmacies indicates the nearest one open outside normal hours. The pharmacies listed below provide a 24-hour service:

Farmacia Comunale no.13 SMN train station, 055 216761
Farmacia all'Insegna del Moro piazza San Giovanni 20r, 055 211343
Farmacia Molteni via dei Calzaiuoli 7r, 055 215472

Helplines

AIDS helpline *800 571661*
Alcoholics Anonymous *055 294417.* AA and Al Anon meetings are held at St James Church *via Rucellai 9, 055 294417/www.stjames.it*
Drogatel *800 016600.* **Open** 9am-8pm daily. A national help centre for drug and alcohol related problems.
Samaritans *800 860022.* Some English-speakers.
Women's Rights & Abuse *800 001122.*

Credit card loss

Most lines are freephone (800) numbers, have English-speaking staff and are open 24 hours daily.

American Express *06 7290 0347/ US card holders 800 874 333*
Diners Club *800 864 064*
CartaSi *800 151616.*
MasterCard *800 870866.*
Visa 800 819 014

Customs

EU nationals are not required to declare goods imported into or exported from Italy for their personal use, if arriving from another EU country. The following limits apply for personal use:

■ 800 cigarettes (200 cigars)

■ 10 litres of spirits, 90 litres of wine (and limits on other alcoholic drinks). US citizens should check their duty-free allowance on the way out. Random checks are made for drugs. For non-EU citizens, the following import limits apply:

- 200 cigarettes or 100 small cigars or 50 cigars or 250g of tobacco
- 1 litre of spirits (over 22% alcohol) or 2 litres of fortified wine (under 22%)
- 50 grams of perfume
- 500 grams of coffee

There are no restrictions on the importation of cameras, watches or electrical goods. Visitors are also allowed to bring in up to €10,329 (or equivalent) in cash without declaring it. For info, call 041 269 9311 or see www.agenziadogane.it.

Dental emergencies

In an emergency, go to the nearest *pronto soccorso* (casualty) department (p183). The following dentists speak English. Always call ahead for an appointment.

Dr Marcello Luccioli *via de' Serragli 21 (055 294847).*
Dr Sandro Cosi *via Pellicceria 10 (055 214238/0335 332055).*

Disabled

All new public offices, bars, restaurants and hotels must be equipped with full disabled facilities. Most museums are wheelchair-accessible. New buses have ramps and a wheelchair area. Trains with wheelchair space and disabled toilets display a wheelchair logo; note there's no wheelchair access up the steps on the south side of the station: use the east or north entrances, or call the information office on 055 2352275 for assistance. Taxis take wheelchairs, but tell them when you book. There are free disabled parking bays all over Florence. There are wheelchair-accessible toilets at Florence and Pisa airports and SMN station, and at many of Florence's main sights. The Provincia di Firenze produces a booklet in English, available from tourist offices, with disabled-aware descriptions of venues across Florence Province; for info, call 800 437631. Wheelchair hire is free from the **Misericordia** (055 212222) and **Fratellanza Militare** (055 26021). See also pp180-182.

Electricity

Most wiring systems work on one electrical current, 220V, compatible with British and US products. A few systems in old buildings are 125V. With US 110V equipment, you'll need a current transformer: buy one before travelling as they can be hard to find. Adaptors can be bought at any electrical shop (look for *elettricità* or *ferramenta*).

Embassies & consulates

There are no embassies in Florence but the consular offices offer some services.

Australian Embassy *via Antonio Bosio 5, Rome (06 852721/www.italy. embassy.gov.au).*
British Consulate *lungarno Corsini 2 (055 284133/www.britishembassy. gov.uk).* Out of hours, a message will tell you what to do in an emergency.
Canadian Embassy *via Zara 30, Rome (06 854441/www.dfait-maeci. gc.ca/canada-europa/italy/menu-en.asp).*
Irish Embassy *piazza Campitelli 3, Ghetto, Rome (06 6979121/www. europeanirish.com/Embassies).*
New Zealand Embassy *via Zara 28, Rome (06 4417171/ www.nzembassy.com).*
South African Consulate *piazza dei Salterelli 1, Duomo & Around (055281863/www.dfa.gov.za/foreign/ sa_abroad/sai.htm).* No office; call to make an appointment.
US Consulate *lungarno A Vespucci 38 (055 2398276/www.florence.us consulate.gov/english).* Out of hours a message will refer you to the current emergency number.

ESSENTIALS

Internet

Almost all hotels provide internet access and free Wi-Fi hotspots are in several *piazze*, with more due. Some cafés also provide Wi-Fi access. There are internet points all over the city centre; most charge around €5/hour, with discounts for students. Remember to take ID – you'll need it to register.

Internet Train *via Porta Rossa 38r (055 2741037), via de' Benci 36r (055 2638555/www.internettrain.it) and 7 other locations.* Helpful English-speaking staff, shipping and museum tickets.
Intotheweb *via de' Conti 23r (055 2645628).* PCs and Macs, international phone cards, faxes and mobile phone rental.
The Netgate *via Sant'Egidio 10r (055 2347967/www.thenetgate.it).*

Opening hours

Regular bank opening hours are 8.20am-1.20pm and 2.35pm-3.35pm Mon-Fri. All banks are closed on public holidays. Most post offices open 8.15am-1.30pm (an hour earlier on Saturdays); the main post office opens Mon-Sat 8.15am-7pm. Food shops generally open early morning and close for lunch from 1pm to 3.30pm (though some stay closed till 5pm), then open again until 7.30pm. They generally close on Wednesday afternoons (Saturday afternoons in summer). Other shops open later in the morning and close on Monday mornings. Many shops now stay open all day (*orario continuato*).

Police

In an emergency, go to the nearest *carabinieri* post or police station (*questura*). Staff will either speak English or be able to find someone who does. If you have had something stolen, tell them you want to report a *furto*. A statement (*denuncia*) will be taken, which you'll need for an insurance claim. Lost or stolen passports should also be reported to your embassy or consulate (p184). See also p183 Emergencies.

Comando Provinciale Carabinieri *Borgo Ognissanti 48 (055 2061).* **Open** 24hrs daily. The best place to report the loss or theft of personal property.
Ufficio Denuncie *via Duca D'Aosta 3 (055 49771).* **Open** 24hrs daily. Ufficio Stranieri 8.30am-12.30pm Mon-Fri. The best place to report a crime.
City Police *via Pietrapiana 50r (055 203911).* **Open** 8.30am-7.30pm Mon-Fri; 8.30am-1.30pm Sat.

Post

Stamps (*francobolli*) are sold at *tabacchi* and post offices. Most post boxes are red and have two slots: *Per la Città* (for Florence) and *Tutte le Altre Destinazioni* (everywhere else). There is only one class of post (*posta prioritaria*). Mail can be also be sent registered (*raccomandata*) or insured (*assicurata*). The Italian post call centre number is *803 160*. Poste restante (general delivery) letters (in Italian, *fermoposta*) should be sent to the main post office (*see above*), addressed to Fermoposta and the code and address of the post office to pick up from (list available at www.poste.it/online/cercaup/elenco_dati.php). You need a passport to collect mail and a small charge is made.

Post offices

Main post office:
- *via Pellicceria 3 (055 2736481)*
Branches:
- *via Cavour 71A (055 463501)*
- *via Pietrapiana 53 (055 2674231)*
- *via Barbadori 37r (055 288175).*

ESSENTIALS

Public toilets

A network of public toilets has disabled access and nappy-changing tables. The cost is 50-60¢. All bars are also obliged by law to let you use their loos. Ask for *il bagno*; in some bars you'll be given the key.

Smoking

A law bans smoking in all public places. This includes bars, restaurants and clubs, although there is a clause that allows some venues to set aside a smoking room, with various pre-requisites. Owners who allow customers to smoke are fined heavily, the smoker can also be fined. Cigarettes are on sale at *tabacchi* and *bar-tabacchi*; both have a blue/black and white sign outside.

Telephones

There are phone centres throughout the city centre, often combining phone services with internet services and faxes. Faxes can be sent from some photocopying outlets and internet points, at most hotels and from large post offices (p185). Telegrams can be sent from main post offices.

Dialling & codes

The international code for Italy is 39. To dial in from other countries, preface it with the exit code: 00 in the UK and 011 in the US. All normal Florence numbers begin with the area code 055. All Italian codes must always include the zero; for mobile phone numbers there is no initial zero. To make an international call from Florence, dial 00, then the country code (Australia 61; Canada 1; Irish Republic 353; New Zealand 64; United Kingdom 44; United States 1), followed by the area code (for

calls to the UK, omit the initial zero) and individual number. The same pattern works to mobile phones. All numbers beginning 800 are free lines (*numero verde*). For numbers that begin 840, the charge is one unit. Phone numbers starting 3 are mobile numbers; 199 codes are charged at local rates; 167 numbers at premium rates.

Directory enquiries

Italian info can be accessed online at www.1254.it or www.pagine bianche.it. All hotels and most restaurants and bars have phone books (*elenco telefonico*) and *Yellow Pages* (*Pagine Gialle*). Phone services are 1254 (Italian and international numbers, in Italian) and 892 412 from mobile phones (international numbers, in Italian and English).

Mobile phones

Pay-as-you-go mobiles and SIM cards are available from phone shops. Buy top-up cards from *bar-tabacchi* or news stands; either call the number on the card, or use the electronic top-up facility in many bars. Some internet points hire out phones (p185).

TIM, Telecom Italia Mobile *via de' Lamberti 12-14 (055 2396066)*.
Vodafone *via de' Martelli 25-31r (055 2670121)*.

Operator services

For reverse-charge (collect) calls, dial 170 for the **international operator**. To be connected to the operator in the country you want to call, dial 172 followed by the number including codes.

Public phones

Some bars, main city squares, stations and airport still have payphones which accept phone

ESSENTIALS

cards (*schede telefoniche*), not coins; some accept credit cards. Cards are available from *tabacchi*, some news stands and bars, as are the pre-paid phone cards offering access via an 800 number to domestic and international calls.

Tickets

For pre-booking of museum tickets see page 10. **Box Office** (via Alamanni 39, 055 210 804/www. boxol.it) sells tickets for concerts, plays and exhibitions.

Time

Italy is one hour ahead of London, six ahead of New York and eight behind Sydney. Clocks go forward an hour in spring and back in autumn.

Tipping

The 10-15 per cent tip customary in many countries is considered generous in Florence. Locals sometimes leave a few coins on bars and €1-€5 for the service after a meal. Some larger restaurants add a 10-15 per cent service charge onto the bill automatically. Taxi drivers will be surprised if you add more than a euro.

Tourist information

The Italian tourist board, **ENIT** sends out info packs (UK: 0800 00482542/020 7408 1254, www.en it.it; US: 212 245 4822, www.enit.it/ www.italiantourism.com). Florence's provincial tourist board, the **Azienda Promozionale Turistica**, APT (www.firenze turismo.it), and the council-run **Ufficio Informazioni Turistiche** both have helpful, multilingual staff. Tourist information offices are in via Cavour 1r (055 290832), borgo Santa Croce 29r (055 2340444), piazza della Stazione 4A (055 212245). Hotel bookings can be made through free service Florence Promhotels (info@promhotels.it; www.promhotels.it), or through the tourist offices. A sporadic summer service runs from three vans: in piazza della Repubblica, via Calzaiuoli and in via Guicciardini. APT personnel and the municipal police provide help and information. You can also register complaints about restaurant or hotel charges.

Visas & immigration

Non-EU citizens and Britons require full passports to travel to Italy. EU citizens are permitted unrestricted access to travel to Italy; citizens of the USA, Canada, Australia and New Zealand do not currently need visas for stays of up to three months, but all non-EU visitors should check about visa requirements at an Italian embassy or consulate in their own country before setting off for Italy. All non-EU citizens planning to stay for more than three months should register with the police within eight days of arrival and then apply for their permits. If you're staying in a hotel, this will be done for you.

What's on

The best listings mags are *Firenze Spettacolo* (www.firenze spettacolo.it); *Florence Concierge Information* from tourist offices (www.florence-concierge.it); and free English-language newspaper *The Florentine* (www.theflorentine.net). The Florence editions of *Corriere della Sera* (www.corriere.it), *Il Giornale* (www.ilgiornale.it), *La Nazione* (http://qn.quotidiano.net) and *La Repubblica* (www.repub blica.it) also publish comprehensive listings for local events.

ESSENTIALS

Vocabulary

Italian is a phonetic language, so most words are spelled as they're pronounced (and vice versa). Stresses usually fall on the penultimate syllable.

Pronunciation

Vowels
a – as in apple
e – like a in age (closed e),
or e in sell (open e)
i – like ea in east
o – as in hotel (closed o)
or in hot (open o)
u – like oo in boot

Consonants
c – before a, o or u: like the c in cat;
before e or i: like the ch in check
ch – like the c in cat
g – before a, o or u: like the g in get; before e or i: like the j in jig
gh – like the g in get
gl – followed by 'i': like lli in million
gn – like ny in canyon
qu – as in quick
r – is always rolled
s – has two sounds, as in soap or rose
sc – followed by 'e' or 'i': like the sh in shame
sch – like the sc in scout
z – has two sounds, like ts and dz
Double consonants are sounded more emphatically.

Useful phrases

hello and goodbye (informal) *ciao*; **good morning, good day** *buongiorno*; **good afternoon, good evening** *buona sera*; **I don't understand** *non capisco/non ho capito*; **do you speak English?** *parla inglese?*; **please** *per favore*; **thank you** *grazie*; **you're welcome** *prego*; **when does it open?** *quando apre?*; **where is... ?** *dov'è...?*; **excuse me** *scusi* (polite), *scusa* (informal); **open** *aperto*; **closed** *chiuso*; **entrance** *entrata*; **exit** *uscita*; **left** *sinistra*; **right**

destra; **car** *macchina*; **bus** *autobus*; **train** *treno*; **ticket/s** *biglietto/i*; **I would like a ticket to...** *vorrei un biglietto per...*; **postcard** *cartolina*; **stamp** *francobollo*; **glass** *bicchiere*; **coffee** *caffè*; **tea** *tè*; **water** *acqua*; **wine** *vino*; **beer** *birra*; **the bill** *il conto*; **single/twin/double bedroom** *camera singola/a due letti/matrimoniale*;

Days of the week

Monday – *lunedì*
Tuesday – *martedì*
Wednesday – *mercoledì*
Thursday – *giovedì*
Friday – *venerdì*
Saturday – *sabato*
Sunday – *domenica*
yesterday – *ieri*
today – *oggi*
tomorrow – *domani*
morning – *mattina*
afternoon – *pomeriggio*
evening – *sera*
night – *notte*
weekend – *fine settimana, weekend*

Numbers & money

0 *zero*; 1 *uno*; 2 *due*; 3 *tre*; 4 *quattro*; 5 *cinque*; 6 *sei*; 7 *sette*; 8 *otto*; 9 *nove*; 10 *dieci*; 11 *undici*; 12 *dodici*; 13 *tredici*; 14 *quattordici*; 15 *quindici*; 16 *sedici*; 17 *diciassette*; 18 *diciotto*; 19 *diciannove*; 20 *venti*; 21 *ventuno*; 22 *ventidue*; 30 *trenta*; 40 *quaranta*; 50 *cinquanta*; 60 *sessanta*; 70 *settanta*; 80 *ottanta*; 90 *novanta*; 100 *cento*; 1,000 *mille*; 2,000 *duemila*; 100,000 *centomila*; 100,000 *un milione*. **how much does it cost/is it?** *quanto costa?/quant'è?*; **do you have any change?**; *ha da cambiare?* **do you accept credit cards?** *si accettano le carte di credito?*; **can I have a receipt?** *posso avere una ricevuta?*

Index

Notes

GabrioStaff
OLIMPO
Hair SPA - Wellness Center

a real hair SPA
massages and wellness rituals . beauty privè

via dè tornabuoni 5 . firenze . 055/214668 . www.gabriostaff.it